THE CANDLE OF THE LORD

THE
CANDLE OF THE LORD

Studies in the Cambridge Platonists

BY THE REV.
WILLIAM CECIL de PAULEY

The spirit of man is the candle of the Lord, searching all the inward parts of the belly.—PROVERBS xx. 27

Essay Index Reprint Series

originally published by
SOCIETY FOR PROMOTING CHRISTIAN KNOWLEDGE

BOOKS FOR LIBRARIES PRESS
FREEPORT, NEW YORK

First Published 1937
Reprinted 1970

STANDARD BOOK NUMBER:
8369-1496-1

LIBRARY OF CONGRESS CATALOG CARD NUMBER:
75-107693

PRINTED IN THE UNITED STATES OF AMERICA

If you desire a larger view of the parts of Morality; I know not where you will find them so well and distinctly explained, and so strongly inforced ; as in the practical Divines of the Church of England. The Sermons of Dr. Barrow, Archbishop Tillotson, and Dr. Whichcote, are master-pieces in this kind : not to name abundance of others who excel on that subject.

JOHN LOCKE.

CONTENTS

CHAP.		PAGE
I.	Benjamin Whichcote	1
II.	Benjamin Whichcote and Jeremy Taylor	39
III.	John Smith	67
IV.	Ralph Cudworth	89
V.	Henry More	115
VI.	Richard Cumberland	149
VII.	Nathanael Culverwel	161
VIII.	George Rust	175
IX.	Edward Stillingfleet	187

ADDITIONAL NOTES

I.	John Calvin	231
II.	Lancelot Andrewes: Excerpt on the Candle of the Lord	245
III.	William Laud: Excerpt on Scripture	246
	Index	247

I
BENJAMIN WHICHCOTE

Whitchcot was a man of a rare temper, very mild and obliging. He had great credit with some that had been eminent in the late times, but made all the use he could of it to protect good men of all persuasions. He was much for liberty of conscience: and being disgusted with the dry systematical way of those times, he studied to raise those that conversed with him to a nobler set of thoughts, and to consider religion as the seed of a Deiform nature, (to use one of his own phrases.) In order to this, he set young students much on reading the ancient philosophers, chiefly Plato, Tully, and Plotin, and on considering the Christian religion as a doctrine sent from God both to elevate and sweeten human nature; in which he was a great example, as well as a wise and kind instructor.

BURNET.

THE CANDLE OF THE LORD

CHAPTER I

BENJAMIN WHICHCOTE [1]

'THE times, wherein I live, are more to mee; than anie else: the workes of God in them, which I am to discerne; direct in mee both principle affection and action.' [2] So in 1651 Benjamin Whichcote defended his presentation of the Gospel against the anxious charges of Antony Tuckney, who had been his tutor at Emmanuel College, the 'Seminary of Puritans.' [3] The times were troubled by Hobbes, who had made man out to be a rascal, and by the Puritans, who, relying upon passages from Scripture, could show that he was wicked; and Whichcote arises in his generation to demonstrate that man has a spiritual quality which enables him to know God and to take his peaceable place in the human family. Shaftesbury's characterization of him is true, as far as it goes—'The Preacher of Good-Nature'; [4]

---

[1] 1609–83.
[2] *Moral and Religious Aphorisms. Collected from the Manuscript Papers of the Reverend and Learned Doctor Whichcote ; . . . To which are added, Eight Letters : which passed between Dr. Whichcote, Provost of King's College ; and Dr. Tuckney, Master of Emmanuel College, . . . London :* MDCCLIII, p. 115.
[3] *Ib., The Preface* (by Samuel Salter), p. ii.
[4] *Ib., Testimonies*, p. xxxii. In his preface to Whichcote's *Works* (Edition, 1751), Shaftesbury says of Hobbes: 'This is *he*, who reckoning up the passions or affections by which men are held together in society, live in peace, or have any correspondence one with another, forgot to mention kindness, friendship, sociableness, love of company and converse, natural affection, or any thing of this kind; I say *forgot*, because I can scarcely think so ill of any man, as that he has not by experience found any of these affections in himself, and consequently, that he believes none of them to be in others.'

but clearly in Whichcote's view all the good in human nature is of God.

The times had already begun to be agitated by motions from yet a third quarter, and it is hard to resist the conclusion that Whichcote was influenced negatively at least, if not positively, by Descartes.[1] For, apart from the evidence afforded by certain remarks scattered here and there in his sermons,[2] there is a pertinent objection made by Tuckney in the course of his complaint that Whichcote had been guilty of exalting the powers of reason at the expense of the claims of faith. Reason, Tuckney holds, ought to be content to work for 'more full clearing of receeved truths; and finding-out others, that itt may bee, yett lie hid; without such a libertie of opposing, or doubtfullie disputing, περὶ τῶν πεπληροφορουμενών, much more without a Cartesian ἐποχή or supposing them for errours, or not established truths; till I coming *de novo*, without anie prepossession of them, shall study and reason my selfe into a beleife of them. And somthing sounding this way, I thought I heard, within this twelvemonth, out of the pulpitte.'[3] The following passages taken from the sermons are significant. 'It is commendable, therefore, when men come to years of understanding, to examine all the principles of their education; and to enquire into all matters of their former supposition: and if upon impartial examination, truth appear to the contrary; if there appear a mistake, an error; we must lay it aside and entertain truth.'[4] 'We should doubt and deliberate, before we resolve and determine. Nothing are we so sure of, as of that which

---

[1] *Cf.*, however, J. H. Muirhead, *The Platonic Tradition in Anglo-Saxon Philosophy*, p. 25.

[2] W. Fraser Mitchell, *English Pulpit Oratory from Andrewes to Tillotson*, p. 286, points out that the sermons 'clearly belong to the days of Whichcote's London ministry, after the Restoration. . . .'

[3] Tuckney's *Third Letter*, pp. 85-6.

[4] *The Works of the Learned Benjamin Whichcote, D.D.*, Aberdeen, 1751, vol. iv. p. 337.

we are sure of after doubting. Where this is not done, there are easy perswasions, credulity, lightness of faith: whence it comes to pass, that men are greatly possessed, strangely persuaded in matters where there is very good assurance that things are otherwise.'[1] 'Now if I may not believe the reason of my mind, in conjunction with three or four of my senses, how shall I know any thing to be this or that? And if I do not know any thing to be true or good, I am not obliged, as to practice.'[2] 'This I account: that, in morality, we are as sure as in mathematics.'[3] 'The whole motion of the world below men, is nulled upon a moral consideration; and no morality to be found in any agent below man: the motions of all else, are no better than mechanick.'[4] Then there are numerous passages in which our author proves the existence of God; and his method is always to reason from effect to cause. 'If there were no other argument in the world, to prove there is a God, a man is an argument sufficient to himself. For thus, a man feels that he is; and he doth prove that by his acting: I act, therefore I am; I do, therefore I have being: and if I am, either I made myself, or was made by another. I did not make myself: for if I had made myself at my own will, I could continue myself in being during my own pleasure; and this I know I cannot: and this is great reason, because it is an exercise of less power, to continue a thing in being which hath being, than to call a thing out of nothing, into being: therefore I made not myself

---

[1] *Ib.*, ii. pp. 37-8.
[2] *Ib.*, i. p. 170.
[3] *Ib.*, iv. p. 264. In his *First Letter* Tuckney writes: 'I have seldom hear'd you preach; but that something hath bin delivered by you, and that so authoritatively, and with the big words, sometimes of "divinest reason," and sometimes of "more than mathematical demonstration"; that hath very much grieved me; and, I believe, others with me: and yesterday, as much as any time.' Whichcote's reply repeats the offence: 'And this is a demonstration in Divinity; beyond which no demonstration in Astronomie is more certain.'
[4] *Ib.*, i. p. 69.

but was made by another. And then that other must neither be my equal, nor inferior; for I can do as much as my equal, more than my inferior; therefore I was made by a greater than myself, a greater both in wisdom and power: and this first independent being I call God. Thus is a man an argument to himself, of the existence of a Deity.'[1] 'We prove a cause antecedent, by an effect consequent: and this is the best argument in the world.'[2] 'God is fairly knowable by the works of his creation, if we awaken our faculties, if we call ourselves to consideration.'[3] 'Now since this scripture,[4] and other scriptures, use no other arguments to prove there is a God (for revelation cannot prove it, revelation supposes it;) therefore I shall forbear all other reasons: for tho' I might produce many metaphysical things; yet because they are abstract from sense, they shall not be named.'[5] If Whichcote is referring here to the ontological argument employed by Descartes, we can see why he declines to make use of it, namely, because natural theology, as outlined in Holy Scripture, makes no mention of it. But if this is not what he has in mind, it is clear at least that his arguments for the existence of God accord with the methods of proof laid down by St. Thomas.

Our reference to St. Thomas suggests that this will be a convenient point to introduce Whichcote's teaching on the subject of man's knowledge of God. In what sense or senses can man be said to know God, and how far does his knowledge take him? Formally, as we have seen, man reaches the knowledge that there is a first cause by considering things, the things around him and the thing he calls himself; but, more particularly, he learns about the character of this cause by considering the things which he knows as good. He comes to entertain an idea of the Being who is supremely good in two ways: first, by conceiving

---

[1] *Ib.*, iii. pp. 241-2.   [2] *Ib.*, ii. p. 233.   [3] *Ib.*, iii. p. 196.
[4] *Rom.* i. 19-20.   [5] *Works*, iii. p. 164.

the first cause in terms of the best that it lies within his power to represent to himself,[1] and second, by 'the way of negation,' for he 'can never remove imperfection, contraction, circumscription, limitation, far enough from him.'[2] But there is a necessary condition to be observed; for if he would entertain a worthy notion of Him who is perfection, he must needs endeavour after this perfection in so far as he can: 'for it is found by experience, that the malignity of the heart doth blind the understanding: and true wisdom will never abide in a malicious and wicked soul.'[3] And it must be admitted that man's knowledge of God can never be complete, because finite perfection, assuming that we had attained to it, cannot, in the nature of things, comprehend infinite perfection. God made man, Whichcote says, 'so as to know *that he is*; and in some measure, to conceive *what he is*, and what are his essential perfections. . . .'[4] The essential perfections are classified as either 'natural' or 'moral.' Among the first are infiniteness, omniscience, omnipotence, omnipresence, eternity, immensity, and ubiquity; and among the second are holiness, faithfulness, righteousness, goodness, truth, kindness, beneficence, clemency, mercy, and compassion.[5] God's natural perfections are 'incomprehensible,' and move man to adoration of Him; but His moral perfections are 'communicable,' and man is at liberty to imitate them. Of the latter Whichcote says: 'I am sure that God is not known by any thing more to us, than by these.'[6] 'And though we cannot comprehend the being of God (for finite cannot comprehend infinite), yet if we do acknowledge God the first and chiefest goodness, and ascribe all excellency and perfection to him, we do him as much right as we are capable of.'[7]

[1] *Cf. Ib.*, iii. p. 177: 'If we would express a notion of our maker, we should employ our mind and understanding to find out what is best and what is most perfect, and then attribute and ascribe it to God.'
[2] *Ib.*, p. 178. [3] *Ib.*, p. 99. [4] *Ib.*, iii. p. 195.
[5] *Ib.*, i. pp. 381-2; ii. p. 385; iv. p. 198. [6] *Ib.*, iv. p. 198.
[7] *Ib.*, ii. p. 233.

It follows, therefore, that the line, if indeed there be one at all, which divides philosophy from religion is a very thin one;[1] and that Whichcote holds that a knowledge of God lays man under a double obligation of worship and obedience. Man, he would say, does not really know God until his whole being has become responsive to His presence, and mere reasonings about Him are fruitless speculations. 'Religion,' he says, 'though it begins at knowledge, it proceeds to temper, and ends in practice';[2] and again, 'religion in that subject where it is, doth not only illuminate the mind and understanding, and give conviction to a man's reason, but also renews the heart and affection; and so there becomes a transformation of the whole man, so that if a man be really under the power of religion, the virtue of his religion reacheth all his faculties.'[3] And though in one sermon he falls back upon what is virtually the principle of the analogical knowledge of God, or as he terms it, the 'way of metaphor,'[4] on the ground that Holy Scripture 'is abundant in the use of it,' he is careful to show that knowledge of God expressed in metaphor is but a conceptual representation of God's presence felt and recognized within the soul. 'And when it is said, *we are an habitation of God through the Spirit*;[5] this represents to us . . . That God is present with us, as a man is in his house.'[6]

---

[1] *Ib.*, i. p. 37: '. . . so soon as a man is able to make use of reason and judgment, he ought to put himself upon motion of religion, for we are as capable of religion, as we are of reason. . . .'

[2] *Ib.*, ii. p. 18.

[3] *Ib.*, ii. p. 142. *Cf.* Calvin, *Institutes*, III. ii. 36: 'For the word of God is not throughly received by faith, if it swim in the top of the braine, but when it hath taken roote in the bottome of the heart that it may be an invincible defence to beare and repulse all the engines of tentations. Now if it be true, that the true understanding of the minde is the enlightning thereof, then in such confirmation of the heart, his power much more evidently appeereth, even by so much as the distrustfulnesse of the heart is greater than the blindnesse of the wit: and as it is harder to have the mind furnished with assurednesse, than the wit to be instructed with thinking' (Trans. by T. Norton, 1611).

[4] *Ib.*, ii. p. 383.   [5] *Eph.* ii. 22.   [6] *Works*, ii. p. 384.

Knowledge of God turns out to be a man's own rational interpretation of his own religious experience; and what Whichcote is concerned to preach is not so much a philosophy of religion as a philosophy of religious experience.[1] He has as little use for speculative knowledge *about* God which fails to influence life and conduct, as he has for an unreflecting religion in which men give themselves over to indulgence of pious emotions. And it is to Scripture that he goes for justification of his view: 'knowledge in scripture-sense, is an effectual principle, and rests not in any notion of the head, or in any simple apprehension: . . . so that when you are called upon to know God, you are required to love and delight in him, which are affections connatural to the knowledge and perception of God.'[2] He can quote, in defence of a warm natural religion, from a speech made by St. Paul, even as St. Paul himself quoted from the Greeks: 'God is more inward to us than our very souls; so the apostle saith, *in him we live, and move, and have our being, we are his offspring.*'[3] The doctrine of Plato's *Eros* can be combined with the doctrine of the new science in order to illustrate the soul's innate tendency to move towards God: 'it is as natural and proper, for mind and understanding in man, to tend towards God, as for heavy things to tend towards their center: for God is the center of immortal souls.'[4] So it turns out that the demand of reason for a first cause is but the blind yearning of the soul for good now become articulate. 'If any man

---

[1] J. H. Muirhead, *op. cit.*, p. 28, notes that Cudworth appears to have been the first to use the phrase 'philosophy of religion.' Calvin has *christiana philosophia* (*Institutes*, III. vii. 1). Jeremy Taylor speaks of 'the whole system and collective body of Christian philosophy' (*Works*, ii. p. 5), and of 'the charity of Christian philosophy, which expounds the sense of the divine providence fairly' (iii. p. 88). Tillotson says that 'Christianity is the best philosophy' (*Works*, ix. p. 34). Locke holds that 'Christian philosophers have much outdone' those that were 'before our Saviour's time' (*Works*, 1823, vii. p. 140).
[2] *Works*, iv. p. 287.   [3] *Ib.*, iii. p. 178; *Acts* xvii. 28.
[4] *Ib.*, p. 144.

will grant me that one principle,' says Whichcote, 'which is certain and we know it by experience, I shall sufficiently secure religion by it; for *intellectus quaerit Deum*, it is the nature of our mind and understanding to seek after God: therefore though a man be never so well accomplished, if he be devoid of sense and apprehension of God, he must be unfurnished; for he is unsatisfied, he hath not enough to satisfy the connatural desires of his immortal soul.' [1]

It is not easy to fix upon a precise meaning for the term 'reason' as Whichcote employs it. It would appear, to begin with, that he makes it include both the mental processes by means of which we arrive at a conclusion, and also the insight we possess into the self-evident principles which condition these processes. It seems to stand too for our capacity to appreciate values, and in particular for our capacity to acknowledge God, the source and sustainer of all that is good and beautiful and true. Furthermore, it is reason which appropriates these values and incorporates them within the soul in such wise that they form its disposition and become its temper; and so it is the governing principle which directs our appetites and controls our passions. Reason is 'the highest and noblest of our faculties,' [2] and it must, therefore, be the faculty which marks us off from all other created beings as personal and fits us to enter into happy fellowship with God. There is one circumstance about reason, however, to which Whichcote repeatedly draws the attention of his hearers, and one which, in view of his own and later times, we must dwell upon, namely, that it is no self-sufficient endowment equipped either by God or by nature to fulfil its own functions. It has been adapted to work with God and in harmony with Him to reflect His mind. Reason, in so far as it speaks true, is the voice of God speaking within the human soul; and, contrariwise, it is man's witness that

[1] *Ib.*, iv. p. 286.   [2] *Ib.*, i. p. 172.

what God says is good and true.¹ Should proof of this be demanded, Whichcote would probably reply that he is enunciating a first principle, and that a rational being, provided that he is in a God-like frame of mind, is aware of God, and that nothing further can be said.

Our author loves to justify the derivative sufficiency of reason by appealing to a text in *Proverbs*: 'The spirit of man is the candle of the Lord.' ² Reason is *lux illuminata et lux illuminans*. The lighting is effected 'by divine influences,' ³ in order to show man the way to God. In this light he can discover beneficent providence at work in the course of nature,⁴ and interpret also the motions that stir within his own soul. The 'light of nature' declares what a man needs to know, in order that he may know God.

The *Proverbs* text had been a favourite with Whichcote even in the days when he gave his Sunday afternoon sermons at Cambridge. Tuckney charges him with exalting the powers of reason so high that the auditory might be led to entertain false notions about the office of faith in the realm of revealed truth: this crying-up of reason, he writes, is a case of '*crambe*, not *bis* but *centies cocta*.' ⁵ He prefers to understand that the candle searches the secret places of man's heart, and not the mysteries of 'divine truths.' ⁶ Whichcote asks in reply: 'Do I dishonour my faith, or do anie wrong to itt; to tell the worlde, that my minde and understanding are satisfied in itt? I have noe reason against itt; yea, the highest and purest reason is for itt! What doth God speak to, but my reason?' ⁷ In the third letter Tuckney repeats that both sense and context show that the candle is *rimari res hominum, non Dei*; and

---

¹ *Ib.*, iii. p. 163: 'Conscience is knowledge in us with God: we know, and God knows.'
² *Prov.* xx. 27.   ³ *Works*, iii. p. 187.
⁴ *Ib.*, iii. p. 190: 'No voice in nature so loud, no language so easy to be understood: every herb, every plant imparts something of God.'
⁵ Tuckney's *Second Letter*, p. 19.   ⁶ *Ib.*, p. 20.
⁷ Whichcote's *Second Letter*, p. 48.

that we cannot argue that since a candle suffices to light up a dark corner in a room, it will avail to light up the heavens on a dark night.¹ But he goes on to say that some interpreters admit a larger sense, 'yett they explain themselves to meane that Grace, which out of his love hee reveleth by his worde; and infuseth by his spirit; . . . so being by the spirit illuminated, wee denie not but it can perceeve the things of God; which otherwise it cannot.'² Whichcote's final rejoinder is calculated to appeal to the sentiments of his opponent, when he points out that if you weaken man's rational capacity to know God, you inevitably lessen the degree of his sin and guilt. 'I allwayes consider, and so express, the mind of man in conjunction with the good spirit of God. I abhorre and detest from my soule all creature-magnifying self-sufficiencie.'³ 'I count itt true sacriledge, to take from God; to give to the Creature: yett I look at itt, as a dishonouring God, to nullify and make base his workes; and to think Hee made a sorrie worthless peece, fitt for no use; when hee made man.'⁴

Having noted what reason is, we ask what it does towards securing the good life. Whichcote's sermons, beyond pointing out that we ought to learn all we can about the nature and character of God from His works, do not discuss the function of reason in the field of science. The mind, to begin with and prior to action, is darkness and not light, *rasa tabula*, a sheet of white paper whereon nothing is written;⁵ and neither light nor writing, when they appear, God's action being waived for the moment, come from without. 'Knowledge is fetch out of us, not brought into us': in other words, the meaning which we place upon what comes from without comes from within. There are

---

¹ Tuckney's *Third Letter*, p. 72. He adduces *Zeph*. i. 12: 'I will search Jerusalem with candles, and punish the men that are settled on their lees.'
² *Ib.*, p. 73.
³ Whichcote's *Third Letter*, p. 100.
⁴ *Ib.*, p. 112.   ⁵ *Works*, ii. p. 4; iii. p. 215.

'common notions,'[1] or 'notions of truth,'[2] which light up and adorn the mind. These are said to be 'principles of action'; for Whichcote is a preacher of practical sermons, and instead of speculating about categories which condition a knowledge of things, he treats of primary virtues which condition our relations with God, our neighbour, and ourselves.

Whichcote has his own peculiar designation for these virtues. They are 'truths of the first inscription.'[3] The phrase is suggested, no doubt, by Scripture, because he says that, apart from the 'connatural' knowledge of virtue imparted by them, neither the Ten Commandments inscribed on tables of stone, nor the more exacting law of 'after-revelation' to be written in the heart, could have been understood. 'For had we not principles that are concreated; did we not know something, no man could prove any thing.' The principles are three in number, and avowedly taken from Scripture, namely, to *live soberly, righteously, and godly, in this present world*';[4] and they can be comprised conveniently under an extended sense of the second, for it is written that *'when thy judgments are in the earth, the inhabitants of the world will learn righteousness.'*[5]

There is no occasion to delay over Whichcote's discussions of these virtues; but it is necessary to observe that every possible interpretation of any one of the three will be guided by the extent of our rational insight into the immutable relations which in 'the nature of things' exist ideally between the rational beings concerned. Piety towards God, justice towards a neighbour, and sobriety in oneself,[6] will rise or fall in their demands in proportion to

---

[1] *Ib.*, ii. p. 13. [2] *Ib.*, iii. p. 215.
[3] *Ib.*, iii. p. 20; p. 120. Calvin appears to restrict these virtues to the elect, and says that 'when they be knit together with an unseparable knot, make a full perfection' (*Institutes*, III. vii. 3; *cf.* III. xvi. 2 and xxv. 1). [4] *Tit.* ii. 12. [5] *Is.* xxvi. 9.
[6] *Works*, ii. p. 59: '. . . these acts of sobriety and temperance are grounded upon the constitution of man, as he doth consist of body and spirit.'

our knowledge of the manifold relations in which we stand to God, to men, and to ourselves. The three virtues 'are rooted in the intellectual nature'; [1] they are as natural to man as light is to the sun; they are 'catholick,' [2] and 'have testimony in all nations, in all places, at all times'; [3] and they are 'ends themselves.' [4] Whichcote's idea of the good life is determined by a reasoning consideration about things that are unalterably fixed, and 'vice is contrary to nature.' [5] Nevertheless, he sees clearly, as Cudworth possibly did not, that reason oftentimes will be deeply concerned to know just exactly how to apply an eternal standard to individual problems of conduct, and accordingly a fair proportion of the sermon material is occupied with expositions of special cases. 'If a man will observe the rule of equity,' for example, 'he must take the case into consideration, and cloath it with all circumstances that belong to it, and give all allowance to the person concerned, for sudden surprisals, for invincible ignorance, for contracted necessity, for unavoidable accident, for something which might befal him that he could not foresee: and if you would extend your goodness to the utmost, give something to the frailty of human nature; where there is no other consideration, cast something in for the frailty of human nature.' [6]

Now, although our moral problems arise in the main from our constitution as embodied souls, there are, by way of compensation, certain helps to be credited to this creature state of ours in the life of moral endeavour. For if, on one side, our natural passions, when left uncontrolled, are liable to develop into unnatural perturbations, certain of our appetites, on the other side, have been designed to take up with their fit and proper objects in this world of our environment, and to contribute in this way their share towards that assemblage of goods called happiness. Whichcote seems to have decided that the human soul has some

[1] *Ib.*, ii. p. 59. [2] *Ib.*, p. 313. [3] *Ib.*, p. 319.
[4] *Ib.*, p. 237. [5] *Ib.*, i. p. 132. [6] *Ib.*, iv. p. 17.

appetites, more or less blind in themselves, which make for the realization of its perfection; and that the several ends to which they impel are made clear in the light of the candle of the Lord. Earlier in this study it has been shown that a man comes to be aware of the existence within him of a God-ward motion, and that he can give sound rational justification for this interpretation of what he feels; and now we are to note that a man is moved from within to seek also his own good and the good of his kind. These two movements come to be known respectively as self-love and benevolence; and all that any one can truly *know* about them emerges during a painstaking investigation into the factors which compose his experience of life. We tend to advance our own interest, and we tend to advance the interests of others; but what we actually accomplish in either direction will depend upon whether or not we know what we are about. Evidently, too, these three tendencies, pertaining as they do to the chief objects to which we are related, are answered by three virtues, namely, godliness, sobriety, and righteousness.

What is this good that all men seek? Whichcote's reply is that a creature having spiritual capacity can find complete satisfaction in none but a spiritual object, and that this object must be God. It is only 'local happiness'[1] that comes by pursuing objects less than God, unless peradventure they be pursued in company with God.[2] To indulge in a particular and selfish career is to behave like a snail that carries its little house with it wherever it goes.[3] A man must 'universalize himself,' if he would be happy; that is to say, he must envisage his good in terms of God and the 'publick good.'[4] The true ideal is 'to serve God and the publick, not to promote our own ends and little designs.'[5] And when this ample standard prevails, it is legitimate to say that 'to enjoy a man's self, is the greatest

---

[1] *Ib.*, iii. p. 48.   [2] *Ib.*, i. p. 197.   [3] *Ib.*, iii. p. 326.
[4] *Ib.*, pp. 325-6.   [5] *Ib.*, i. p. 37.

good in the world,'[1] and that happiness and goodness, or holiness, are materially the same.[2] The upshot of Whichcote's teaching on self-love seems to be that a man attains happiness in so far as he has divested himself of irreligious and unsocial practices and adjusted himself in partnership with the family of God; and that what Hobbes failed to see is that the interest to which self-preservation[3] points is secured by whole-hearted surrender to God and not by mutual compromise with men.

It is just as natural for a man to promote the common good as it is for him to promote his own: for 'there is in man, a secret genius to humanity; a biass that inclines him to a regard of all of his own kind';[4] and though it may not be this or that man's settled disposition to do so, he cannot but 'approve'[5] when he sees another man do a generous deed. Furthermore, to live a neighbourly life is to live in accordance with the nature of things; because the function of every created thing is twofold, namely, to be perfect in its own nature, and to contribute towards the perfection of all other things. A principle of 'universal benevolence' holds throughout the entire creation, and in the superior world of intelligence each man is free to find out how he can best serve mankind.[6] 'Righteousness,' says Whichcote, is 'fair and equal dealing with a man's neighbour,'[7] and it will take different forms in different cases, as, for example, keeping one's word, or being candid.[8] God is good to all men; and 'it should be, one man a God to another: but we, thro' our degeneracy, make it to be, every man a wolf to another.'[9] 'Wherefore, we may detest and reject that doctrine which saith, that God made man in a state of war. Undoubtedly, man, if he have not abused himself, is the mildest creature under heaven.'[10]

---

[1] *Ib.*, p. 117. [2] *Ib.*, p. 235; p. 316. [3] *Ib.*, iii. p. 329.
[4] *Ib.*, iv. p. 212. [5] *Ib.*, p. 213. [6] *Ib.*, ii. p. 222; iv. p. 44.
[7] *Ib.*, ii. p. 227. [8] *Ib.*, p. 222.
[9] *Ib.*, iv. p. 107. Cf. *Ex.* vii. 1: 'And the Lord said unto Moses, See, I have made thee a god to Pharaoh.' [10] *Ib.*, iv. p. 213.

We shall bring to a close this short account of Whichcote's idea of good nature as foundation for the good life by remarking that his ethical theory is worked out within a theological frame: virtue, for him, is 'the moral part of religion.'[1] He takes this view because his reasoning begins with the fact of *good* nature: for if there is, in his own admirable phrase, 'a difference in things,'[2] there must be a Providence whose interest creates and furthers the good; and since good nature possesses tendencies towards its complete perfection, there must be a spiritual final cause. And possibly in this circumstance lies an explanation of why he includes the whole range of duties under a Biblical set of virtues, *godliness*, righteousness and sobriety, instead of under the traditional scheme of the cardinal virtues, prudence,[3] justice, temperance and fortitude. Each group, to be sure, is designed to make clear the conditions which will ensure a harmonious and contented life. But the members of the first group, including sobriety, are calculated to carry their possessor, as it were, out of himself, and to help him achieve a harmonious life in company with all spiritual beings of whom God is chief,[4] whereas the second group might conceivably become detached from any wider reference, social or religious, and become self-regarding. In consequence, when Whichcote is dealing with the special marks of the Christian life, instead of falling back on the theological virtues, faith, hope and love, he is free to retain his favourite group. 'Therefore talk no more against moral preachers,' he says, 'for they who call upon men to live godly, righteously, and soberly, they carry on the work of Christ, and these men preach Christ.'[5] 'Christianity comprehends in it, the moral part of religion, as well as the

---

[1] *Ib.*, ii. p. 59.   [2] *Ib.*, i. p. 70.
[3] Whichcote records agreement with Aristotle that all the virtues are 'conjoined in prudence' (ii. p. 52) and holds, consistently with this, that all truths 'hang together, mutually depend each on other' (ii. p. 14).
[4] *Ib.*, ii. p. 52.   [5] *Ib.*, iii. p. 263.

instituted part thereof, viz. going to God in and through Christ.'[1] The Christian virtues are simply the original virtues widened and deepened, because revelation has widened and deepened our knowledge of God, and placed us under new obligations to Him, to our neighbour and to ourselves. He does not cease to be 'the author of nature,' because we know Him now in Christ as 'the giver of grace.'[2]

This teaching was not without influence upon Anthony, third Earl of Shaftesbury, who served the public good when he published the sermons of our 'truly christian philosopher,' 'written after him at church.' But he was a 'miscellaneous writer,'[3] who, as Professor Laird says, 'conjoined in the smoothest fashion, what his successors were at pains to separate';[4] and it is not easy to detect precisely to what extent he was profited by the preacher. His interest fixes chiefly on man, or rather on man as a member of good society, and not on theological subjects, which he believes had better be left to the study of professional theologians under the guardianship of the state;[5] but, as we shall see, he holds that religion of the proper sort plays an important part in furthering the realization of his social ideal.

In Shaftesbury's scheme there are two 'affections' which make us candidates for happiness, or its equivalent, virtue. They are the 'natural,' or 'public,' affections, and the 'self,' or 'private,' affections;[6] and when the two sets do not combine in comfortable alliance, this is because their subject has not understood the meaning of good as it pertains to rational beings. Good is said to qualify primarily a whole, and only secondarily a part, which means that we must understand the good of an individual in the light of the good of the whole to which he belongs. It would not be correct to speak of a lone man as being good or enjoying it,

---

[1] *Ib.*, ii. p. 235.   [2] *Ib.*, p. 75.
[3] *Characteristics*, Edited by J. M. Robertson, ii. p. 161.
[4] *The Idea of Value*, p. 188.   [5] *Characteristics*, i. p. 231.
[6] *Ib.*, i. pp. 286 ff.

without reference to the good of any other, because there is no such thing as a self-sufficient man.[1] So it follows that although private affection ought to be made compatible with public, it may not be weakened unduly, else the subject would have little or no care to make himself fit to contribute his part towards the good of his kind.[2] The affections of a good man will be suitably balanced, and he will secure his own good when he has learned to subordinate it to the good of society. He must therefore have insight into what constitutes this larger good, and bring 'right reason'[3] to bear upon the problem of ordering his internal 'economy.'[4] He will require to 'reflect'[5] upon his affections, and 'judge'[6] whether the ends to which they move him are to the advantage of society; for even though 'natural affection' should of itself do what is in effect the right thing, he has not acted virtuously, unless he has been moved also by his own choice of what he knows to be good. He can no more escape from the necessity of passing judgment upon the worth of his affections, than he can avoid registering like and dislike for the beautiful and the ugly, and for the sweet and the bitter. And why not? For the morally good *is* beautiful, and the bad *is* ugly; and the awareness that they are is just as immediate to our minds as is our perception of differences among colours and sounds. Shaftesbury says that 'the heart cannot possibly remain neutral; but constantly takes part one way or other. However false or corrupt it be within itself, it finds the difference, as to beauty and comeliness, between one heart and another, one turn of affection, one behaviour, one sentiment and another; and accordingly, in all disinterested cases, must approve in some measure of what is natural and honest, and disapprove of what is dishonest and corrupt.'[7] He explains that 'by means of this reflected sense, there arises another kind of affection towards those

---

[1] *Ib.*, p. 244.   [2] *Ib.*, p. 287.   [3] *Ib.*, p. 75.   [4] *Ib.*, p. 289.
[5] *Ib.*, p. 253.   [6] *Ib.*, p. 295.   [7] *Ib.*, p. 252.

very affections themselves (i.e. *pity, kindness, gratitude, and their contraries*), which have been already felt, and are now become the subject of a new liking or dislike.'[1] And a review of his terminology will show that all the higher faculties are involved in the exercise of human nature's moral talent: he speaks of a 'moral artist,'[2] of 'natural moral sense,'[3] 'common sense,'[4] 'sense of right and wrong,'[5] of 'rational affections,'[6] 'moral affections,'[7] and of 'taste or relish'[8] in matters of virtue.

When we turn back again to the sermons, we find that they throw a good deal of light upon Shaftesbury, and the origins of the 'moral sense' school of ethicists. Whichcote, we have observed, distinguishes very clearly between the 'strong propensions and desires of the soul after a state of happiness' and the direction and control to which they are properly subjected by reason, fortified as it is by knowledge of the difference of things.[9] And we have remarked, too, that by 'knowledge' Whichcote means far more than assent to what is true: we know a thing when we have consented to it, and have been taken with it. In reference to our knowledge—or lack of knowledge—of the character of the resurrection body, he says that 'states are not known by notion and description, but by sense and feeling, and by being in the very state itself';[10] and his remark serves to illustrate what he means by knowing God and the good. Illustration, however, is hardly necessary, for elsewhere, with acknowledgment to Aristotle, he says that 'bare speculation, knowledge and notion, is very little in the way of virtue, unless it be savory knowledge, or knowledge with a sense, when a man hath the gust of the thing as well as a precise separate abstract notion of it.'[11] But in spite of his frequent descriptions, in language restricted customarily to

---

[1] *Ib.*, p. 251. [2] *Ib.*, p. 136. [3] *Ib.*, p. 262.
[4] *Ib.*, p. 88.   [5] *Ib.*, p. 260. [6] *Ib.*, p. 256.
[7] *Ib.*, p. 275. [8] *Ib.*, ii. p. 256. [9] *Works*, iii. p. 329.
[10] *Ib.*, iv. p. 253. [11] *Ib.*, p. 289.

knowledge by sense-perception, of the knowledge that is of 'things above'—*e.g.* 'relish,'[1] 'taste,'[2] 'the palate of the soul,'[3] 'to feel' God 'by a spiritual touch,'[4] 'spiritual sense,'[5] 'sense of Deity'[6]—he is more careful than his admirer to reserve the office of making judgments in moral matters to reason. 'Every faculty of man,' he says, 'hath a natural sense of its own proper object, and perceives it better by its perception and sensation of it, than any philosopher doth by notion and definition'; and it falls to 'mind and spirit' to 'mingle . . . with unbodied and immaterial things.'[7] So we may say that in Whichcote's analysis of moral action, it is reason that deliberates, 'approves'[8] and chooses, and that it is the affections which furnish it with wings.[9]

When Whichcote enlarges upon the beauty of the good life, however, he does not appear to be employing analogies in order to convey his meaning. The good is beautiful. If harmony is the principle of beauty, it is also the principle of the good life, which is life at peace with all that is within and without. There is order, and therefore beauty, in the motions of the heavenly bodies; and there is order, and therefore beauty, in the motions of a good man.[10] When we see a good man or a good action, we see an ordered whole, and we experience an aesthetic enjoyment. When we envisage the moral ideal, we do not feel ourselves coldly repelled as by a standard that we cannot reach; on the contrary, we feel ourselves moved by a living pattern of goodness which waits to transform our ill-shapen lives into its own likeness. It is good Platonism to identify the good with the beautiful; but there is little doubt that Whichcote is taught by the Scriptures when he appeals to our appreciation of the beauty of holiness. It is a favourite thought of

[1] *Ib.*, i. p. 61.   [2] *Ib.*, ii. p. 130.   [3] *Ib.*, i. p. 91.
[4] *Ib.*, iii. p. 186.   [5] *Ib.*, ii. p. 123.   [6] *Ib.*, iii. p. 165.
[7] *Ib.*, iv. p. 313.
[8] *Ib.*, iii. p. 409; iv. p. 213.   *Cf. Rom.* ii. 18; *Phil.* i. 10.
[9] *Ib.*, ii. p. 360.   [10] *Ib.*, p. 395.

his that God compels us by way of attraction, and not by way of power;[1] and it accords with it that the good life, which is the life beautiful, can make its demands upon us in the same gentle tones.[2] Accordingly, he suggests a better rendering of a word in the original of the passage from *Romans*[3] which is associated memorably with St. Augustine's conversion—'*Let us walk with a grace*'; and he paraphrases it thus—'as for the credit of the gospel, beautifully, comely, venerably, suitable and proportionable to the principles of christianity.'[4]

Shaftesbury's divergence from Whichcote, however, turns out to be more extreme than the comparison we have just made, when taken by itself, can show. There is another matter, not of psychological analysis, but of philosophical and theological principle, on which the difference between them is complete. This is the question of the relation of morality to religion. Whichcote states his own view repeatedly. It is that morality constitutes a fundamental part of religion; and that religion constitutes a fundamental part of morality: that God obliges man to obedience; and that conscience obliges man to worship. Natural, or rational, religion and natural, or rational, living are one and the same thing; to live dependently upon God and to live according to nature are one and the same thing. Atheism, therefore, must come under the preacher's censure, and when he deals with it, he clothes himself in the most forbidding of prophet's mantles. An atheist is 'profane,'[5] a 'monster,'[6] a doer of good and evil 'without difference or distinction,'[7]

---

[1] *Ib.*, ii. p. 244: ' . . . there is that in God that is more beautiful than power, than will, and sovereignty, viz. his righteousness, his goodness, his justice, wisdom, and the like.'

[2] *Ib.*, p. 397: 'Therefore of the difference of things; there are some that are comely, beautiful, handsome, graceful, and becoming a person of ingenuity to do them.'

[3] xiii. 13. For εὐσχημόνως the *A.V.* has 'honestly,' and *A.V.M.* 'decently.' J. Moffatt translates—'let us live decorously.'

[4] *Works*, ii. p. 395.   [5] *Ib.*, iii. p. 163.

[6] *Ib.*, p. 32; p. 181.   [7] *Ib.*, i. p. 137.

'vile and contemptible.'[1] What else can be said about men who do not reason, and show themselves to be men? It is true that there are two sorts of atheists: two sorts, if we exclude reprobates (*i.e.* those who 'have wrought out of themselves the sense of human nature'[2]). The first have lost all power to concentrate on serious things, because they have lived carelessly, and for profit and pleasure: 'they never use reason in that that is the peculiar and proper act of reason; but only to keep sense company.'[3] The second are would-be intellectualists, and their attitude to the things of the spirit must surely be a pose; for, so strong are the arguments for the existence of God, that no man in his senses could fail to be convicted by them. The case for a God is 'unanswerable,'[4] and Aristotle's demonstration in the *Metaphysics* is specially commended. It is highly probable, indeed, that nobody who thinks at all is an out-and-out atheist, as is shown by the subterfuges that these professed atheists are driven to; for having sinned against 'an innate sense of God,'[5] they must needs try to show that man's end is the grave, and that the nature of things is synonymous with chance. And argue as they may, they cannot rid their minds of a haunting fear that there may be a God after all! 'Now when he comes to think,' concludes Whichcote of such a man, 'that in his fundamental notion, there may be an error; then he cannot but think: oh, what will become of me, that have taken upon me to remove the old landmarks, and to controul the most famous rights, the most established laws, those things that all mortals do subscribe to, and are fundamental to the safety of the universe! and I have taken upon me to vary from them, and to subordinate them to my will and humour: if all things be not alike, I am ruined to eternity.'[6]

Shaftesbury discusses the matter at some length, and though his conclusion is favourable on the whole to religion,

[1] *Ib.*, p. 144.   [2] *Ib.*, iii. p. 165.   [3] *Ib.*, p. 237.
[4] *Ib.*, p. 185.   [5] *Ib.*, p. 238.   [6] *Ib.*, p. 240.

by which in its genuine form he means communion with God, he appears to hold that it is of value primarily because it helps to sustain the moral stability of the community. He employs Whichcote's terms, but sometimes with different meanings and usually in different relations. All our knowledge of God is based upon our knowledge of what is good; but this turns out to be what is good for the public. It is just as natural for us to know that there is a God, as it is for us to know that there is a public good; but we come to know the latter, in process of our temporal development as well as in process of logic, *before* we come to know the former. Give a creature a reflecting faculty, says Shaftesbury, and 'it will at the same instant approve of gratitude, kindness, and pity; be taken with any show or representation of the social passion, and think nothing more amiable than this, or more odious than the contrary. . . . Before the time, therefore, that a creature can have any plain or positive notion one way or other concerning the subject of a God, he may be supposed to have an apprehension or sense of right and wrong, and be possessed of virtue and vice in different degrees . . .'[1] Our author is obviously at pains to separate what Whichcote had conjoined.

But what precise bearing has religious belief or unbelief upon the moral sense? Shaftesbury distinguishes three instances before giving his answer. In the first case, sense of right and wrong is as natural as natural affection, and therefore it cannot be eradicated directly by acceptance of either theism or atheism. In the second case, ineradicable sense of right and wrong can be either impaired by allegiance to a God of 'ill character,'[2] or stabilized by allegiance to a God who is benevolent towards all; and so 'religion is capable of doing great good or harm, and atheism nothing positive in either way.'[3] In the third case, ineradicable sense of right and wrong may be opposed and deadened

---

[1] *Characteristics*, i. p. 266.   [2] *Ib*., p. 264.   [3] *Ib*., p. 265.

indirectly by 'contrary affections,'[1] such as atheism has a 'natural tendency'[2] to beget. What happiness can be gained by exercising benevolence, if there is not concomitant faith in a benevolent principle at work in the universe? 'Nothing indeed can be more melancholy than the thought of living in a distracted universe, from whence many ills may be suspected, and where there is nothing good or lovely which presents itself, nothing which can satisfy in contemplation, or raise any passion besides that of contempt, hatred, or dislike.'[3] On these grounds, therefore, Shaftesbury concludes that morality is advanced by a worthy religion, 'since where the latter is wanting, there can neither be the same benignity, firmness, or constancy, the same good composure of the affections or uniformity of mind.'[4]

The different attitudes of the two men towards religion are thrown into clear relief when we set their views on happiness side by side. Both agree that happiness is a name for contentment of mind, and that it is the fruit of duly ordered affections; but whereas Whichcote would attain to it indirectly by endeavouring after the vision of God, Shaftesbury would find it more nearly to hand by exchanging reciprocal kindnesses among men. Whichcote believes that happiness spans the here and the hereafter, and that our enjoyment of God in this life is of a piece with our enjoyment of Him in the next; Shaftesbury believes that, in God's providence, our present happiness gives promise of our future happiness, and that 'the love of friendship' leads us to hope that we may 'enjoy the same blessed society hereafter.'[5]

Shaftesbury's preoccupation with the human affections is well illustrated by the following passage: 'For where the theistic belief is entire and perfect, there must be a steady opinion of the superintendency of a supreme Being, a

[1] *Ib.*, p. 258. [2] *Ib.*, p. 275. [3] *Ib.*, p. 276.
[4] *Ib.*, p. 279. [5] *Ib.*, ii. p. 59.

witness and spectator of human life, and conscious of whatsoever is felt or acted in the universe; so that in the perfectest recess or deepest solitude there must be One still presumed remaining with us, whose presence singly must be of more moment than that of the most august assembly on earth. In such a presence, 'tis evident that as the shame of guilty actions must be the greatest of any, so must the honour be of well-doing, even under the unjust censure of a world.'[1] What Whichcote had said of a devout man was—'This man thinks I must do my duty, 'tis true, but I am not primarily charged with myself; that belongs to God.'[2] Shaftesbury fashions the first cause in the likeness of 'natural affection';[3] and the first utilitarian takes on the work of helping men to be good humanists.

The remainder of this chapter will deal with Whichcote's exposition of Christianity; and the proportion of space which we have devoted to his treatment of natural religion need not encourage the reader to suppose that our author himself has been guilty of minimizing the supreme importance of revelation. His object, as we have been suggesting, has been to prepare the groundwork of a rational apologetic for the Christian faith, for its existence, and for its content. His aim is to find for Christ a place in the nature of things; for, as he sees the problem, if Christianity cannot be justified, the only remaining rational alternative, philosophy, is unable to satisfy the aspirations of men who have sinned against its light. When Adam disobeyed God's positive commandment by eating the fruit of a tree, he asserted 'self-dependence,' and therein denied the first practical principle of natural religion. And revealed religion—which Whichcote preaches chiefly under the heads of the Incarnation, the Atonement, the Resurrection, and the Holy Spirit—discloses the ways and means which God took for our recovery. His interest in doctrine is practical, and one

---

[1] *Ib.*, i. p. 268.   [2] *Works*, iii. p. 239.
[3] *Characteristics*, i. p. 29.

of his great themes is the pardon of God's love, given in reply to man's need for forgiveness.¹

Divine revelation is recorded in Holy Scripture, which is 'God's instrument in the world,' ² 'the only rule of faith,' ³ and 'the full and adequate rule of faith.' ⁴ It contains, rather than is, 'the word of God.' ⁵ It is an authority set alongside the authority of reason; though when we turn to it for illumination, we do not cease to use reason. On the contrary, we are to understand its meaning by means of reason, and to study it with the aid of the best scholarship: though it will disclose its secrets to unlearned piety and conceal them from an arrogant philosopher.⁶

But how are we to justify the authority of Scripture? How can we be certain that it contains the record of God's Self-disclosure in Christ? Whichcote's reply to these questions is in all essentials the same as that given by Hooker; and it is no wonder that Tuckney complains that his old pupil had been reading the works of both Hooker and Chillingworth.⁷ He is fully alive to the need for demonstration that Scripture is authoritative; for, on his own principles, we may not go beyond the findings of natural light, unless natural light itself can justify us in doing so. The only alternative to the authority of reason is the

¹ *Works*, iii. p. 113: 'There is in the gospel only one great matter of faith, which God proposes to us to believe; the grace of God in Christ, pardon of sin in his blood, acceptance through him, going to God by him.'

² *Ib.*, ii. p. 240.   ³ *Ib.*, i. p. 177.   ⁴ *Ib.*, ii. p. 85.

⁵ Cf. *Ib.*, i. p. 35; iii. 50; *Third Letter*, p. 110. The Hon. Robert Boyle holds that 'as well Philosophers as Physicians' who 'seem to favour that which explicates the Phaenomena of Nature by Atoms' are not necessarily 'Naturalists' or 'Atheists,' and defends the authority of Scripture in *Some Considerations Touching the Style Of the H. Scriptures* (1661), where he says that 'all is not Scripture that is in the Scripture' (p. 19).

⁶ *Ib.*, i. p. 177: 'The reformed church doth hold that the scripture is the only rule of faith: and therefore traditions, councils and fathers, and the writings of learned men, are only to be used as helps, better to understand the scripture.'

⁷ *Third Letter*, p. 80.

authority of God; and it is necessary, therefore, to show that His authority is our authority for the authority of Scripture. No doubt the fundamental principle taught in Scripture, namely, that of mediation between God and man, is likely to be true, as some philosophers saw; [1] and no doubt the manner of life which it holds before us for imitation is in keeping with our nature and aspirations: but these considerations in themselves are insufficient to warrant the conclusion that Scripture is entitled to share with reason in the work of ruling our thought and conduct.

In his third reply to Tuckney, Whichcote lays down 'three heads of arguments, whereby to prove the authoritie of scripture,' [2] and in the sermons he has a good deal to say about each of them. The first is the witness which Scripture bears to its own message: *insita argumenta*. He notes under this head, in addition to the two more commonly recognized internal evidences from prophecy and miracle, ten others. Among these the following are worthy of mention: *harmonia singularum partium inter se; continuatio doctrinae successivis temporibus; enarratio invictae fidei, quae ubique in Martyribus triumphans suis;* and *pietas scriptorum, et candor; in agnoscendis infirmitatibus suis, et in dando gloriam Deo*. The second head is the testimony which the Holy Spirit bears to the message of Scripture; and the third, upon which he does not comment, is tradition. In his second letter to Tuckney, he had expressed himself less formally, and in language which shows that he does not treat the problem of the credentials of Scripture in disinterested fashion. Its message is of such a nature that the inquirer cannot view it with absolute detachment. What it has to say is what every serious man wants to be told.

---

[1] *Works*, ii. p. 302: 'Those men that have been the wisest of men among the philosophers, they had a great conceit of this truth, of a mediation between God and man; and thought the pure deity was so high and lofty, so pure and abstract, that we, in our meanness, could not have access (*Platon. Symp.*).'

[2] P. 110.

And to *know* what it says is to have closed with it. 'And I endeavoured to make it appeare,' he writes, 'that the truth declared by God, concerning our relief by Christ, was amiable, gratefull, acceptable to minde and understanding, and such as spake ittselfe from God; as our Saviour spake himselfe to be Christ, to the inward sense of the Samaritans. And to this purpose reason was made use of, as a receiver, as a discerner, as a principle to be instructed and taught; not as an author or inventer or controuler of what God speakes: Divine truth allwaies carrying it's own light and evidence; so as that the mind receiving itt is illuminated, edified, satisfied. . . . I adde allsoe; that the persuasion of the holie spirit contributes to the minde's assurance and satisfaction.'[1]

Let us observe how these heads are dealt with in the sermons. In connection with the first, two passages, in which the unity of natural with revealed truth is stated, may be quoted. 'The great materials of natural light, are first in reason, and then reinforced in scripture. The articles of faith are first in scripture, and being there revealed, are after justified in reason: there is no true reason against them, but there is full satisfaction in them.'[2] 'There is nothing of after-light of God in Christ reconciling, subject to reproof of the former light of God creating.'[3]

In illustration of the second head, reference may be made to two passages: the first suggests that Scripture is a sacrament of the Holy Spirit; and the second secures its internal unity by the authorship of the same Spirit. 'For God sends not his truth into the world alone and unaccompanied, but having done one thing, will also do another to make the former effectual. Now they that have not the divine spirit, want the great interpreter upon the words of God, the great commentator upon divine truth in the world; and therefore their minds are left unsatisfied

[1] *Second Letter*, pp. 47-8. [2] *Works*, i. p. 380. [3] *Ib.*, ii. p. 8.

and unresolved.'[1] The 'inspired' writers of the New Testament quote from the Old, says Whichcote, in order 'to shew the unity of the spirit: the same spirit spake by Moses, and the prophets, and the apostles.'[2]

We cannot leave this head without drawing attention to the restraint which Whichcote lays upon the influence of the Spirit; for although he is well aware that all the Christian graces in human life are the fruit of the Spirit,[3] he must show that the Spirit verifies His presence by making Himself known to reason. For if revealed religion does not conform to the normal requirements of order and proportion, its claim to be the Divine extension of natural religion is made void, and a door is opened for all manner of extravagance. Whichcote's practical test for the identification of a genuine religious experience is that it should be in keeping with the experience of the Spirit as recorded in Scripture. God cannot contradict His written word. 'So that to secure ourselves from dreams, and enthusiasms, let us confine ourselves to the dictates of reason, and letter of scripture; which gives joint assurance and acknowledgment to morals. Now, if any man pretend a revelation from heaven, and do not shew his warrant from holy scripture, which is God's instrument in the world; this we have to say, you come in the name of God, you say you have a revelation from him, but I must then have a revelation too, before I can believe you.'[4] To be unable to justify God's call by Scripture is to make of it 'a partial rule of faith,' 'to make a new religion,'[5] and to assert 'self-sufficiency.'[6] Moreover, we are not entitled to claim that any given passage in Scripture obliges us, unless our own peculiar circumstances are similar to those described in the context: 'commands that are in scripture, are not general; but when

---

[1] *Ib.*, iii. p. 55.   [2] *Ib.*, p. 113.
[3] *Cf. Third Letter*, p. 108: 'I oppose not rational to spiritual; for spiritual is most rational.'
[4] *Works*, ii. p. 240.   [5] *Ib.*, p. 86.   [6] *Ib.*, i. p. 209.

they are given upon a common reason, and such as will hold in all times, and circumstances of life.'[1]

With regard to the third argument for the authority of Scripture, namely, tradition, it is important, in view of Westcott's verdict that Whichcote 'had an imperfect conception of the corporate character of the Church, and of the Divine life of the Christian Society,'[2] to note the following passage: 'So that when I read the 17th verse,[3] I wonder that any one that lives within the pale of the visible church, and takes the bible into his hand, and once looks upon this text; that he is not, not only almost, but altogether persuaded to become a christian.'[4] But the explanation of Whichcote's reticence is to be found probably in his dread that any man should pay formal deference to the authority of the Church and remain unvitalized by its Gospel.[5] He holds that a thing is not accepted as true, until it has been seen with its own light; that there is no knowledge, unless there is 'concomitant affection.'[6]

Among the rules given for right interpretation of Scripture, there is one which involves important consequences for Church polity. We are, says Whichcote, to look to the sense rather than to the words of Scripture;[7] and we are to compare passages, instead of building doctrine upon

[1] *Ib.*, ii. p. 146.
[2] *Essays in the History of Religious Thought in the West*, p. 393.
[3] *Rom.* i.
[4] *Works*, iii. p. 131. *Cf.* Hooker, *Ecclesiastical Polity*, III. vii. 14: 'And by experience we all know, that the first outward motive leading men so to esteem of the Scripture is the authority of God's Church. For when we know the whole Church of God hath that opinion of the Scripture, we judge it even at the first an impudent thing for any man bred and brought up in the Church to be of a contrary mind without cause. Afterwards the more we bestow our labour in reading or hearing the mysteries thereof, the more we find the thing itself doth answer our received opinion concerning it.'
[5] *Cf.* i. p. 180: 'But an implicit faith in men, or in the church, this is popery.'
[6] *Ib.*, iv. p. 287.
[7] *Cf.* St. Augustine, *De Catechizandis Rudibus*, ix. 13: 'esse prae ponendas verbis sententias.'

isolated proof-texts. He confronts himself with a difficulty: passages quoted in the New Testament from the Old are sometimes given a new meaning. St. Matthew, for example, applies the text '*When Israel was a child, then I loved him, and called my son out of Egypt,*'[1] to an event in the life of the Holy Child; but, in doing so, is dealing with Scripture quite legitimately, since what is true of the type must be true also of its anti-type: and 'most of the things in the old testament were types of Christ, or something belonging to him.'[2] And when St. Paul extends the meaning of the words '*the just shall live by faith,*'[3] his action also is to be approved; because his doctrine of justification by faith is consistent with the sense of the original. So we note the 'great liberty and latitude holy men have taken, when they have applied the old testament to the new.'[4] And as it is in the Bible, so it ought to be in the Church. Only those points of doctrine which are necessary for salvation—and they are both few in number and clear of apprehension—may be made obligatory: all else is instrumental, and diversity of opinion in unessentials is of less moment than a tolerant disposition born of Christian charity.

Whichcote gives his account of the mind of 'the reformed church,' that is to say, the Church of England, in four particulars.[5] (1) It is rational religion (*Rom.* xii. 1), observing all Divine requirements known to natural light. (2) It adds to these, by warrant of Scripture, three things: 'we go to God by the mediation of Christ; we receive bread and wine in memory of Christ's death and passion; and we use water in baptism, to acknowledge Father, Son, and Holy Ghost.' (3) It obliges to godliness, righteousness and sobriety. (4) It treats every matter of belief and practice not covered by the foregoing as 'circumstantial.' 'God

---

[1] *Hos.* xi. 1.   [2] *Works*, iii. p. 116.
[3] *Hab.* ii. 4; *Rom.* i. 17; *Gal.* iii. 11.
[4] *Works*, iii. p. 116.   [5] *Ib.*, ii. pp. 324-5.

hath not secured the christian church that it shall ever have the protection of government, and among christians at liberty, there was, in matters of indifferent nature, a very great latitude.'

There is little to record on the distinctive notes in (2). Our author is perhaps a little too anxious to state a completely intelligible doctrine of Atonement. His view combines Anselmic and Abelardian elements: Jesus Christ in His death on the Cross offered the sacrifice [1] and satisfaction [2] of perfect obedience, paid the whole debt [3] and made restitution [4] for man's sin, and secured God's honour; [5] and accordingly man is 'moved to repentance, to disclaim whatsoever he hath done amiss, to look upon sin as an ugly and an abominable thing.' [6] There is no thought of an implacable God who waits to be appeased; for the Father is 'the first mover towards our recovery.' [7] 'Our recovery began at God himself: our Saviour was not the first moving cause; but, rather, a promoting cause.' [8]

The ninety-seven sermons contain no exposition of sacramental doctrine, and the preacher's infrequent references to the sacraments, as in the passage quoted above, are incidental to his treatment of other themes. In one passage he brackets 'the sacramental elements' along with 'the ministerial office' and the Lord's Day, as instruments of religion, 'holy because of their ends,' 'set apart for purposes supernatural,' and 'not for common use.' [9] The institution of the Lord's Supper, he says, was simple in the extreme: the Saviour, when participating in the Passover, 'puts a new notion upon one of the cups, and one of the breads.' [10] But all questions as to preparation, frequency, posture, and the like, have been left for determination by sober judgment informed by charity.

[1] *Ib.*, p. 79. [2] *Ib.*, p. 78. [3] *Ib.*, p. 266.
[4] *Ib.*, p. 266. [5] *Ib.*, p. 268. [6] *Ib.*, p. 265.
[7] *Ib.*, p. 96. [8] *Ib.*, iv. p. 161. [9] *Ib.*, iv. p. 68.
[10] *Ib.*, p. 180.

The fact is that Whichcote's faith in the Christian temper is as deep as his faith in reason; and he believes that when the two are combined, peace will come to the Church. Where differences prevail, the first thing to be done is to secure agreement upon essentials: and these have been taught clearly in Scripture. Then it must be recognized that the only unessentials worth discussing are those which can be employed to further the end for which the essentials stand. And if agreement cannot be arrived at concerning them, the only course is to agree that there are many ways of achieving the same end.[1] This procedure is truly Scriptural.

One further matter remains for discussion. Up to this point we have set Whichcote's views against a background of Scripture; and we have tried to show that he interprets his experience of God and man in the light of its teaching. But by common consent he is described as a Christian Platonist, and the father of Cambridge Platonism; and we must inquire into the question of his debt to Platonism.

We begin by repeating once more that Whichcote venerates reason, because he finds it venerated in Scripture: the book of *Proverbs* extols it, and Jesus Christ appeals to it. He argues that if nature's best faculty cannot be trusted, revelation will have nothing to graft on, and its case will go by default. He justifies this claim for natural light, not by referring to the Prologue of the Fourth Gospel, as a Platonically-minded theologian might be expected to do, but by adducing passages from the first stages of St. Paul's argument in *Romans*. Here is to be found the *locus classicus* of natural religion. It declares that God speaks to man's conscience, and makes him to perceive His invisible things through the things that are made; and that all who live

---

[1] *Cf.* ii. 35: 'Archbishop Laud says, the church of England is not such a shrew to her children, as to deny her blessing, or to denounce anathema against them, if some peaceably dissent in some particulars remoter from the foundation.'

contrary to reason and against nature are without excuse. Of certain verses in chapters i. and ii., Whichcote says that they 'have forced upon me all those notions I do entertain, or have publiquely delivered; concerning natural light, or the use of reason.'[1] And the sum and substance of what reason has delivered throughout the ages has been comprised in a well-attested tradition: for in 'the great matters of natural knowledge' it is just as incredible that men should have persistently mistaken lies for truth, as it is that a religion, 'being above sixteen hundred years old,'[2] should be false. The assured conclusions of reason and the *philosophia perennis* are one and the same thing.

Whichcote is free, therefore, to borrow from Platonism, and also to discount the theory that the Greeks borrowed from the Christians; and he thinks that the fidelity of philosophers to the light that is in them often puts Christians to shame.[3] But he borrows on principle, and his work shows no trace whatever of being a synthesis of Scriptural ideas with philosophical, such as we find in Clement's *Stromateis*; and, as Dr. Powicke says, when the Cambridge men quote the Platonists, it is 'generally by way of illustration on some aspect of the religious life, or some principle of moral conduct.'[4]

But Whichcote is free to borrow from Aristotle also, to whom he refers explicitly in the sermons about eighteen times, sometimes by name, and sometimes in traditional fashion as 'the philosopher,' or 'the great philosopher,'[5] the exact reference often being given. The newly aroused interest in Plato did not lead him to repudiate the master of his early training; and in spite of his dislike for petrified systems of thought, whether Scholastic or Calvinist, he will not hesitate to draw upon the life that is in them. Aristotle,

---

[1] *First Letter*, p. 9. [2] *Works*, iii. pp. 34-5. [3] *Works*, ii. p. 173.
[4] *The Cambridge Platonists*, p. 21.
[5] *Works*, i. p. 334. *Cf.* ii. p. 36: 'In matters of philosophy there are different opinions: Aristotelians, and Platonists.'

he says, is 'credible in matters of nature and reason.'[1] He is claimed as authority for many points in the moral life, such as the following: a good man stands 'four-square,'[2] behaving consistently in all situations; deliberates only on things within his power;[3] delights in doing right;[4] overlooks an injury;[5] and seasons justice with equity.[6] And moreover, Aristotle teaches that every thing has a nature of its own and tends to fulfil its own end,[7] that a man will realize his nature within the sphere of the body politic by translating into action the truths he has learned in contemplation,[8] and that his worth ought to be estimated not so much by his peculiar talent, as by the use that he has made of it.[9] Finally, and most important of all, Aristotle established a proof for the existence of the first cause: 'he saith "that the heavens could not move, because they are inanimate beings, if they were not assisted by a superior and intelligent agent."'[10]

But if there are fewer references to Plato and 'the noble Platonists' than there are to Aristotle, there is a great deal more of their spirit in evidence; and the epithet 'eagle-eyed,'[11] which Whichcote applies to them, might well be applied to himself. Like Plato, he saw; and if he saw more than Plato saw, it is not that his vision is clearer, but that God in Christ enabled him to entertain an ampler view. What he saw he has tried to make others see, not by the method of argument, but by clarity of statement. Reason, in his hands, is not a tool which reaches conclusions, but one that discloses truth by clearing away from it erroneous growths. In making his positive assertions about God and the good, he hopes that his hearers will be stimulated, first, to meditate upon their significance, and, then, to put them into practice. Plato challenges his readers to exercise their

---

[1] *Ib.*, i. p. 168.　　[2] *Ib.*, ii. p. 141.　　[3] *Ib.*, i. p. 334.
[4] *Ib.*, iv. p. 288.　　[5] *Ib.*, p. 218.　　　[6] *Ib.*, p. 18.
[7] *Ib.*, iii. p. 246.　　[8] *Ib.*, i. p. 168; ii. p. 4.　[9] *Ib.*, i. p. 314.
[10] *Ib.*, iii. p. 187.　　[11] *Ib.*, ii. p. 172.

powers of thinking by putting them to school under Socrates and the dialogue; Whichcote arrests his hearers by his aphorisms. Great thoughts were great things to him, and he expresses them with directness as they come to him. He would have said, doubtless, that full and complete truth exceeds the span of our minds, but that its several portions, as we discuss and apply them, become easily articulated, each one with another; and that though we cannot entertain all truths codified in a thoroughgoing system, we are not hereby hindered from living the several truths we know. And if we should give way to imagining that we have reached the point of being able to define with exactness the truths which he delivered, this will be a warning to us that we have been absurdly trying to treat a living thing as though it were dead.

II
BENJAMIN WHICHCOTE AND JEREMY TAYLOR

I made a visit to Dr. Jeremy Taylor, to confer with him about some spiritual matters, using him thenceforward as my ghostly father. I beseech God Almighty to make me ever mindful of, and thankful for, His heavenly assistances!

JOHN EVELYN.

CHAPTER II

BENJAMIN WHICHCOTE AND JEREMY TAYLOR [1]

DISCUSSION about values and the meaning of value in general assumes that man is a dependent creature; for however sturdily the inquirer lays stress upon his own power to create values, it seems to be a fact that, apart from the existence of some conditioning environment, he cannot experience values at all. The poetic voice that stirs within him cannot sing, unless nature's, or some other's, self sets at least the theme. The two thinkers with whom this chapter will deal, while emphasizing the necessity of that give and take which obtains between a man and all that he is not, see, in their theory of value, that the ultimate *datum* in all values is God. And they both assure us that, although we must perforce start with ourselves when we would make an attempt to give meaning to our lives, we are compelled by the exigencies of our nature to go outside ourselves and to make a fresh beginning from God. 'To begin the history of a man's reason and the philosophy of his nature, it is not necessary for us to place him there where without the consideration of a God or society or law or order he is to be placed, that is, in the state of a thing rather than a person,' [2] says Jeremy Taylor; and Whichcote's echo is—'He that will make his reckoning of himself, and leave out God, he must reckon again.' [3] About this

[1] 1613–67.
[2] *Works*, Eden's edition, vol. ii. p. 8.
[3] *Works*, Aberdeen, 1751, vol. i. p. 282. *Cf.* Stillingfleet, *Irenicum*, I. ii. p. 2: 'A state of Nature I look upon only as an imaginary state, for better understanding the nature and obligation of Laws. For it is

method of procedure there is nothing new, and it belonged to the spirit of the times, for Hobbes passed from the supposedly original Right of Nature to the Law of Nature, known to right reason, enforced by his social deity, the Great Leviathan, and ultimately promulgated by the Governor of all; and Descartes, having set out from the *datum* of his own self-consciousness, moved outwards to God and His goodness, in order to dispel his doubt.

Taylor is not a speculative thinker, but essentially a practical man, bent upon living the good life: his interest is to unravel from life's tangled skein the great truths which enable a man to find happiness. And the impression left upon the mind of a reader who has perused his thousands of pages, in which tedious commonplaces are often relieved by penetrating epigrams and pertinent illustrations, is that he is one of those 'once-born' souls to whom it comes easily to clothe facts in spiritual principle. So convinced is he that experience bears its own justification or condemnation, as the case may be, on its very face, that he ransacks all literature, the Bible included, in order to show that wise men have found the true way of life to be as he finds it. He believes that God, present in His goodness, is an ultimate *datum*, and the condition of all our experience of goodness. 'That God is present in all places, that He sees every action, hears all discourses, and understands every thought, is no strange thing to a christian ear, who hath been taught this doctrine, not only by right reason, and the consent of all the wise men in the world, but also by God himself in holy scripture.'[1] But if Scripture takes chief place among the written records of religious experience, since it tells, at the prompting of the Holy Spirit, of the mightiest acts of God that men have known, its message

confessed by the greatest Assertors of it, that the relation of Parents and Children cannot be conceived in a state of natural liberty, because Children as soon as born are actually under the power and authority of their Parents.'

[1] Taylor's *Works*, iii. p. 22.

can be grasped only by a mind made discerning by the light of the same Spirit. 'For although the scriptures themselves are written by the Spirit of God, yet they are written within and without: and besides the light that shines upon the face of them, unless there be a light shining within our hearts, unfolding the leaves, and interpreting the mysterious sense of the Spirit, convincing our consciences and preaching to our hearts; to look for Christ in the leaves of the gospel, is to look for the living amongst the dead.'[1] It is in the conscience that God is pre-eminently present to man, and if He be not known within, He will not be known without in 'the glass of creation':[2] for God's presence is an immediacy made concrete in all experience of the good. 'That the sun is to rule the day, the moon and the stars to govern the night, I see and feel: that God is good, that He is one, are prime principles.'[3] Apart from the idea of the good, moral experience would not be possible; the moral law is in man's heart 'antecedently to all our actions,'[4] and bears witness to Him from whom it derives. When a man acts, he makes an attempt to realize some good which, though it is not yet his, is already and originally God's. And that this good that he seeks, and in the light of which he assesses the value of his life, is not of his own devising, but of God's gift, is to Taylor a self-evident truth.

Whichcote's more philosophical, though not less practical, mind sees in man's inherent sense of value a witness to his divine origin and destiny: for man's search is for something beyond what mere nature can give him, and he finds 'a difference of things.' Reason, Whichcote urges, is not a faculty fit merely to deal with mental counters corresponding to extra-mental objects in which it has no share; reason is the whole of a man affirmed and found in what he knows. His prerogative is to enter into communion with the known; and should he be content to remain aloof from

[1] *Ib.*, viii. p. 379. [2] *Ib.*, iii. p. 26.
[3] *Ib.*, ix. p. 60.   [4] *Ib.*, ix. p. 142.

what he tries to know, a logical subject confronted by an external thing, he knows only *about* it. True knowledge involves the action of the entire man: thinking, supposedly isolated from willing and feeling, can do no more than syllogize about abstractions. 'I say, if so be a man doth not admit what he receives, with satisfaction to the reason of his mind; he doth not receive it as an intelligent agent, but he receives it as a vessel receives water; he is *continens* rather than *recipiens*.'[1] But 'let understanding go before and affections follow after,'[2] and then the whole man is enriched by what he has grasped, and knowledge has her perfect work. And since it is only in spiritual realities that the whole man can dwell with complete satisfaction, Whichcote holds that God and His goodness comprise together the sum-total of what man can be said really to know. 'For the use of judgment is to observe the difference of things, which he doth not, that knows not how to value spiritual and eternal things before those that are present and temporal';[3] and 'mind and spirit are of so pure a complexion, that they cannot mingle, save only with unbodied and immaterial things.'[4]

Whichcote advances some proofs for the existence of God, and like Descartes he sees that they presuppose an innate idea of the Being whose existence they are designed to establish: but the proofs are intended not so much to lead to a God hitherto unknown, as to show His primacy of place in experience; and it is understood that no experience has been understood until it has been given religious setting. Having exhorted his hearers to reverence God, he adds that the obligation to do so 'is founded upon this innate sense that we have of God, or the possibility there is to come to know there is a God, by our own being, and the being of the residue of our fellow-creatures.' Our case stands thus: we cannot experience value, unless we have

[1] Whichcote's *Works*, iv. p. 142.
[2] *Ib.*, ii. p. 360.
[3] *Ib.*, i. p. 197.
[4] *Ib.*, iv. p. 313.

a scale of values, and when we name 'the first and chiefest good,'[1] we have named God.

The theme of the following proof is that man's insufficiency is sufficient to convince him intellectually and convict him morally of the existence of the self-sufficient God. 'For thus, a man feels that he is; and he doth prove that by his acting: I act, therefore I am; I do, therefore I have being: and if I am, either I made myself, or was made by another. I did not make myself: for if I had made myself at my own will, I could continue myself in being during my own pleasure; and this I know I cannot: and this is great reason, because it is an exercise of less power, to continue a thing in being which hath being, than to call a thing out of nothing, into being: therefore I made not myself but was made by another. And then that other must neither be my equal, nor inferior; for I can do as much as my equal, more than my inferior; therefore I was made by a greater than myself, a greater both in wisdom and power: and this first independent being I call God. Thus is a man an argument to himself, of the existence of a Deity. This is the first point of all religion, and that that is fundamental to conscience; which if it be acknowledged, all other things will follow. Here we do begin; and at the day of judgment, God will make this out against his creation, that he made every intelligent and voluntary creature capable of knowing that he is.'[2]

This limited power of acting which a man identifies with himself is teleological in character; for he acts not for the sake of acting merely, but with a view to preserving his being. Everything in nature fulfils its own nature: 'all things must work according to their natural principles (nor can they do otherwise), as heavy bodies must tend downwards';[3] but human nature knows a moral *ought* as well as a natural *must*. Self-preservation, where there is a self to preserve, comes to mean the conservation of value; and

[1] *Ib.*, iii. pp. 234-5.   [2] *Ib.*, iii. pp. 241-2.   [3] *Ib.*, p. 328.

the end for which a man works is happiness. 'The most universal principle belonging to all kind of things, is self-preservation; which, in man, being a rational agent, is somewhat farther advanced to strong propensions and desires of the soul after a state of happiness, which hath the predominancy over all other inclinations; as being the supreme and ultimate end to which all his designs and actions must be subservient by a natural necessity.'[1] But what is this happiness which man is driven from within to seek? It is not something to be interpreted as the whim of the moment may suggest: it consists in the fruition of having directed one's life towards God. Too often a man proposes for his end something other than God disposes, and his reason employs itself in discovering means towards such ends as culture and comfort; but this is to prostitute reason to uses incompatible with its power of insight into the best, which is his birthright. 'Because all these accomplishments are inadequate and not proportionable to our capacities. For intellectual nature is capable of being more highly raised and of nobler endowments, of higher perfections. Intellectual nature hath a secret desire and thirst after God; and therefore it cannot be accomplished, neither can it be satisfied, unless it find out and pitch upon that object which is most proper and peculiar. If any man will grant me that one principle, which is certain and we know it by experience, I shall sufficiently secure religion by it; for *intellectus quaerit Deum*, it is the nature of our mind and understanding to seek after God; therefore though a man be never so well accomplished, if he be devoid of sense and apprehension of God, he must be unfurnished; for he is unsatisfied, he hath not enough to satisfy the connatural desires of his immortal soul.'[2]

The initial proposition, 'I act,' yields the inference that God is my efficient cause, and, once teleological import reveals itself, the further inference that God is my final

[1] *Ib.*, p. 329.   [2] *Ib.*, iv. p. 286.

cause: and in passing from the first to the second an imperative emerges—'That God that is original to me, I ought to make him final to me; and if I receive all from God, I ought to refer to him, and rest in him.'[1]

'It was never God's intention when he made man at first, to put him into a state of absolute independency, or self-sufficiency.'[2] Man stands to God, not in the relation of an effect launched out upon its own independent career by a remote cause, but in the relation of a derivative being who enjoys some knowledge of the character of his divine source: his own act of self-recognition is a reflection, as it were in a mirror, of an Other Self, who is and has and gives all the good that he would fain see in himself. All created things are dependent; but when a created self reflects upon himself, he becomes aware of what he is and of what he needs, and it is in terms of these that he names his Creator. Whichcote's thinking is paralleled by Descartes's, when, towards the conclusion of his Third Meditation, he finds a movement within himself which directs him to God. 'When I make myself the object of reflection,' he writes, 'I not only find that I am an incomplete (imperfect) and dependent being, and one who unceasingly aspires after something better and greater than he is; but, at the same time, I am assured likewise that he upon whom I am dependent possesses in himself all the good after which I aspire (and the ideas of which I find in my mind), and that

---

[1] *Ib.*, iii. p. 374. *Cf.* Hooker, *Ecc. Pol.*, I. xi. 1: 'But we must come at length to some pause. For, if every thing were to be desired for some other without any stint, there could be no certain end proposed unto our actions, we should go on we know not whither; yea, whatsoever we do were in vain, or rather nothing at all were possible to be done. For as to take away the first efficient of our being were to annihilate utterly our persons, so we cannot remove the last final cause of our working, but we shall cause whatsoever we work to cease. Therefore something there must be desired for itself and for no other. That is simply for itself desirable, unto the nature whereof it is opposite and repugnant to be desired with relation to any other.'

[2] *Ib.*, i. p. 218.

not merely indefinitely and potentially, but infinitely and naturally, and that he is thus God.'

Now if man looks backwards to his origin and forwards to his destiny, and discovers God at either end of his pilgrimage, he will inquire about His guidance along the way; and both our authors teach that any good thing understood and enjoyed is of God's gift. When we think of God as our goal, we do not give up thinking of Him as our guide; and at all times He shows Himself immanent in our enjoyment of life.

It is a favourite thought with Taylor that God awakens in man a recognition of His presence, a recognition which is also a response to His own invitation, by appealing to his interest in whatever he happens to find useful to him, as well as in whatever he finds valuable in its own right as an end. In *Holy Living* he says—'there can but two things create love, perfection and usefulness; to which answer on our part, first, admiration, and secondly, desire; and both these are centred in love';[1] and again, in the preface to *The Great Exemplar*—'it was natural to Adam to love God, who was his father, his creator, the fountain of all good to him, and of excellency in Himself; and whatsoever is understood to be such, it is as natural for us to love, and we do it for the same reasons, for which we love any thing else; and we cannot love for any other reason but for one or both these in their proportion apprehended.'[2] And in the *Ductor Dubitantium* we are warned against responding to God's appeal by way of an attitude of detached admiration which stops short of adopting God's good for our very own spiritual principle. 'For there can be but two causes of amability in the world, perfection and usefulness, that is, beauty and profit; that in the thing itself, this as it relates to me. Now he that says a man may love virtue for its own sake without consideration of the reward, says no more than that a man may love a flower which he never hopes

[1] Taylor's *Works*, iii. p. 156.   [2] *Ib.*, ii. p. 7.

to smell of; that is, he may admire and commend it, and love to look on it; and just so he may do to virtue. But if he desires either, it is because it is profitable or useful to him, and hath something that will delight him; it cannot else possibly be desired. Now to love virtue in the first sense is rather praise than love; an act of understanding rather than of the will; and its object is properly the perfections of the flower or the virtue respectively: but when it comes to be desired, that is, loved with a relation to myself, it hath for its object other perfections, those things that please and delight me; and that is nothing but part of the reward, or all of it.' [1]

There is a vast difference between acknowledging that God is worthy to be loved and actually loving Him: the first is an assertion by the logical faculty that a certain proposition is true, and the second is an expression by the whole self of active interest in God. Contrariwise, apart from rational insight into God's perfection, desire of itself moves blindly as the impulse of the passing moment directs. It is not possible to bear witness to the reality of value without admitting it into one's life; and experience cannot simultaneously hold itself aloof from what it embraces.

We find that Whichcote draws a like distinction between God's intrinsic goodness and the goodness which He bestows upon man; but he sees more clearly that the first of these is the ground of the second, and that, when meditated upon, it is more potent to arouse a definitely religious response. His second sermon on the text, '*For our conversation is in heaven ; from whence also we look for the Saviour, the Lord Jesus Christ,*' begins as follows: 'First, what he is in himself, his excellency, majesty, and greatness; he is a being of all perfection. Secondly, what he is to us; by whom, for whom, and to whom are all things. As we are to make acknowledgments and confession, that all that we are or have to expect, or look for; all is of free

[1] *Ib.*, ix. p. 316.

grace and mercy. As for the former, if we employ mind and understanding, to search after God, our noble and highest faculties to take cognisance of God, this will employ our thoughts to the utmost, because of the excellency, and transcendency of the object; here is work enough for eternity, to make search and enquiry after God. . . . And then to employ ourselves about the latter, to think what God is to us, how he stands in all relation to us; original to our being, father to our spirits, a center of our souls, our utmost end; this will engage our affections, and so make our religion pleasurable and delightful to us; and so no motion towards God or application to him, will either be tedious, or burdensome. . . . Now this is the way to put the soul of man into an holy exstasy and rapture; the soul exercised in divine contemplations, inflamed with heavenly affections transported beyond the lower world, caught up for a while beyond the third heaven, sees and feels far beyond all language. This is the reason why we drudge in the world, and make ourselves slaves to the things here below, because of our alienation and estrangedness from God: but if we did but convert our mind and understanding to God, and did enquire what he is in himself, and what he is to us, we should be swallowed up into heavenly exercise, experience and acquaintance with things that are excellent and transcendent, keep us from doating upon, and admiring things that are ordinary, and transient.'[1] Elsewhere the same warning against cupboard love is repeated: we have not really loved God, until we have gone out from ourselves and found behind His gifts the Giver Himself. 'It is greatly to the shame of human nature, that we seem rather to love God, for what he is to us, than for what he is in himself. We love him, because he may be good to us; rather than because he is the most lovely object in himself, the first and chiefest goodness: rather as he is necessary to our happiness; than because of his own loveliness,

[1] Whichcote's *Works*, ii. pp. 186-8.

excellency, and beauty. Therefore we consider ourselves even there, where we mind God. . . . We should be wholly taken with God, possess't and transported with him: the contemplation and thought of his excellency, goodness, and perfection, should so fill our souls, that foreign things should be driven away, and be as it were nothing, in this order and competition.'[1]

It turns out, then, that there are two senses in which God is the author of the values we enjoy: for, in the first place, He created them, although we may not always see that what we enjoy is from the first giver; and, in the second place, He has made us fit to enjoy what He gives. God made, as it were, the beauty and the eye of the mind that sees the beauty. Our thirst for value, as we have noted, is due to our Creator even more than to the value which satisfies it: and God's hand lies hidden only to be discovered in our receiving as well as in His giving. So when on our side there is lacking insight into what we are and what we are for, evil may be mistaken for good, bitter for sweet; and we shall be misfits in God's scheme of things.

The following is one statement of Taylor's theory of value, which may be styled one of correspondence by dependence: 'For since God gave (man) proper and peculiar appetites with proportion to their own objects, and gave him reason and abilities not only to perceive the sapidness and relish of those objects, but also to make reflex acts upon such perceptions and to perceive that he did perceive, which was a rare instrument of pleasure and pain respectively: it is but reasonable to think that God, who created him in mercy, did not only proportion a being to his nature, but did also provide satisfaction for all those appetites and desires which Himself had created and put into him. . . . Therefore that this intendment of God and nature be effected, that is, that man should become happy, it is naturally necessary that all his regular appetites should have an object

[1] *Ib.*, iii. pp. 327-8.

appointed them, in the fruition of which felicity must consist: because nothing is felicity but when what was reasonably or orderly desired is possessed; for the having what is not desired, or the wanting of what we desired, or the desiring what we should not, are the several constituent parts of infelicity; and it can have no other constitution.'[1] The full force of this passage will be understood by supplementing it by another taken from a sermon entitled *The Foolish Exchange*, in which Taylor explains that a lost soul suffers greater ill than deprivation of a spiritual environment. Such a soul becomes invested with 'contrary objects, and cross effects, and dolorous perceptions: for the will, if it misses its desires, is afflicted; and the understanding, when it ceases to be ennobled with excellent things, is made ignorant as a swine, dull as the foot of a rock; and the affections are in the destitution of their perfective actions made tumultuous, vexed and discomposed to the height of rage and violence.'[2]

Whichcote, who lays stress upon man's ability to see and approve what is good, says likewise: 'The eye could never behold the sun, if it were not like it. The mind of man could never contemplate God, if it be not God-like; for (as in nature) there must be a suitable disposition of the faculty to the object. . . . As to instance; the understanding takes cognisance of things as they are intelligible, the will moves towards things as they are desirable; the sight looks after things as they are visible; the hearing receives what is audible: every faculty hath a tendency to its object, under that precise formal notion whereby it appropriates that object to that faculty. . . . Therefore we are said to be partakers of the divine nature; otherwise we shall not relish heavenly things.'[3]

---

[1] Taylor's *Works*, ii. pp. 6-7.   [2] *Ib.*, iv. p. 562.
[3] Whichcote's *Works*, ii. p. 189. *Cf.* J. Smith, *Select Discourses* (Edition, 1859), p. 425: 'True delight and joy is begotten by the conjunction of some discerning faculty with its proper object.'

But man knows that his response to God's appeal is not of the same kind as a physical, or even a psychological, reaction to an external stimulus. So Whichcote explains that 'in intellectual nature, the way of motion is to propose, declare and shew, to excite by reason and argument, to warn, to admonish, to foretell, to convince, to promise, to threaten, to reward, to punish, to enlighten the understanding, to move the will, to affect the conscience, and the like. . . . Every creature according to its nature, is affected, moved, and suffers under God. Now intellectual nature is moved in this way, in a way of illumination, persuasion, mental conviction and satisfaction; for this you must know and understand, that intellectual nature, remaining such, cannot be divested of intelligence and freedom; for those are its necessary and essential perfections, and a man ceaseth to be a man, if divested of these, and turned out of intellectual nature; he ceaseth to be a man.'[1] The difference between a thing's reaction to stimulus and human nature's response to God is set out in this way: 'God doth order nature so, that things in this lower world have sundry virtues lying hid, and do not appear till things meet with their mates, and then there is a motion by consent. The soul of man otherwise is not matched, and, therefore is not at all excited nor sufficiently drawn forth, save in conjunction with God; but then it doth soon display its liveliness and sprightfulness. . . . This argument the mind of man hath of its divinity, its divine original, that it is remarkably from God himself, that the things of God delight it, and take with it; and spiritual things it converses withal, not as things that are foreign and strange, but as things that are natural to it. . . . And all true delight and joy is begotten by a conjunction of some discerning faculty with its proper object. . . . Now mind and spirit are of so pure a complexion, that they cannot mingle, save only with unbodied and immaterial things; . . . These two things are

[1] *Ib.*, i. pp. 336-7.

of certain resolution: nothing that is apprehensive of God, or capable of God, can enjoy him in any state, without ineffable sense of pleasure: nothing that is apprehensive of God, or capable of God, can be without him or lose him, without inward bitterness, discontent and dissatisfaction.'[1]

That man is not free who has not distinguished good from evil, welcomed good as his own, and determined to live for it. To be free is to be unwilling to choose anything but good. On this point our authors are in all but verbal agreement. 'It is not power,' says Whichcote, 'to be able to do that which ought not to be done; for ungoverned appetite is not power but weakness. It is not power to do evil, but impotency, weakness and deformity. Free-will, which we so much contend for, and brag so much of, it is no absolute perfection, and we need not be so proud of it. For free-will, as it includes a power to do wrong, as well as right, is not to be found in God himself; and therefore it is no perfection in us.'[2] 'Our very will,' says Taylor, 'in which mankind pretends to be most noble and imperial, is a direct state of imperfection; and our very liberty of choosing good and evil is permitted us, not to make us proud, but to make us humble; for it supposes weakness of reason and weakness of love. For if we understood all the degrees of amability in the service of God, or if we had such love of God as He deserves, and so perfect a conviction as were fit for His services, we could no more deliberate: for liberty of will is like the motion of a magnetic needle toward the north, full of trembling and uncertainty till it were fixed in the beloved point; it wavers as long as it is free, and is at rest when it can choose no more.'[3]

When value is interpreted within the frame-work of this divine scheme, it serves to denote the point of meeting between God and man; and, remembering that man is a spiritual being, value marks, on the one side, God's penetra-

---

[1] *Ib.*, iv. pp. 312-4.   [2] *Ib.*, i. p. 251.
[3] Taylor's *Works*, viii. p. 395.

tion of man and, on the other side, man's self-disposal to God. The tone of man's life becomes spiritual, when his interest has moved from himself to something in which he sees that God delights. Communion with Him comes with man's concentration upon something which is known to derive from His eternally creative act. The question is not, What can man make? but, What can man take? And the answer involves abandoning self-reliance for self-dedication, the result being that man's life becomes a channel for receiving God's best gifts. So Whichcote speaks of man as an 'instrumental' cause. 'God,' he says, 'always did intend, that his creatures should depend upon him, and hold of him: for man was made but in the place and order of a second cause, and a second cause is no cause divided from the first.'[1] Unfortunately, seeing that men behave as they do, we are minded to compare their fickleness with nature's constancy; but men might be consistently good if they would only express what is principal to human nature, namely, God and His goodness. Freedom of will means submitting oneself to God, the original and final Cause; and if it were not so, intelligence and will could never enter upon their inheritance. 'For if God do make a creature that is voluntary and intelligent; we must leave him to the direction of his faculties, otherwise he should controul his own workmanship.'[2] In this way Whichcote would resolve the antinomy between man's freedom and God's grace; he draws attention to the living relation in which man is bound to God; and he explains that although man is an effect in God's hand, he has not been created to act passively in obedience to a law-giver's demands, but in answer to a Father's love. Theologians would have been saved a deal of trouble, had it been seen that grace is not the antithesis to free-will, but the sphere in which free-will is developed and exercised. The initial 'I act' points me to One who made me and receives me; and my will

[1] Whichcote's *Works*, i. p. 218.   [2] *Ib.*, p. 252.

achieves its commensurate end by sharing in a spiritual whole. Whichcote affirms that our moral 'virtues' are God's 'graces,'[1] an identification in which Taylor concurs.[2]

Once man accepts God's will, as he sees it, for his end, and embodies it in his life, he enjoys the freedom for which he was made; and all the conative tendencies which saturate his nature find due fulfilment. For human nature is appetitive throughout, and not only in its instinctive complement. It is, indeed, because man is rational, that he thirsts for God. Taylor says that 'the first appetite man had in order to his great end was, to be as perfect as he could, that is, to be as like the best thing he knew as his nature and condition would permit,' in fact, 'to be like God.'[3] And this appetite includes insight into the character of the good to which it aspires. In keeping with this, in his exhaustive treatment of conscience, Taylor impresses upon us that he is dealing with the entire 'mind of man' and, surpassing St. Augustine who discovered so many psychological adumbrations of the Holy Trinity, he notes that conscience is an image of God, because it includes understanding which is the home of its principles, memory which is the place of its approval or disapproval, and will which is the cause of its actions.[4] God is known when He is loved, and loved when He is known; and the knowing and the loving are one. But it is after God has made the advances that man's discernment is evoked; for unless goodness were proffered, it could not be discerned. 'For as the sun sends forth a benign and gentle influence on the seed of plants, that it may invite forth the active and plastic power from its recess and secrecy, that by rising into the tallness and dimensions of a tree it may still receive a greater

---

[1] *Ib.*, iv. p. 122. *Cf.* St. Bernard, *De Gratia et Libero Arbitrio*, vi.: 'Nor, indeed, is the case otherwise than that grace ordereth aright what creation hath bestowed, so that the virtues are none else than the affections rightly ordered ' (Trans. by W. W. Williams).
[2] Taylor's *Works*, vii. p. 148.   [3] *Ib.*, ii. p. 7.
[4] *Ib.*, ix. p. 3 ff.

and more refreshing influence from its foster-father, the prince of all the bodies of light; and in all these emanations the sun itself receives no advantage but the honour of doing benefits: so doth the almighty Father of all the creatures; He at first sends forth His blessings upon us, that we by using them aright should make ourselves capable of greater. . . .'[1]

How far, we inquire, can man's understanding reach, and where are the limits to his understanding set? Apparently, the sole path towards God open to man is by way of goodness; and whatever else can be known of God can be described only by one who walks along that way: for, says Taylor, 'He who might have made ten thousand worlds of wonder and prodigy, and created man with faculties able only to stare upon, and admire, those miracles of mightiness, did choose to instance His power in the effusions of mercy, that at the same instant He might represent Himself desirable and adorable, in all the capacities of amability; that is, as excellent in Himself, and profitable to us.'[1] Again, as if he would say that a God uncomprehended were no God, he shows that godly fear belongs only to the man who fears the good God; and in a sermon he advises to 'heighten our apprehensions of the divine power, of His justice and severity, of the fierceness of His anger and the sharpness of His sword, the heaviness of His hand and the swiftness of His arrows, as much as ever you can; provided the effect pass on no further but to make us reverent and obedient.'[2] When we turn to Whichcote, we find that God's power is adjectival to His goodness; for he says that 'his prime perfection is goodness, and our truest notion of him is, that he is almighty goodness.'[3] Indeed, it is in goodness that all God's attributes cohere, for 'there is that in God himself that is more beautiful than will. It is not majesty and glory divided from goodness, that is the divine perfection; but that wisdom and power are in immutable

[1] *Ib.*, iv. p. 471.   [2] *Ib.*, p. 92.
[3] Whichcote's *Works*, i. p. 22.

conjunction in goodness, for where wit and power are without goodness, there may be a diabolical nature.'[1] Again, he says, 'by this, we may be assured, that goodness is the excellency of the divine nature; because all other perfections become divine, as they are in conjunction with goodness.'[2] Impotent goodness, he believes, is a contradiction in terms: God's essence is communicative, and the whole creation in all levels, from highest to lowest, receives of His goodness. Of God's 'natural perfections,' *e.g.* His 'infiniteness, eternity, omniscience, omnipotence, omnipresence, his immensity, ubiquity,' men may not partake; but in His 'moral perfections,' *e.g.* His 'holiness, righteousness, goodness and truth,' it is their glory to share.[3] And it is in terms of the latter that we know what we may know of the former; for God's infinite attributes express His goodness. Wherever we observe nature at work, we see God's goodness; and the universe around us in the eye of a prophet becomes a parable of His love. When a mother in the animal kingdom displays affectionate care for her young, she offers us a token of Him whose impress is stamped throughout His entire creation; and 'even the stupid earth that we tread upon maintains the grass, and all that grows upon it.'[4] To this belief in transcendent goodness made immanent in nature, Jeremy Taylor also pledges himself, when he illustrates the peculiar fitness of the Word made flesh to be our example: 'for the first in every kind is in nature propounded as the pattern of the rest; and as the sun, the prince of all the bodies of light, and the fire of all warm substances, is the principal, the rule and the copy, which they in their proportions imitate and transcribe; so is the Word incarnate the great example of all the predestinate. . . .'[5]

God's goodness issues in many streams, and to one of them Whichcote delights to point; for although every man

[1] *Ib.*, ii. p. 398. [2] *Ib.*, iv. p. 159. [3] *Ib.*, ii. 385.
[4] *Ib.*, iv. p. 162. [5] Taylor's *Works*, ii. p. 40.

is bathed in goodness, there is no certainty that individual men will all use their gifts well. That God should continue to make His sun to rise on the evil is proof enough of His mercy; but that He should welcome penitent sinners is something we might not dare to expect. But Whichcote argues that if the path of a sinner's return to God had been irrevocably barred, He cannot then be 'the first and chiefest goodness.' 'Nothing worse can be put upon God, than to be represented implacable and irreconcilable.'[1] But a place for repentance does not mean either that a sinner easily secures it, or that God easily grants it; effectual repentance will have to show its temper in good works. Death-bed repentance, therefore, is 'very hazardous and uncertain,' says Whichcote; and he inquires—'Is the time of sickness a time for men to learn? when men should come to practice, is that a time to be taught? when men are put upon the very last nick of acting?'[2] That it is open to a bad man to repent and obtain Divine forgiveness is the furthermost limit to which Divine immanence can reach; and in saying this, we are exalting Divine transcendence to the utmost limit of our thought, if not beyond it. That God enters into one who is at that far remove from Him called sin, and draws him to Himself, is the most compelling instance of the truth that He passes our understanding. Whichcote says: 'Holiness, as attributed to God, doth denote God's peerless majesty, together with infinite power and wisdom, as it is in conjunction with righteousness and goodness. And it is well for us, that God is cloathed therewith; for it gives us the greatest security imaginable; for if you could divide almightiness from goodness, you would destroy holiness; for the other are perfections only as they are in conjunction with goodness. There is no true excellency if goodness be not in conjunction with it.'[3]

So to the principle of self-preservation, according to which everything, unless it be violated by another thing,

---

[1] Whichcote's *Works*, i. p. 7.   [2] *Ib.*, p. 181.   [3] *Ib.*, iv. p. 57.

tends to remain in possession of its own proper nature, Whichcote adds a second, namely, 'a principle of restoration and recovery.' 'In nature there are many disturbances through change of weather, through winds and storms and tempests; yet in nature, there is still a principle of recovery to calmness, and clearness, when the heavens are masked with clouds';[1] and in human nature this principle takes the form of repentance, whereby man wins peace of mind.

Taylor's teaching on the need for repentance is no less strong than Whichcote's; though his more rigorous view is not due to a more intense conviction of sin's heinous character. It is rather to his conception of Holy Baptism that we must look for an explanation of the great wealth of meaning which he attaches to repentance and to the restrictions with which he hedges it about. A baptized person, he holds, has been taken within God's 'covenant of grace,' which has been made to supplement the original 'covenant of works,' broken by Adam's transgression. On man's side, answering to the redemption wrought by Christ, two conditions are called for, namely, faith and repentance.[2] At Baptism every trace of sin has been done away, and a complete break has been made with the past and all that it holds against a sinner; and it is an entirely new man who goes forward to live an entirely new life. But if a convert should fall into sin, his condition is a more serious one than it would have been if he had not repented. In committing sin, he has, in effect, repudiated his part in a covenant with God; and to that covenant he is obliged to return. 'A man can be regenerated but once': 'but if we be overtaken by infirmity, or enter into the marches or borders of this estate, and commit a grievous sin, or ten, or twenty, so we be not in the entire possession of the devil, we are for the present in a damnable condition if we die; but if we live, we are in a recoverable condition; for so we may repent often.'[3] The way of recovery will be long and tedious,

[1] *Ib.*, ii. p. 181.   [2] Taylor's *Works*, ii. p. 346.   [3] *Ib.*, iii. p. 206.

BENJAMIN WHICHCOTE AND JEREMY TAYLOR 61

for 'all our life we are working ourselves into that condition we had in baptism, and lost by our relapse.'[1] 'Repentance is the institution of a philosophical and severe life, an utter extirpation of all unreasonableness and impiety, and an address to, and a final passing through, all the parts of holy living.'[2] Its moments are four in number: first, godly sorrow, which is its 'frontispiece or title-page'; second, deliberate forsaking of sin done, which must be more than 'the vomits of intemperance, which ease the stomach that they may continue the merry meeting'; third, such acts, including restitution, as will embody an otherwise imperfect resolution to lead the good life; and, fourth, the consummation of all these in a life which has 'acquired the habits of all those christian graces which are necessary in the transaction of our affairs, in all relations to God and our neighbour, and our own person.'[3] These, and all other stages of a prodigal's return, are the means towards, and the expression of, a goodness in the soul, awakened there by Him whose saving power promises restoration; but sorrow for sin in itself is not a good, unless it becomes taken up into the soul's Godward flight.[4] A good life, in short, is one of *penitence*; and therein a repentant sinner declares the glory of God. If Whichcote, as we saw, finds the goodness of God shown signally in His recovery of a sinner, Taylor finds the very image of God portrayed in penitent obedience. Here is a passage, glittering with neo-Platonic hues, taken from a sermon upon repentance, and it illustrates the place of good works in the life of one who formerly disowned them: 'For if God is glorified in the sun and moon, in the rare fabric of the honeycombs, in

[1] *Ib.*, ii. p. 358.
[2] *Ib.*, iv. p. 396. *Cf.* Calvin, *Institutes*, III. iii. p. 5: 'Wherefore in my judgement, repentance may thus not amisse be defined: that it is a true turning of our life unto God, proceeding from a pure and earnest feare of God, which consisteth in the mortifying of the flesh and of the olde man, and in the quickening of the Spirit.'
[3] *Ib.*, iv. pp. 385-92.   [4] *Ib.*, ii. p. 376.

the discipline of bees, in the economy of pismires, in the little houses of birds, in the curiosity of an eye, God being pleased to delight in those little images and reflexes of Himself from those pretty mirrors, which, like a crevice in a wall, through a narrow perspective transmit the species of a vast excellency: much rather shall God be pleased to behold Himself in the glasses of our obedience, in the emissions of our will and understanding; these being rational and apt instruments to express Him, far better than the natural, as being nearer communications of Himself.'[1]

Turning to Whichcote, we observe that in his view repentance on its positive side depends upon a continuous exercise of the rational power in virtue of which man is man. It is natural that man should lead a spiritual life, because his is a spiritual nature. He must 'exercise his naturals.' He will set his life towards the only end ample enough to satisfy him. He will find in God not merely an object, but a presence. God is found everywhere or nowhere; and if there is any virtue to be found, it will be discovered by an eye which has pierced through to virtue's source. 'The state of religion,' says Whichcote, 'lies, in short, in this; a good mind, and a good life. All else is but about religion, and hath but the place of means or an instrument.'[2] There are some who suppose mistakenly that religion is a 'system of certain maxims and propositions';[3] but religion rests upon moral conviction as to what is good, and not upon intellectual assent: and there are some who foolishly regard religion as concerned about 'certain usages and performances'; but this is to confuse negative inhibitions with positive principle.[4] On the contrary, the religious life is active throughout; it is dutiful, because it is first devotional: and in these twin activities 'the whole man'[5] finds harmony within and without. Conformance to tradition in itself can never prove a satisfying substitute for

---

[1] *Ib.*, iv. p. 382.   [2] Whichcote's *Works*, ii. p. 391.
[3] *Ib.*, ii. p. 387.   [4] *Ib.*, iv. p. 193.   [5] *Ib.*, ii. p. 142.

immediate acquaintance with God; and it is man's business to think, and to explore, though not out of curiosity, the character of God from whom all good things come. Too often man has employed himself with ends that fit ill with his capacity; and there are too many 'intellectual Gibeonites,' pragmatists, who make themselves servants to two unrelenting task-masters, *bonum utile* and *bonum jucundum*. What is required is more of the 'Bereans temper,' and examination of religious principles, 'tho' never so certainly grounded.'[1]

Once man's reason has been awakened to meditate upon God, there emerges within him a sense of direction; and his basic desire for happiness which, as we have noted, is the form taken by the instinct of self-preservation in his case, becomes a desire for God. Whereas, to begin with, urged along by the cravings of nature, he would ally himself now with this interest and now with that, hoping for a permanent home in the scheme of things; now, he knows and loves One who has made him for Himself. Instead of making demands upon life, he waits for Another to make demands upon Him. He has been transported from the realm of natural necessity into the ampler realm of freedom, which lies beyond the intervening territory of moral obligation. He lives under the constraint of love, rather than under the compulsion of moral law; for the religious life takes the moral life into partnership, and uses it as a means for expressing devotion to God. The religious life knows one motive, namely, doing God service; and this is a motive which can mix with every morally good motive, and assign to it a due place in a coherent life. If any act proposed as the one morally fitting can be deemed worthy of being offered to God, it can express the worshipful life. Accordingly, Whichcote can say that 'religion is not a particular good only; as meat against hunger; or drink against thirst; or cloaths against cold; but it is universally good; a good,

[1] *Ib.*, iv. p. 291.

without limitation or restraint.'[1] And it would seem that along this line of thought lies the solution of the problems raised by the relations between means and end, duty and self-realization, right and good. Whichcote's ethical theory is intuitional on two counts; for he holds that a man can discover what is his true end, and that he can decide which acts he is bound to perform. And though he speaks as if particular acts were means to an ultimate end, it would be a mistake to put him down as teaching that it is this end which constitutes their worth. He is one of those whose emphasis falls upon the side of the ultimate end, rather than upon the immediately demanded act; but he warns that there cannot be steadfast intention to pursue life's good, unless this good finds expression in congruous deeds. The end is not so much a terminus to be reached by means of so many successive steps, as a strenuous game in the course of which a player displays his skill in meeting situations as they arise. 'For holiness and purity of mind, is the self-same thing to the mind, that health and strength is to the body.'[2]

The moral life, in serving the religious life, comprises duties towards oneself and one's neighbour as well as duties towards God; and without sobriety terminating in oneself, and righteousness terminating in one's neighbour, there will not be holiness terminating in God. 'Wherefore sobriety, righteousness, and godliness, are the due perfections of an intellectual nature, upon a moral account. For these are the things that are good in themselves, and sanctify by their presence, and are necessary and indispensable. . . . These are the things that make men God-like; these are the things that are final and ultimate; these are the things that do sanctify human nature by their presence.'[3]

Jeremy Taylor places the scope of the moral life under the same three heads: 'these are the three natural laws, described in the Christian doctrine, that we live godly,

---

[1] *Ib.*, iv. p. 190. [2] *Ib.* [3] *Ib.*, ii. p. 237.

soberly, and righteously'; [1] and 'the final cause of conscience,' he says in another treatise, is 'to conduct all our relations and entercourses between God, our neighbours, and ourselves; that is, in all moral actions.' [2] As for the first of these, every action is to be made an oblation to God,[3] undue scrupulosity being eschewed; as for duty towards oneself, every man's own value is measured by what he himself values, and it is presumed that every man will have in him 'sufficient stock of self-love to serve the ends of his nature and creation.' [4] In *Holy Living* we read that 'every man hath desires of his own, and objects just fitted to them, without which he cannot be, unless he were not himself. And let every man that loves himself so well as to love himself before all the world, consider if he have not something for which in the whole he values himself far more than he can value any man else.' [5] Finally, man's duty towards his neighbour answers to man's need of man: 'and thus God gave necessities to men, that all men might need: and several abilities to several persons, that each man might help to supply the public needs, and by joining to fill up all wants, they might be knit together by justice, as the parts of the world are by nature.' [6] These three ends are proposed, because man's innate capacity for love is touched by God's disposing love; and all duties, even as the laws embodying them, are expressions of man's love.

---

[1] Taylor's *Works*, ii. p. 12.   [2] *Ib.*, ix. p. 15.
[3] *Ib.*, iii. p. 18.
[4] *Ib.*, ii. p. 12. *Cf.* Calvin, *Institutes*, II. viii. 54: 'And the Lord, the more to expresse with how great earnestnesse we ought to be led to the love of our neighbours, appointed it to be measured by the love of our selves (*ad nostri amorem*) as by a rule, because he had no vehementer or stronger affection to measure it by. . . . For God doth not make the love of our selves, a rule whereunto charitie toward other should be subject, but whereas by perversenesse of nature the affection of love was wont to rest in our selves, he sheweth that now it ought to be else-where spread abroad, that we should with no lesse cheerefulnesse, ferventnesse, and carefulnesse be readie to doe good to our neighbour than to our selves.'
[5] *Ib.*, iii. p. 89.   [6] *Ib.*, p. 115.

This helps to explain why it is that the good life can be consistently good. If the good life is begotten in good motives, some one principle must comprehend them; but if good motives cannot be produced to order, it seems that they can be nurtured by happy inadvertence, when reason and affections are ever directed towards the wonder of God's love.

III
JOHN SMITH

I never got so much good among all my books by a whole day's plodding in a study, as by an hour's discourse I have got with him. For he was not a library locked up, nor a book clasped, but he stood open for any to converse withal that had a mind to learn. Yea, he was a fountain running over, labouring to do good to those who perhaps had no mind to receive it.

SIMON PATRICK.

CHAPTER III

JOHN SMITH [1]

THE reader who turns to the *Select Discourses* of John Smith, expecting to find there a system of philosophical theology, will be disappointed; but he will know the joy of being in touch with a mind convicted of spiritual truth. The author is more concerned to give a reasonable account of the faith that is in him, than to win acceptance for a theory of life by means of logical argument. Of mere speculation he is distrustful, and for curiosity he has contempt. The good life, he would persuade us, is a serious endeavour and not a pass-time; and it requires a skill such as marks an artist off from minds made common by commerce, and a loyalty weaned through much patience from enthusiasm to devotion.[2] In the pages of the *Discourses* there are many intuitive flashes which illuminate the dark secrets of human life and the purpose of God; but their advent, we are made to feel, was upon a soul well disciplined in intellect and will. Here is faith confirmed by reason.

John Smith, unfortunately, did not live to complete his projected treatment of revealed religion, which, doubtless,

---

[1] 1616–52.
[2] *Select Discourses : by John Smith, M.A.* Edited by H. G. Williams, Cambridge, 1859, p. 1: 'Were I indeed to define divinity, I should rather call it a *divine life*, than a *divine science*; it being something rather to be understood by a spiritual sensation, than by any verbal description, as all things of sense and life are best known by sentient and vital faculties; γνῶσις ἑκάστων δι' ὁμοιότητος γίνεται, as the Greek Philosopher hath well observed—every thing is best known by that which bears a just resemblance and analogy with it: and therefore the Scripture is wont to set forth a good life as the prolepsis and fundamental principle of divine science. . . .'

would have contained much material on the theme of the life which is 'hid with Christ in God';[1] and we are dependent upon other essays for his views about the subject, including two which deal with natural religion, entitled respectively, *A Discourse on the Immortality of the Soul*, and, *A Discourse of the Existence and Nature of God*. From these we learn of his cherished conviction that the good life, in its genesis and quality, will become apparent to all who will go to school with themselves, with their longings and reasonings, and that its meaning will be disclosed from within the soul itself.

What, then, can an interrogator who stands upon the plain of nature know about the origin and destiny of his soul? Like Whichcote, Smith refers to the passage in *Romans* i.—the visible creation points to its invisible Creator; and, like Whichcote, he holds that God is known also by means of His reflection in the mirror of the soul: but he prefers to transfer the emphasis to the interior partner. He says that 'though the whole fabric of this visible universe be whispering out the notions of a Deity, and always inculcates this lesson to the contemplators of it—ὡς ἐμὲ πεποίηκε ὁ θεός—as Plotinus expresseth it; yet we cannot understand it without some interpreter within';[2] and he welcomes the schoolmen's distinction between the sensible *vestigia Dei* and the intelligible *faciem Dei*. He says elsewhere that 'God hath copied out Himself in all created being, having no other pattern to frame any thing by, than His own essence . . .: but true religion is such a communication of the Divinity, as none but the highest of created beings are capable of.'[3] And yet again: 'But how to find God here, and feelingly to converse with Him, and, being affected with the sense of the Divine glory shining out upon the creation, how to pass out of the sensible

---

[1] *Col*. iii. 3. The substance of revelation is comprised in *The communication of God to mankind through Christ* (p. 61).
[2] *Select Discourses*, pp. 129-30.   [3] *Ib*., p. 390.

world into the intellectual, is not so effectually taught by that philosophy which professed it most, as by true religion: that which knits and unites God and the soul together, can best teach it how to ascend and descend upon those golden links that unite, as it were, the world to God.'[1] So in keeping with these sentiments our author turns to the *Epistle to the Hebrews* for his *locus classicus* of natural religion; for 'the necessary foundation of all religion' is 'That God is, and That He is a rewarder of them that seek Him,'[2] the latter proposition being taken to include the immortality of the soul. There is no hint at minimizing the function of reason in religion; but there is a stout claim that faith both anticipates and completes its findings.[3] Faith is a more inward activity of soul than reason; and religious faith instigates reason, if need be, to clarify its own vision of the invisible.[4] Religion claims philosophy

---

[1] *Ib.*, p. 439.

[2] *Ib.*, p. 60. *Heb.* xi. 6: 'But without faith it is impossible to please him: for he that cometh to God must believe that he is, and that he is a rewarder of them that diligently seek him.'

[3] Authority is vested in 'the Scriptures, or the reason of the thing itself' (p. 62), 'the common dictate of nature or reason' (p. 64), and 'Scripture' 'reason or experience' (pp. 114 f.); and reason enjoys 'innate notions of divine truth' (p. 6), 'common notions' (p. 6), or 'truths of natural inscription' (p. 392). 'Unreasonableness, or the smothering and extinguishing of the candle of the Lord within us, is no piece of religion, nor advantageous to it: that, certainly, will not raise men up to God, which sinks them below men' (p. 456); and to deny reason 'were to deny a beam of Divine light, and so to deny God, instead of denying ourselves for Him' (p. 399). 'The law of nature . . . is nothing else but a paraphrase or comment upon the nature of God, as it copies forth itself in the soul of man' (p. 138).

[4] He seems to make faith a child of *Eros*. Faith is 'that powerful attractive which, by a strong and divine sympathy, draws down the virtue of heaven into the souls of men; which strongly and forcibly moves the souls of good men into a conjunction with that Divine goodness by which it lives and grows: this is that Divine impress that invincibly draws and sucks them in, by degrees, into the Divinity, and so unites them more and more to the Centre of life and love: it is something in the hearts of men which, feeling, by an occult and inward sensation, the mighty insinuations of the Divine goodness, immediately complies with it, and, with the greatest ardency that may

for handmaid; and the self-searchings of a religious man will discover things for which a rationalist does not look. We are told that 'the first and most ancient wisdom amongst the heathens was indeed a philosophical divinity, or a divine philosophy, which continued for divers ages; but, as men grew worse, their queasy stomachs began to loathe it: which made the truly wise Socrates complain of the sophists of that age, who began to corrupt and debase it; whereas heretofore the spirit of philosophy was more generous and divine, and did more purify and ennoble the souls of men, commending intellectual things to them, and taking them off from settling upon sensible and material things here below, and still exciting them to endeavour after the nearest resemblance to God, the supreme goodness and loveliness, and an intimate conjunction with Him; which, according to the strain of that philosophy, was the true happiness of immortal souls.' [1] There is no mistaking John Smith's idea of the scope and business of philosophy; and we shall not expect that, with him for guide, 'a view of our own souls' [2] will show precisely what Descartes saw in his meditations.

The second of the two propositions taken from *Hebrews* calls for treatment first: 'for, indeed, the chief natural way whereby we can climb up to the understanding of the Deity, is by a contemplation of our own souls.' [3] But before setting out to *prove* that the soul is immortal, our author premises that the proposition 'doth not absolutely need any demonstration to clear it, but might be assumed rather as a principle or postulatum, seeing the notion of it is apt naturally to insinuate itself into the belief of the most vulgar

be, is perpetually rising up into conjunction with it; and, being first begotten and enlivened by the warm beams of that goodness, always breathes and gasps after it for its constant growth and nourishment. It is then fullest of life and vivacity when it partakes most freely of it; and perpetually languisheth when it is in any measure deprived of that sweet and pure nourishment it derives from it' (p. 348). *Cf.* p. 332.

[1] *Ib.*, p. 442.   [2] *Ib.*, p. 138.
[3] *Ib.*, p. 62.

sort of men.'[1] It is an all but universally accepted notion, and that, too, 'with a kind of repugnancy to sense, which shews all things to be mortal';[2] and this goes to indicate that, despite its illegitimate associations in the minds of some with such ideas as materiality and traduction, the notion may be, and indeed probably is, one of our 'common notions.'[3] 'For we cannot easily conceive how any prime notion, that hath no dependency on any other antecedent to it, should be generally entertained, did not the common dictate of nature or reason, acting alike in all men, move them to conspire in the embracing of it, though they knew not another's minds.'[4]

Four arguments are put forward in order to show 'that the soul of man is something really distinct from his body, of an indivisible nature, and so cannot be divided into such parts as should flit from one another; and, consequently, that it is apt of its own nature to remain to eternity, and so will do, except the decrees of heaven should abandon it from being.'[5] The first, in mathematical fashion, considers the absurdities which follow upon supposition that the soul is a product of the same matter and motion which constitute its body: 'so that the very grass we walk over in the fields, the dust and mire in the streets that we tread upon, may, according to the true meaning of this dull philosophy, after many refinings, macerations, and maturations, which nature

---

[1] *Ib.*, p. 63. Scripture supposes that we have 'antecedent knowledge' of the soul's immortality, and 'principally teaches us the right way and method of providing in this life for our happy subsistence in that eternal estate' (p. 115).

[2] *Ib.*, p. 65.   [3] *Ib.*, pp. 64, 107.   [4] *Ib.*, p. 64.

[5] *Ib.*, p. 69. The following account of *substantial being* ought to be compared with the view of Henry More: 'That it is either body, and so divisible, and of three dimensions; or else it is something which is not properly a body or matter, and so hath no such dimensions as that the parts thereof should be crowding for place, and justling one with another, not being all able to lodge together, or run one into another: and this is nothing else but what is commonly called spirit. Though yet we will not be too critical in depriving every thing which is not grossly corporeal of all kind of extension' (pp. 68 f.).

performs by the help of motion, spring up into so many rational souls, and prove as wise as any Epicurean, and discourse as subtilely of what it once was, when it lay drooping in a senseless passiveness.'[1] 'The power itself of sensation'[2] cannot arise out of matter and motion 'any more than vision can rise out of a glass'; for sensation 'is not the motion or impression which one body makes upon another, but a recognition of that motion'; and, furthermore, sensation itself is only so much material presented to reason, which is a judging, comparing,[3] and retaining[4] faculty, 'whereby we know what it is to know.'[5]

The second proof considers the soul in partial abstraction from its body; for although some of the motions which it feels within itself have been transmitted to it from the body, or through the body, from the external world, there are others which originate in its own free will. 'We know we commonly meditate and discourse of such arguments as we ourselves please: we mould designs, and draw up a plot of means answerable thereto, according as the free vote of our own souls determines; and use our bodies many times, notwithstanding all the reluctance of their nature, only as our instruments to serve the will and pleasure of our souls. All which, as they evidently manifest a true distinction between the soul and the body, so they do as evidently prove the supremacy and dominion which the soul hath over the body.'[6] The third proof makes a yet further abstraction of soul from body, and considers it in its capacity of originating 'mathematical notions,' such as notions of perfect figures, infinite divisibility, and proportion, notions which no piece of matter is fit to embody. 'For, though we could suppose our senses to be the school-dames that first taught us the alphabet of this learning; yet nothing else but a true mental essence could be capable of it, or so much improve it as to unbody it all, and strip it naked of any

---

[1] *Ib.*, p. 71.   [2] *Ib.*, p. 73.   [3] *Ib.*, p. 82.
[4] *Ib.*, p. 83.   [5] *Ib.*, p. 77.   [6] *Ib.*, p. 89.

sensible garment, and then only, when it hath done it, embrace it as its own, and commence a true and perfect understanding of it.'[1] The final proof makes a last abstraction, and points out that the soul, in spite of its bondage to time and the fluctuations that go with it, can intuit eternal truth, which it knows with a clarity lacking in knowledge of material things; and that this noble power bespeaks its kinship with God. All first principles, such as justice, wisdom, goodness and omnipotency, 'we always find to be the same, and know that no exorcisms of material mutations have any power over them: though we ourselves are but of yesterday, and mutable every moment, yet these are eternal, and dependent not upon any mundane vicissitudes; neither could we ever gather them from observation of any material thing, where they were never sown.'[2] Our reason can transcend the distortions of its own making, whereby it separates justice from goodness, and power from wisdom, and contemplate a 'perfect simplicity'[3] wherein all are knit together.

These arguments, we have noted, are speculative discussions designed by reason in order to clear a conviction entertained by faith that the soul is immortal; but it is necessary to point out also that in our author's estimate their cogency depends upon the value which the seeker sets upon his own immortality. Nobody can be deeply interested in the problem of immortality, unless he be interested in goodness; because nobody desires assurance of certain immortal misery. And, conversely, a sincerely good man lives so close to God that he will not have to rely upon any speculative proofs: his is an assurance of the experience of God's love. 'Though every good man is not so logically subtile as to be able, by fit mediums, to demonstrate his own immortality, yet he sees it in a higher light. His soul, being purged and enlightened by true sanctity, is more capable of those divine irradiations, whereby it feels itself

[1] *Ib.*, p. 95.   [2] *Ib.*, p. 98.   [3] *Ib.*, p. 99.

in conjunction with God, and by a συναύγεια, (as the Greeks speak), the light of divine goodness mixing itself with the light of its own reason, sees more clearly, not only that it may, if it please the supreme Deity, of its own nature exist eternally, but also that it shall do so: it knows it shall never be deserted of that free goodness that always embraceth it; it knows that Almighty love which it lives by, to be stronger than death, and more powerful than the grave; . . . He would not raise it up to such mounts of vision, to shew it all the glory of that heavenly Canaan, flowing with eternal and unbounded pleasures, and then precipitate it again into that deep and darkest abyss of death and non-entity.'[1]

These arguments, to be sure, are not novel; but their special significance in Smith's *Discourses* becomes apparent, when we regard them as so much Platonism packed round the following Cartesian paragraph:—'If we reflect but upon our own souls, how manifestly do the species of reason, freedom, perception, and the like, offer themselves to us, whereby we may know a thousand times more distinctly what our souls are than what our bodies are? For the former we know by an immediate converse with ourselves, and a distinct sense of their operations; whereas all our knowledge of the body is little better than merely historical, which we gather up by scraps and piecemeal from more doubtful and uncertain experiments which we have made of them: but the notions which we have of a mind, *i.e.* something within us that thinks, apprehends, reasons, and discourses, are so clear and distinct from all those notions which we can fasten upon a body, that we can easily conceive that, if all body-being in the world were destroyed, yet we might then as well subsist as we now do. For whensoever we take notice of those immediate motions of our own minds, whereby they make themselves known to us, we find no such thing in them as extension or divisibility, which are

[1] *Ib.*, p. 103 f.

contained in every corporeal essence: and having no such thing discovered to us from our nearest familiarity with our own souls, we could never so easily know whether they had any such things as bodies joined to them or not, did not those extrinsical impressions, that their turbulent motions make upon them, admonish them thereof.'[1]

We find, on turning to the *Discourse* which treats of the other fundamental truth of natural religion, that the author undertakes to prove rather *what* God is than that He is; and that he will do this by reflecting upon his experience of what the soul is.[2] He is conscious of grave privation in each of the soul's characteristic excellencies, and in the very consciousness he is aware of the existence of a Being in whom they exist and function without let or hindrance. Thus reason, in confessing the limitations which enmesh it in temporal process and require that it shall struggle on from *data* through argument to conclusions, is aware of the existence of Supreme Reason which sees all truths together and eternally one. 'There is nothing whereby our own souls are better known to us, than by the properties and operations of reason: but when we reflect upon our own idea of pure and perfect reason, we know that our souls are not it, but only partake of it; and that it is of such a nature that we cannot denominate by it any other thing of the same rank with ourselves; and yet we know certainly that it is, as finding, from an inward sense of it within ourselves, that both we and other things else beside ourselves partake of it, and that we have it κατὰ μέθεξιν, and not, κατ' οὐσίαν, neither do we, or any finite thing, contain the source of it, within ourselves: and, because we have a distinct notion of the most perfect mind and understanding, we own our deficiency therein. And as that idea of understanding, which we have within us, points not out to us this or that particular,

---

[1] *Ib.*, pp. 98 f.
[2] 'The common notions of a Deity' are 'strongly rooted in men's souls' (p. 31).

but something which is neither this nor that, but total, understanding; so neither will any elevation of it serve every way to fit and answer that idea.'[1] In similar fashion, again, our author finds that he is conscious of possessing free will which enables him to pursue and achieve rational ends: 'so, indeed, we know it must be a mighty, inward, strength and force that must enable our understandings to perform their proper functions, and that life, energy, and activity can never be separated from a power of understanding.'[2] And yet again, he is aware that the stream of his love tends to ebb and flow, and to become fouled by his passions, because he experiences the love of Another, a love which is 'perpetually most infinitely ardent and potent' and 'always calm and serene.'[3] Finally, he tells of how he feels himself impelled from within unceasingly to move out from himself towards some self-sustaining good in which he will find all his own emptiness made full. 'It is not the nimbleness and agility of our own reason which stirs up these eager affections within us, (for then the most ignorant sort of men would never feel the sting thereof) but indeed some more potent nature which hath planted a restless motion within us that might more forcibly carry us out to itself; and, therefore, it will never suffer itself to be controlled by any of our thin speculations, or satisfied with those airy delights that our fancies may offer to it: it doth not, it cannot, rest itself any where but upon the centre of some Almighty good, some solid and substantial happiness; like the hungry child that will not be stilled by all the mother's

---

[1] *Ib.*, p. 130 f. Mr. Basil Willey observes in *The Seventeenth Century Background* (p. 142) that Smith's is a version of the ontological argument. It is also interlocked with the demand for a first cause or prime mover. *Cf.* p. 148: 'The Deity, indeed, is the centre of all finite being, and entity itself, which is self-sufficient, must, of necessity, be the foundation and basis of every one of these weak essences, which cannot bear up themselves by any central power of their own; as we may also be most assured of, from a sensible feeling of all the constant mutations and impotency which we find both in ourselves and all other things.'
[2] *Ib.*, p. 132.   [3] *Ib.*, p. 133.

music, or change its sour and angry looks for her smiling countenance: nothing will satisfy it but the full breasts.'[1]

John Smith deals with the canon of 'clearness and distinctness' as we should expect a mystic to do. Our 'common notions' are 'clear and distinct,' provided that they are not blurred by passion;[2] and the knowledge which we reach by means of the understanding, or discursive reason, is so also, unless it is clouded by self-interest.[3] But the highest knowledge that lies open for appropriation, our author holds, is not comprehensible in conceptual form; knowledge of this order obtains only within the sphere of personal relationship with God, and is enjoyed in communion with Him.[4] This is that knowledge referred to in Scripture, when it speaks of 'seeing' God; and by Plotinus, when he makes mention of 'an intellectual touch' (νοερᾷ ἐπαφῇ).[5] 'But how sweet and delicious that truth is, which holy and heaven-born souls feed upon in their mysterious converse with the Deity, who can tell but they that taste it? When reason once is raised, by the mighty force of the Divine Spirit, into a converse with God, it is turned into sense: that which before was only faith well built upon sure principles (for such our science may be), now becomes vision.'[6] The vision in its perfection is

---

[1] *Ib.*, pp. 139 f.

[2] We read (p. 15) that 'the clearest and most distinct notions of truth that shine in the souls of the common sort of men, may be extremely clouded, if they be not accompanied with that answerable practice that might preserve their integrity.' *Cf.* pp. 19 and 129.

'But since man's fall from God, the inward virtue and vigour of reason is much abated, the soul having suffered a πτερορρύησις, as Plato speaks—a *defluvium pennarum*; those principles of divine truth, which were first engraven upon man's heart with the finger of God, are now, as the characters of some ancient monuments, less clear and legible than at first' (p. 393).

[3] 'We may carry such an image and species of ourselves constantly before us, as will make us lose the clear sight of the Divinity, and be too apt to rest in a mere "logical life," . . . without any true participation of the divine life. . . .' (p. 20).

[4] *Ib.*, pp. 20, 166. [5] *Ib.*, p. 3. [6] *Ib.*, p. 17.

reserved for the disembodied state, when those who behold it shall experience the *beatitudo* which it brings; but in this life a measure of it is granted to all who have already entered upon the divine life. 'And so, when Moses desired to behold the face of God, that is, as the Jews understand it, that a distinct idea of the Divine essence might be imprinted upon his mind, God told him, "No man can see me, and live."'[1] When Scripture records that God spoke with him 'face to face,'[2] it means ('I should rather think') 'to import the clearness and evidence of the intellectual light wherein God appeared to Moses';[3] and 'this clear, distinct, kind of inspiration,'[4] known as *gradus Mosaicus*, vouchsafed to him, is distinguished from all lower forms in that God worked upon his intellect alone, and not upon his imagination also, as He did in the case of other prophets. It was given to One only to know the Divine essence: 'St. John, that lay in the bosom of Christ, who came from the bosom of the Father, and perfectly understood His eternal essence, hath given us the fullest description that he could make of Him, when he tells us that "God is love; and he that dwelleth in love, dwelleth in God."'[5]

The sum and substance of revelation is comprised in 'the communication of God to mankind through Christ.'[6] It was conveyed to men originally in the 'doctrine, life, and death'[7] of Christ, the Saviour, who conversed with men, 'not so much "face to face," as "mind to mind"';[8] and we have it declared to us now in Scripture, which has been written *doctis pariter et indoctis*;[9] because God saw fit 'to accommodate His truth to our weak capacities,'[10] and because 'truth is content, when it comes into the world, to

---

[1] *Ib.*, p. 166. *Ex.* xxxiii. 20.   [2] *Ex.* xxxiii. 11.
[3] *Select Discourses*, p. 273.   [4] *Ib.*, p. 275.
[5] *Ib.*, p. 434. 1 *John* iv. 16.   [6] *Ib.*, p. 61.
[7] *Ib.*, p. 358.   [8] *Ib.*, p. 276.
[9] *Ib.*, p. 300. *Cf.* p. 456: 'Certainly, a man may as well read the Scriptures as study a piece of Aristotle, or of natural philosophy, or mathematics.'   [10] *Ib.*, p. 388.

wear our mantles, to learn our language; to conform itself, as it were, to our dress and fashions.'¹ In Christ we have One 'that partakes every way of human nature,'² and shares in all the conditions of its frailty, 'our sinfulness excepted.'³ He is the Mediator between God and men, who denied Himself to the extent of giving up His life 'for the good of mankind.'⁴ He washed away our sins in His blood;⁵ He took away 'our guilt and cancelled that handwriting that was against us, which bound us over to eternal condemnation';⁶ and '"He spoiled all the principalities and powers of darkness, and made a show of them openly, triumphing over them in (or by) it," that is, His cross, as the apostle speaks.'⁷

But we err greatly, if we imagine that mere assent to the historicity of this revelation will earn salvation; for to entertain such a view would be to relapse into the Jewish belief which St. Paul was obliged to combat.⁸ The righteousness of faith means more than credal acceptance of Christ's sacrifice; it means the assimilation of His life. 'The Scripture,' writes Smith, 'speaks of Christ, not only as a particular person, but as a Divine principle in holy souls';⁹ and elsewhere he says that 'the gospel or evangelical administration must be an internal impression, a vivacious and energetical spirit and principle of righteousness in the souls of men, whereby they are inwardly enabled to express a real conformity thereto.'¹⁰ In so far as this level of life has been

---

[1] *Ib.*, p. 173. The following is an interesting instance of analogical knowledge: 'when the Scripture would intimate God's seriousness and reality in any thing, it brings Him in as ordering it a great while ago, before the foundation of the world was laid, as if He more regarded that than the building of the world' (p. 177).
[2] *Ib.*, p. 358.   [3] *Ib.*, p. 122.
[4] *Ib.*, p. 358. *Cf.* p. 410: 'This was the grand lesson that our great Lord and Master came to teach us, viz. To deny our own wills; neither was there anything that He endeavoured more to promote by His own example. . . .'
[5] *Ib.*, p. 343.   [6] *Ib.*, p. 345.   [7] *Ib.*, p. 466. *Col.* ii. 15.
[8] *Ib.*, pp. 302 ff.   [9] *Ib.*, p. 470.   [10] *Ib.*, p. 327.

reached, the soul is become divine, or 'deified,'[1] because made partaker of the divine nature;[2] and, 'by the Platonist's leave,'[3] it can be received only by gift from Christ. 'This life is nothing else but God's own breath within him, and an *infant-Christ* (if I may use the expression) formed in his soul.'[3] For 'as Christ was in His bodily appearance, still increasing in wisdom, and knowledge, and favour with God and man, until He was perfected in glory; so is He also in His spiritual appearance in the souls of men; and, accordingly, the New Testament does more than once distinguish between Christ in His several ages and degrees of growth in the souls of all true Christians.'[4] And though it be legitimate to inquire into one's own assurance of salvation, it is surely 'more desirable to find a revelation from within, arising up from the bottom and centre of a man's own soul,'[5] than to hear a voice from heaven.

The idea of 'immensity,' as Hume saw,[6] is a stock one in Platonism; and, seeing that Smith appears to have made more use of it than his Cambridge contemporaries, we shall do well to deal with it here. Whichcote, we have pointed out, regards it as one of the 'natural,' as opposed to the moral, 'perfections' of the Deity, which we are not under obligation to imitate,[7] and numbers it among His 'incomprehensible' attributes.[8] Jeremy Taylor treats of the subject of the Divine presence after his own fashion in a section of his *Holy Living*, where he says that 'God is present by His essence; which, because it is infinite, cannot be contained within the limits of any place'; and that, since He is essen-

---

[1] *Ib.*, p. 416. Henry Hallywell (*A Defence of Revealed Religion*, London, 1694, p. 194) objects to the expressions, 'Godded with God,' and 'Christned with Christ,' as used by Enthusiasts.
[2] 2 *Pet.* i. 4.   [3] *Select Discourses*, p. 21.
[4] *Ib.*, p. 448.   [5] *Ib.*, p. 435.
[6] Essay on *The Platonist*: 'The Divinity is a boundless Ocean of Bliss and Glory: Human Minds are smaller Streams, which, arising at first from this Ocean, seek still, amid all their Wanderings, to return to it, and to lose themselves in that Immensity of Perfection.'
[7] *Works* (1751), ii. p. 385.   [8] *Ib.*, p. 381.

tially pure, He cannot be contaminated in a sinful place, any more than can the light of the sun when it shines upon mud. 'So that we may imagine God,' he explains, 'to be as the air and the sea, and we all enclosed in His circle, wrapped up in the lap of His infinite nature; or as infants in the wombs of their pregnant mothers: and we can no more be removed from the presence of God than from our own being.'[1] Cudworth says that when we have been exercising our minds in the contemplation of the Being who is 'incomprehensible to our finite understandings,' and have 'filled up all their capacity, there is still an immensity of it left without, which cannot enter in for want of room to receive it . . .;[2] and he argues that space is 'the infinite extension of an incorporeal Deity.'[3] Henry More holds that the idea of 'omnipresence or ubiquity' is necessarily included in the idea of a Perfect Being; that a contradiction is implied in the thought of an absolutely perfect essence which is limited in presence or subject to change of place; and that God is like 'a Circle whose Centre is every where and Circumference no where.'[4] Culverwel says that 'the Indians have a customs, once a year to cast a golden bushel into the Sea: and thus they think they set a measure and bound to its proud waves, so as it shall not invade their land. Their custome is ridiculous enough,' he continues, 'and yet they are far more vain that go about *Deum suo modulo metiri*, to circumscribe an Immense being with the narrow compasse of their reason.'[5] 'Origen,' writes George Rust, 'according to the philosophicalness of his excellent spirit had asserted God to be purely incorporeal and immense, and that it was an impious derogation to his most

---

[1] I. iii.

[2] *The True Intellectual System. . . ,* 1845, ii. pp. 519-20.

[3] *Ib.,* iii. p. 232.

[4] *A Collection of Several Philosophical Writings of Dr. Henry More,* 1662, *The Immortality of the Soul,* pp. 23-4.

[5] *An Elegant and Learned Discourse . . .* (*Spiritual Opticks*), 1652, p. 194.

perfect Essence, to be limited by any form whatever, and therefore not by humane shape, however the Scripture does ascribe to him the several parts of humane bodies.'[1] And Stillingfleet undertakes to show that 'it is repugnant to the immensity of God' to hold that He created this world out of an eternal matter.[2]

The proposition, God is immense, *i.e.* without measure, will mean one or other of two things, according as we lay emphasis upon the subject or the predicate. In the first case, we have in mind chiefly the positive thought of God's transcendence; in the second case, we have in mind chiefly the negated thought of the measure which He transcends. And God being Creator of all, it is denied that He is measured either by the space-time universe or by the mind of man.

The immensity of God, however, has a second positive meaning, namely, that He is the ever-present Measure of all created measures, active in all spheres of the created order—material, living, rational and spiritual. It means, in short, that God is immanent in the universe which He transcends.

John Norris, who discusses immensity at some length, distinguishes it from 'incomprehensibility,' with which it is often identified.[3] Divine immensity, he says, is 'no other than the Substance of God as it is universally diffused, intirely present in, and filling all places without being

[1] *A Letter of Resolution Concerning Origen* . . . 1661, p. 8.
[2] *Origines Sacrae*, III. ii. 10. In the event of God being material: 'For either he must then recede from that part in which he was, and contract himself into a narrower compass that he might fashion that part of the world which he was about, or else he must likewise frame part of himself with that part of the World which he was then framing of, which consequence is unavoydable on the Stoical Hypothesis of Gods being corporeal and confined to the World as his proper place.'
[3] In dealing with the meaning of 'incomprehensible' in a version of *Quicunque Vult*, Ommanney (*A Critical Dissertation on the Athanasian Creed*, pp. 312-3) writes: 'There can be little doubt that the word *incomprehensible* was suggested to the translator by the Greek ἀκατάληπτος, but was understood by him and should be understood by us to mean, not that which is incapable of being grasped by the intellect, but that which cannot be contained within the limits of space. In this sense

circumscribed by any, yet without any Local Extension': [1] and consistently he speaks of it alongside 'Self-existence' and 'Eternity' as one of God's 'incommunicable Attributes.'[2] The idea of immensity, therefore, unlike the idea of extension, 'has nothing clear and distinct in it';[3] and the proposition, God is immense, is 'an Infinite and Incomprehensible Truth.'[4]

These thoughts, however, are no monopoly of Platonism, for we find them frequently in Calvin's *Institutes*, where they are related to the teaching of Scripture, and in one instance to the thought of Irenaeus.[5] God is said to be 'immense'[6] and 'incomprehensible'[7] in His essence, and 'immense' in His attributes.[8] When we say that He is in

the word was received and used in the sixteenth century, as for instance by Hooker very distinctly: "That presence everywhere is the sequel of an infinite and *incomprehensible* substance, for what can be everywhere but that which can nowhere be comprehended?" (*E.P.*, V. lv. 4). At the same time, while the word was chosen by the translator as the most literal and exact interpretation of ἀκατάληπτος, it would appear probable that it also commended itself to his mind as embracing and representing the various renderings of the Latin in previous English versions—the "mychel" of that attributed to Schorham, the Wycliffite "without mesure myche," the "immensurate" of Hilsey, and the "without mesure" of the version which followed Hilsey's.' But the passage in Hooker immediately preceding that just quoted seems to require the other sense: 'He filleth heaven and earth, although he take up no room in either, because his substance is immaterial, pure, and of us in this world so incomprehensible, that albeit no part of us be ever absent from him who is present whole unto every particular thing, yet his presence with us we no way discern farther than only that God is present, which partly by reason and more perfectly by faith we know to be firm and certain.' Cf. Calvin, *Institutes* (I. xiii. 1): Etsi enim, ut est incomprehensibilis, terram quoque ipsam implet. . . .

[1] *An Account of Reason and Faith : In Relation to the Mysteries of Christianity*, London, 1697, p. 195.
[2] *Ib.*, p. 328. [3] *Ib.*, p. 203. [4] *Ib.*, p. 209. [5] II. vi. 4.
[6] *Ib.*, I. xiii. 1. *Cf.* I. xi. 2; xv. 2; III. xxiii. 4; IV. xvii. 10.
[7] *Ib.*, I. xi. 3; III. xx. 40.
[8] *Ib.*, II. iii. 5; III. xxiv. 2: *immensa Dei bonitas*.

Ib., III. xviii. 5: *immensa benignitate*. *Cf.* Irenaeus, *Adv. Haer.*, III. xxxviii. 2: *immensam benignitatem*.

Ib., III. xx. 40: *immensae potentiae*.

Cf. Article I : *immensae potentiae, sapientiae ac bonitatis*.

heaven, we do not understand 'that he is bound fast inclosed and compassed with the circle of heaven, as within certain barres. For Salomon also confesseth that the heavens of heavens cannot containe him. And he himselfe saith by the Prophet that heaven is his seate, and the earth his footestoole. Whereby verily he signifieth that he is not limited in any certaine coast, but is spread abroad throughout all things. But because our minde (such is the grossenesse of it,) could not otherwise conceive his unspeakable glory, it is signified to us by the heaven, than which there can nothing come under our sight more ample or fuller of majestie. Sith therefore wheresoever our senses comprehend any thing, there they use to fasten it: God is set out of all place (*extra omnem locum Deus statuitur*), that when we will seeke him, we should bee raised up above all sense both of bodie and soule. Againe by this maner of speaking he is lifted above all chaunce of corruption and change: finally it is signified that he comprehendeth and conteineth the whole world and governeth it with his power. Wherefore this is all one as if he had been called of infinite greatnesse or height, of incomprehensible substance (*incomprehensibilis essentiae*), of unmeasurable power (*immensae potentiae*), of everlasting immortalitie.'[1]

God, in Smith's view, is the identical metaphysical, physical, and spiritual first principle; and although our minds cannot fully understand His essence, our knowledge of Him grows more ample according as we bring clarity of thought to bear upon our experience of Him in the religious life. He is not, as we have seen, a principle that merely awaits to be cognized, but the Person who moves us to love and understand Him. And all these ideas appear to be gathered up in the single concept 'immensity.' 'The Divinity,' we read, 'comprehends its own essence, penetrating all that immensity of being which itself is';[2] and again—although the term 'comprehends' is usually taken

[1] *Ib.*, III. xx. 40. [2] *Select Discourses*, p. 166.

in the intellectual sense [1]—we read that 'as it comprehends all things, and sums them up together in its infinite knowledge, so it must also comprehend them all in its own life and power.' [2] God's 'own unbounded being and goodness is the primary and original object of His immense and Almighty love'; [3] 'and therefore the Deity is so boundlessly happy, because it is every way one with its own immense perfection.' [4] God did not create a world only to throw it back upon its own resources: 'He is that Omnipresent Life that penetrates and runs through all things, containing and holding all fast together within Himself'; [5] 'that, as the first production and continued subsistence of all things are from Himself, so the ultimate resolution and tendency of all things might be to Him.' [6] But His omnipresence is in virtue of His 'unlimited power,' and not by reason of 'infinite expanse or extension of essence.' [7] It falls to us, therefore, to realize that we are bounded by divine immensity, and that we are called upon to live the divine life; for, though every created thing must live and move and have its being in God, 'yet it is only true religion that can give us a more feeling and comfortable sense of it.' [8]

The divine life is the happy life, because its end and aim is God, the origin of all good; and where this universal end has been well sustained, interest in 'a particular life' [9] flags. The earth-bound life, on the contrary, brings misery: this is a contacted life, where the soul tries to attain the unattainable end of having itself for centre in a self-contained world. To sin is 'to endeavour after a divorce between

---

[1] *Ib.*, pp. 134-5: 'That which first begets the notion of time in us, is nothing else but that succession and multiplicity which we find in our own thoughts. . . . Whereas, an infinitely comprehensive mind hath a simultaneous possession of its own never-flitting life; and because it finds no succession in its own immutable understanding, therefore it cannot find any thing to measure out its own duration.'
[2] *Ib.*, p. 132.   [3] *Ib.*, p. 341.   [4] *Ib.*, p. 150.
[5] *Ib.*, p. 148.   [6] *Ib.*, p. 409.   [7] *Ib.*, p. 136.
[8] *Ib.*, p. 401.   [9] *Ib.*, p. 415.

God and His creation.'[1] And the ruling principle of sin turns out to be identical with that which St. Augustine discerned at the foundation of the earthly city, and Erasmus named first among the companions of Folly, namely, self-love. Self-love is the supreme case of idolatry,[1] because it denies that God is immense. It is one thing with 'self-enjoyment,' 'self-feeling,' 'self-sufficiency,' 'self-conceit,' 'self-will' and 'self-seeking':[2] for all are opposed to 'self-nothingness,'[3] which characterizes the Christian temper. 'That bravery and gallantness, which seem to be in the great Nimrods of this world, are nothing else but the swelling of their own unbounded pride and vain-glory.'[4]

[1] *Ib.*, p. 409.   [2] *Ib.*, pp. 133, 355, 368, 369, 415.
[3] *Ib.*, p. 158. *Cf.* p. 400: 'But by self-denial I mean, the soul's quitting all its own interest in itself, and an entire resignation of itself to Him, as to all points of service and duty: and the soul loves itself in God, and lives in the possession, not so much of its own being, as of the Divinity.'
[4] *Ib.*, p. 411.

IV
RALPH CUDWORTH

To give anything like an adequate account of Cudworth's two principal works would be to review all the ancient philosophies and estimate his criticisms upon them.

MARTINEAU.

CHAPTER IV

RALPH CUDWORTH [1]

RALPH CUDWORTH was not content simply to commend the good life and its claims in sermons and discourses as Whichcote and Smith had done. He set himself to search into the very ground and possibility of the thing; and in the two treatises, *The True Intellectual System of the Universe*, and *A Treatise Concerning Eternal and Immutable Morality*,[2] he offers a philosophical vindication of man's place and function in the whole created order. We are not, therefore, unprepared for the change of climate awaiting us, when we turn to the three large volumes in which these treatises —one being uncompleted—are contained; though the sermons of the man reveal that the warmth of his religious devotion can have been no less forceful than the keenness of his intellect.[3] 'Christ was a master of life, not of the schools,' he once told a congregation, 'and he is the best Christian, whose heart beats with the purest pulse towards heaven; not he, whose head spins out the finest cobwebs.'[4]

---

[1] 1617–88.

[2] 'The Lawes of Nature are immutable and eternall,' said Hobbes (*Philosophical Rudiments*, III. xxix). *Cf.* J. Laird, *Hobbes*, p. 62: 'Hobbes even called them (*the laws of Nature*) "eternal," partly, no doubt, because, being matter of reason, they had the timelessness of logical implications, partly to show that there need be no magic or religiosity about the idea.'

[3] W. Fraser Mitchell, *English Pulpit Oratory from Andrewes to Tillotson*, p. 295: 'The finest achievement of "Platonic" preaching must, however, be considered to belong to Ralph Cudworth (1617–88), whose wonderful sermon, preached before the House of Commons on the 31st March, 1647, has earned a belated eulogy in Professor Grierson's recent study of religion and culture in the seventeenth century.'

[4] On the text 1 *John* ii. 3-4.

But Descartes had reduced the material world to a mechanical system, and had explored, in exclusively logical fashion, problems about God and the soul concerning which theology has many things to say; while Hobbes had entangled the soul in mechanism, and in the name of philosophy had renounced intellectual inquiry into matters of faith. The times demanded a rational defence of religion. And Cudworth's position is that if there is a Copernican system of heavenly bodies, there must be an intellectual system of the universe; and that reason may be guided by faith, as surely as faith can learn from reason.

Of these two adversaries against truth as Cudworth knows it, Hobbes must have seemed to him the more dangerous. This contender for right and law, in his eyes, had proved traitor to both man and God. He had taken his departure from fiction, not from fact; he had begun with man regarded in isolation from God and also from himself, that is to say, from his reason. Man is basically a concupiscible animal, said Hobbes, and enjoys the right to possess whatever his strong arm can secure; and every single man is at war with any other man who may possess something which the two cannot share. In this condition of affairs there are no law-breakers, because there are no laws to be broken; and there are no men *by nature* wicked, 'for the affections of the minde which arise onely from the lower parts of the soule are not wicked themselves.'[1] But this quasi-historical individualism is not as extreme as it appears to be; and beneath the wolf's clothing there hides a soul having some affinities with other souls and even with God. '. . . it is true indeed, that to Man, by nature, or as Man, that is, as soone as he is born, Solitude is an enemy; for Infants have need of others to help them to live, and those of riper years to help them to live well, wherefore I deny not that men (even nature compelling) desire to come together.'[2]

---

[1] *Philosophical Rudiments concerning Government and Society*, London, 1651, *Preface*.   [2] *Ib.*, I. ii.

But his gregarious instinct is too limited in its scope to enable him to develop an organized society; it leads at best to an unstable 'Market-friendship.' And although he is impelled by passion to seize what he wants from another, his reason tells him that he is under a law of nature, which is also the divine law, impotent though it be to secure what it commands. 'That which is done out of necessity, out of endeavour for peace, for the preservation of our selves, is done with Right; otherwise every damage done to a man would be a breach of the naturall Law, and an injury against God.' [1]

Hobbes seeks to justify the principle by which his natural man becomes a partner in a rationally constituted society, as well as a member of the Christian Church, namely, the principle of covenant. A city is one body animated by one soul,[2] he explains, because individual rights have been surrendered for one great end of peace. The transition from the original to the ideal condition is due partly to passion and partly to reason. Certain passions, apparently, move men to desire peace; and 'Reason suggesteth convenient Articles of Peace, upon which men may be drawn to agreement.' [3] Hobbes says, more exactly, that the end which men have in view in restraining themselves 'is the foresight of their own preservation, and of a more contented life thereby.' [4] The accepted virtues, therefore, turn out to be means towards furthering peace. And it looks as if the dictates of natural law, which men may know even in the state of nature, do not oblige unconditionally, unless there exists common agreement that they shall. 'It is not therefore to be imagin'd,' says Hobbes, 'that by Nature (that is, by Reason), men are oblig'd to the exercise of all these Lawes in that state of men wherein they are not practis'd by others. We are oblig'd yet in the interim to a readinesse of mind to observe them whensoever their

[1] *Ib.*, III. xxvii.
[2] *Ib.*, IV. xix.
[3] *Leviathan*, I. xii.
[4] *Ib.*, II. xvii.

observation shall seeme to conduce to the end for which they were ordain'd. We must therefore conclude, that the Law of Nature doth alwayes, and every where oblige in the internall Court, or that of Conscience, but not alwayes in the externall Court, but then onely when it may be done with safety.'[1]

The Christian religion, like the social order, originates in a covenant; for God enters into a pact with men in Baptism and promises them entrance into the Kingdom that is to come upon two conditions—obedience to natural law re-affirmed by Christ (including repentance for disobedience), and faith that He is the promised Messiah.[2] Jesus Christ, no doubt, revealed certain 'points of faith which cannot be understood by the naturall reason, but onely by revelation,' such as the following—'that he was the Christ; that his Kingdome was not terrestriall; that there are rewards, and punishments after this life; that the soule is immortall; that there should be such, and so many Sacraments';[3] but the Christian moral code is identical with the original law, which has been evident from time immemorial to all possessed of a 'quiet mind.' 'The Lawes therefore which Christ contracts in one place,[4] and explaines in another,[5] are no other then those to which all mortall men are obliged, who acknowledge the God of Abraham,'[6] to whom, and to whose seed, God once promised the land of Canaan in return for their obedience and faith; and 'it is manifest, that there were no other Lawes, or worship, which Abraham was obliged to, but the Lawes of nature, rationall worship, and circumcision.'[7] The moral law binding upon Christians is thus, as Butler says, a

---

[1] *Rudiments*, III. xxvii.

[2] Hobbes holds that the Apostles' Creed may be contracted into the single proposition that Jesus is the Messiah, on the ground that many, e.g. the dying thief, upon making this confession were admitted into the Kingdom (*Rudiments*).

[3] *Ib.*, XVII. xiii.   [4] *St. Matt.* xxii. 37 f.   [5] *Ib.*, v., vi. and vii.
[6] *Rudiments*, XVII. viii.   [7] *Ib.*, XVI. v.

'republication' of the old; but Hobbes failed to see that the new truths revealed in Christianity brought new obligations. Butler explains that 'the essence of Revealed Religion' consists 'in religious regards to the Son, and to the Holy Ghost'; and therefore the relations in which Christians stand towards these Two Persons are the source of certain 'duties.' These duties, he goes on to say, are primarily the 'inward religious regards' of 'reverence, honour, love, trust, gratitude, fear, hope'; and so he exalts 'internal worship,' an attitude of mind finding expression in external actions and forms.[1] For Hobbes, on the contrary, 'all worship consists either in words or deeds,' and expresses man's fear of God's irresistible power. 'Worship is an outward act, the sign of inward honour; and whom we endeavour by our homage to appease, if they be angry, or howsoever to make them favourable to us, we are said to worship.'[2] As for man's love to God, it is a settled disposition to yield Him the obedience which is His right; 'for he that loves God and his neighbour, hath a minde to obey all Lawes, both divine and humane. But God requires no more than a minde to obey.'[3] Hobbes holds that there is no excuse for denying the existence of God, because the world must have had a cause, but that it is presumptuous for us to claim to know His essence. 'Neither speak they honourably enough of God, who say we have an Idea of him in our mind; for an Idea is our conception, but conception we have none, except of a finite thing.'[4] It is a mark of the humble mind to think of God by way of analogy.

In *The True Intellectual System of the Universe*, Cudworth makes no pretence of hoping to convince every doubter, because, he says, the matters with which he will deal call for more than an inquirer's sympathetic interest. God, to wit, can be known only by those whose vision has not been dimmed by the folly that goes with bad or careless living.

[1] *Analogy*, II. i. 15.
[2] *Rudiments*, XV. viii.
[3] *Ib.*, XVII. viii.
[4] *Ib.*, XV. xiv.

He is known by multitudes who could not follow an argument sustained to prove His existence: 'minds cleansed and purged from vice may, without syllogistical reasonings and mathematical demonstrations, have an undoubted assurance of the existence of a God. . . .'[1] In *A Treatise of Freewill*, he claims to share Plato's belief in the pragmatic value of 'faith and true opinions'; because simple folk, incapable of demonstrating God's existence, must believe that He exists, 'in order to a morally virtuous and good life.'[2] Here is a case in which we are justified in going beyond the evidence, although the source of error in general lies in 'the rash and incautious use' of our power of giving or withholding assent.

A second limitation imposes itself upon our thinking about God. In an argument conclusions are drawn from premisses, and the latter cannot be gleaned and placed in proper sequence, unless certain axioms have been consented to. The first principle of thought is beyond proving, and, therefore, says Cudworth, the existence of God cannot be proved *a priori*, but must be proved 'by necessary inference from principles, altogether undeniable.'[3] 'And whensoever any thing is thus necessarily inferred from what is undeniable and indubitable, this is a demonstration, though not of the $\delta\iota\acute{o}\tau\iota$, yet of the $\acute{o}\tau\iota$ of it; that the thing is, though not why it is.' And by way of reminding us that this infirmity is not peculiar to either philosophy or theology, but pertains also to an intellectual province sometimes held up as the model of perfect thinking, he adds that 'many of the geometrical demonstrations are no other.'[4]

How, then, does reason confirm faith's assurance; and what reasons are there for holding that God exists? Cud-

---

[1] *The True Intellectual System of the Universe : wherein all the Reason and Philosophy of Atheism is confuted, and its impossibility demonstrated, with a Treatise concerning Eternal and Immutable Morality.* Edition by John Harrison, London, 1845, i. p. xlv.
[2] Edition by John Allen, 1838, p. 41.
[3] Harrison, vol. i. p. xliv.   [4] *Ib.*, iii. p. 30.

worth accepts the criterion of Descartes, that whatever is clearly and distinctly known is true, and explains that clearness obtains when no contradiction lurks in the proposition under examination. But when the problem of God's existence comes to be tackled, it becomes evident that while Cudworth regards Descartes as being in the main on the side of the angels, he views his treatment of the ontological proof with suspicion. Both are agreed that the idea of God is innate, and Cudworth defines it thus: 'The true and proper idea of God, in its most contracted form, is this, a being absolutely perfect; for this is that alone, to which necessary existence is essential, and of which it is demonstrable. Now, as absolute perfection includes in it all that belongs to the Deity, so does it not only comprehend (besides necessary existence) perfect knowledge or understanding, but also omni-causality and omnipotence (in full extent of it); otherwise called infinite power.' [1] He explains elsewhere that by perfect knowledge we are to understand 'that which hath no defect or mixture of ignorance with it or the knowledge of whatsoever is knowable'; and likewise by perfect power 'that which hath no defect or mixture of impotency in it; a power of producing and doing all whatsoever is possible, that is, whatsoever is conceivable.' [2] And when we say that the chief attributes of God are perfect goodness, perfect knowledge, and perfect power, we must not let slip the unity of Him whose attributes they are. For the idea of God is 'a natural and most simple uncompounded idea,' [3] not composed in Locke's way by enlarging empirically derived ideas of imperfect goodness, imperfect knowledge, and imperfect power—a 'bundle of unconceivables and impossibles.' Though it ought to be remarked that Locke, in framing his complex idea of God, suggests a principle of selection, when to 'the ideas of existence and duration, of knowledge and power, of pleasure and happiness,' he appends the ideas 'of several

[1] *Ib.*, i. p. 307.   [2] *Ib.*, ii. p. 537.   [3] *Ib.*, p. 559.

other qualities and powers which it is better to have than to be without.'[1]

Cudworth is in agreement with Descartes that whatever is clearly and distinctly known is true. Descartes, however, will make no use of the principle, until he can be sure that God does not deceive him, and proceeds to show that a deceiving God is self-contradictory; but Cudworth holds that even to entertain the supposition that God may deceive vilifies one's thinking. He points out that Descartes involves himself in a circular argument. He allows that if there is not a good God, we cannot be certain of anything; but he maintains that we know Him to be good by insight of the natural light. 'For to say that the truth of our understanding faculties is put out of all doubt and question, as soon as ever we are assured of the existence of a God essentially good, who therefore cannot deceive; whilst this existence of a God is in the meantime itself no otherwise proved, than by our understanding faculties; that is, at once to prove the truth of God's existence from our faculties of reason and understanding, and again to prove the truth of those faculties from the existence of a God essentially good: this, I say, is plainly to move round in a circle, and to prove nothing at all: a gross oversight, which the forementioned philosopher seems plainly guilty of.'[2]

Cudworth goes on to say that Descartes's error goes even deeper: he has not conceived clearly and distinctly his own idea of the perfect Being. He has driven a wedge into the idea, and separated perfect power from perfect knowledge, with the result that the power attributed to God is imperfect. Power divorced from knowledge is irrational, and a God having power to deceive cannot be God. Besides, power cannot exert itself over truth: 'truth is not factitious; it is a thing which cannot be arbitrarily *made*, but *is*.'[3] 'So that conception and knowledge are hereby made to be the measure of all power, even omnipotence or infinite power

[1] *Essay*, II. xxiii. 33.   [2] *Ib.*, iii. p. 32.   [3] *Ib.*, p. 33.

itself being determined thereby; from whence it follows that power hath no dominion over understanding, truth, and knowledge; nor can infinite power make any thing whatsoever to be clearly conceivable, for could it make contradictious things clearly conceivable, then would itself be able to do them; because whatsoever can be clearly conceived by any, may unquestionably be done by infinite power.'[1] 'And, certainly, if any one did desire to persuade the world, that Cartesius, notwithstanding all his pretences to demonstrate a Deity, was indeed but a hypocritical Theist, or personated and disguised Atheist, he could not have a fairer pretence for it out of all his writings, than from hence; this being plainly to destroy the Deity, by making one attribute thereof to devour and swallow up another; infinite will and power, infinite understanding and wisdom.'[2]

Cudworth's point is that the idea of a perfect Being must contain all possible, or clearly conceivable, perfections; and that these perfect attributes cannot contradict one another, else they would not be attributes of a perfect Being. The content of the idea is deducible from the idea; and if we try to construct the idea synthetically, by heaping together the ideas of all conceivable perfections, we are in fact proceeding analytically and asking what is necessary to be conceived as pertaining to the idea of a perfect Being. The idea of a triangle, for instance, contains the ideas of three angles, because the three are necessarily conceived in the simple idea of a triangle. Our author says that 'the genuine attributes of the Deity, namely, such as are demonstrable of an absolutely perfect Being, are not only not contradictious, but also necessarily connected together, and inseparable from one another. For there could not possibly be one thing infinite in wisdom only, another thing infinite only in power, and another thing only infinite in duration or eternal. But the very same thing which is infinite in wisdom, must needs be also infinite in power, and infinite

[1] *Ib.*, p. 35.   [2] *Ib.*, ii. p. 533.

in duration, and so vice versa. That which is infinite in any one perfection, must of necessity have all perfections in it. Thus are all the genuine attributes of the Deity not only not contradictious, but also inseparably concatenate; and the idea of God no congeries either of disagreeing things; or else of such as are unnecessarily connected with one another.'[1] And he takes the wind out of a possible adversary's sails by pointing out that the incomprehensibility of God is an argument in favour of His existence. 'Were there no other being in the world, but what our finite and imperfect understandings could span or fathom, and encompass round about, look through and through, have a commanding view of, and perfectly conquer and subdue under them; then there could be nothing absolutely and infinitely perfect, that is, no God.'[2]

Cudworth's caution will restrain any reader who may be tempted by the cogency of his argument to arrogate too much to human intellect; for he does not let us forget that he is dealing with the clear idea of a perfect Being as it is in the mind of an imperfect being. 'In very truth, all the several attributes of the Deity are nothing else but so many partial and inadequate conceptions of one and the same simple perfect being, taken in as it were by piecemeal, by reason of the imperfection of our human understandings, which could not fully conceive it all together at once; and therefore are they really all but one thing, though they have the appearance of multiplicity to us. As the one simple light of the sun, diversely refracted and reflected from a rorid cloud, hath to us the appearance of the variegated colours of the rainbow.'[3] Our idea of the perfect Being may be clear and distinct; but the perfect Being Himself transcends our clear and distinct idea of Him. We cannot know God clearly by ideas. We apprehend, but do not comprehend, Him.[4] This limitation is not peculiar to our knowledge of God; it distinguishes our knowledge of things from our

[1] *Ib.*, p. 559. [2] *Ib.*, p. 519. [3] *Ib.*, p. 559. [4] *Ib.*, p. 531.

knowledge of ideas. Anticipating Berkeley, Cudworth admits that 'even body itself which the Atheists think themselves so well acquainted with, because they can feel it with their fingers, and which is the only substance that they acknowledge either in themselves or the universe, hath such puzzling difficulties and entanglements in the speculation of it, that they can never be able to extricate themselves from.'[1] Anticipating Kant, he says that 'it is certain, that we cannot fully comprehend ourselves.' 'But though we do not comprehend all truth, as if our mind were above it, or master of it, and cannot penetrate into, and look quite through the nature of every thing, yet may rational souls frame certain ideas and conceptions, of whatever is in the orb of being proportionate to their own nature, and sufficient for their purpose. And though we cannot fully comprehend the Deity, nor exhaust the infiniteness of its perfection, yet may we have an idea or conception of a Being absolutely perfect; such a one as is *nostro modulo conformis*, "agreeable and proportionate to our measure and scantling"; as we may approach near to a mountain, and touch it with our hands, though we cannot encompass it all round, and enclasp it within our arms. Whatsoever is in its own nature absolutely inconceivable, is nothing; but not whatsoever is not fully comprehensible by our imperfect understandings.'[2]

What reasons does Cudworth give for the existence of a God answering to our idea of Him; and how, in his way of thinking, do we know that there is a Being whom to know is not fully to comprehend? In the first place, we note that he refuses to pontificate on the validity of the ontological argument as Descartes states it. He will not discredit it, but he is of opinion that it will fail to carry conviction in quarters where conviction is most needed. He is satisfied to set down side by side its merits and demerits, and then to leave the matter to the judgment of 'the intelligent and impartial reader.'[3] On the negative side, it can be said that

[1] *Ib.*, p. 518.   [2] *Ib.*, p. 518.   [3] *Ib.*, iii. p. 41.

we are 'able to frame in our minds the ideas of many other things, that never were, nor will be';[1] and that although the idea of a perfect Being includes necessary existence within it, so far from being entitled to infer therefrom the existence of a perfect Being, we are entitled merely to conclude 'that whatsoever hath no necessary and eternal existence, is no absolutely perfect Being.'[2] On the positive side, it must be said that when we think of necessary existence in the idea of a perfect Being, we are thinking of 'a necessary schesis or relation to existence,' as contrasted with 'an impossible schesis to existence' in a self-contradictory idea, and as contrasted with 'a contingent schesis to existence' in an imperfect idea: and so of the first we are entitled to conclude that 'it is impossible it should not be.'[3]

There is a hint given in this antinomy of the way in which Cudworth himself prefers to pass from the idea of God to the existence of God. He reasons from imperfect existing things—from himself, the things about him, and the universe around him.[4] The idea of a perfect Being cannot be shelved, he would say, as though it were a figment of imagination; because a Being answering to the idea is demanded by the stubborn fact of existing things. These are not strewn about fortuitously, without relation to each other: they are instances of degrees of value, and significant of the Supreme Value and Creator of all values. 'Wherefore it is certain,' he concludes, 'that in the universe things did not thus ascend and mount, or climb up from lower perfection to higher; but, on the contrary, descend and slide

[1] *Ib.*, p. 38.   [2] *Ib.*, p. 39.   [3] *Ib.*, pp. 39-40.
[4] *Cf.* ii. p. 515: 'Wherefore since the Atheists cannot deny the existence of soul or mind in men, though no such thing fall under external sense, they have as little reason to deny the existence of a perfect mind, presiding over the universe, without which it cannot be conceived whence our imperfect ones should be derived. The existence of that God, whom no eye hath seen nor can see, is plainly proved by reason from his effects, in the visible phenomena of the universe, and from what we are conscious of within ourselves.'

down from higher to lower: so that the first original of all things was not the most imperfect, but the most perfect Being.'[1] Later in the same volume, he returns to his conception of a universe laid out in terraces of value; and he shows that when man divines values in the created order, he is proclaiming his inheritance in the order of being where values have origin. 'Moreover, nothing can be more evident than this, that mind and understanding hath a higher degree of entity or perfection in it, and is a greater reality in nature, than mere senseless matter or bulky extension. And consequently, the things, which belong to souls and minds, to rational and intellectual beings as such, must not have less, but more reality in them, than the things which belong to inanimate bodies. Wherefore, the differences of just and unjust, honest and dishonest, are greater realities in nature, than the differences of hard and soft, hot and cold, moist and dry. He that doth not perceive any higher degree of perfection in a man than in an oyster, nay, than in a clod of earth or lump of ice, in a piece of paste or piecrust, hath not the reason or understanding of a man in him. There is unquestionably a scale or ladder of nature, and degrees of perfection and entity one above another, as of life, sense, and cogitation, above dead, senseless, and unthinking matter; . . . Wherefore there being plainly a scale or ladder of entity, the order of things was unquestionably, in way of descent, from higher perfection downward to lower; it being as impossible for a greater perfection to be produced from a lesser, as for something to be caused by nothing. Neither are the steps or degrees of this ladder (either upward or downward) infinite; but as the foot, bottom, or lowest round thereof is stupid and senseless matter, devoid of all life and understanding, so is the head, top, and summity of it a perfect omnipotent Being, comprehending itself, and all possibilities of things. A perfect understanding Being is the beginning and head

[1] *Ib.*, iii. p. 57.

of the scale of entity; from whence things gradually descend downward, lower from lower, till they end in senseless matter.'[1]

This philosophical argument coincides with a religious attitude; because reason and faith both set out from the same point, namely, experience of value, and reach the same goal, namely, experience of God. The difference is that, whereas reason moves slowly, faith passes more quickly into sight. Accordingly, Cudworth says in the preface to *The True Intellectual System* that 'this divine goodness and perfection, as displaying and manifesting itself in the works of nature and providence, is supposed in Scripture to be the very foundation of our Christian faith; when that is defined to be the substance and evidence *rerum sperandarum*; that is, "of whatsoever is" (by a good man) "to be hoped for."'[2] The religious temper of mind is a medley of faith, hope, and love; and these 'do all suppose an essential goodness in the Deity.'[3]

Among the other arguments for the existence of God advanced by our author, there is one deserving special mention. It has its roots in the affective life. We are, he would say, seekers after value who do not tire in the search, explorers in a sphere of things whose limits lie beyond our farthest adventures hitherto; and our prizes prove always to be earnests of better things yet in store. What we hope to know and enjoy lies above us to be reached, rather than below us to be arranged. And this something more is something akin: so, at least, we explain the peculiar emotion that it evokes. Here is Cudworth's own analysis of what he feels: 'And nature itself plainly intimates to us, that there is some such absolutely perfect Being, which, though not inconceivable, yet is incomprehensible to our finite understandings, by certain passions which it hath implanted in us, that otherwise would want an object to display themselves upon; namely, those of devout veneration, adoration,

[1] *Ib.*, pp. 434-5.   [2] *Ib.*, i. p. xlv.   [3] *Ib.*, ii. p. 576.

and admiration, together with a kind of ecstasy and pleasing horror; which, in the silent language of nature, seem to speak thus much to us, that there is some object in the world, so much bigger and vaster than our mind and thoughts, that it is the very same to them that the ocean is to narrow vessels; so that when they have taken into themselves as much as they can thereof by contemplation, and filled up all their capacity, there is still an immensity of it left without, which cannot enter in for want of room to receive it, and therefore must be apprehended after some other strange and more mysterious manner, viz. by their being as it were plunged into it, and swallowed up or lost in it.' [1] From another passage in which Cudworth replies to some atheists who try to show that God is but a projection of the mind, originating in fear and ignorance, we gather that a *numinous* experience, such as he describes, is reserved for a good and contented man. It is the wonder felt by one bowed in reverence before values which exceed his grasp; if he were not good, he would stand cowed as before an object strange and terrible. The feet of a good man are set 'in a large room'; [2] and he moves freely to and fro in a home. 'Religious fear,' defined as 'an awful regard' of God, 'who is essentially just,' [3] is awakened in him; because he is conscious of a moral realm in which he enjoys a place, and from which he knows that he will not be dislodged. Those who experience this fear, says Cudworth, have already found their chief good 'in that which is most truly their own, namely, the use of their own will.' [4]

What does Cudworth mean by God's goodness? It is His primary attribute, the measure of His wisdom, as His wisdom

---

[1] *Ib.*, pp. 519-20. *Cf.* J. H. Muirhead, *The Platonic Tradition in Anglo-Saxon Philosophy*, p. 48.
[2] *Psalm* xxxi. 8.   [3] Harrison, ii. p. 574.
[4] *Ib.*, p. 569. *Cf.* Kant, *Critique of Aesthetic Judgment*, ii. 28 (Trans. by J. C. Meredith): 'So the righteous man fears God without being afraid of Him, because he regards the case of his wishing to resist God and His commandments as one which need cause *him* no anxiety.'

in turn is the measure of His power. The illustration given of this mystery is that 'of an infinite circle, whose inmost centre is simple goodness, the radii, "rays" and expanded area, "plat" thereof, all comprehending and immutable wisdom, the exterior periphery or interminate circumference, omnipotent will or activity, by which every thing without God is brought forth into existence.'[1] But this representation of inseparable attributes gives way to the more comprehensive truth that the Divine essence is goodness.[2] Cudworth has too strong a hold upon the unity and simplicity of God to leave an impression that perfect goodness could exist apart from perfect wisdom and perfect power. And there is the empirically grounded consideration that knowledge and power do not of themselves constitute the *summum bonum*. It 'may be experimentally found within ourselves . . . that there is a certain life, or vital and moral disposition of soul, which is more inwardly and thoroughly satisfactory, not only than sensual pleasure, but also than all knowledge and speculation whatsoever.'[3] Plato, although he 'sometimes talks too metaphysically and cloudily' of God's goodness, is right when he teaches that therein lies the sufficient reason of creation. And the universe, in which all parts exist for the sake of the whole, shows that God's goodness continues to bless the work of His hand. But Scripture, 'without any metaphysical pomp and obscurity,' brings us nearest to the meaning of God's essence, when it calls Him Love, for this word denotes a living personal Being. And the Love that is God is not the *Eros* lauded by the Greeks. The latter is the desire of an imperfect being, as likely to become perverted through pursuing bad ends, as sublimated through pursuing good ones. A love which originates with the wants of a creature 'therefore could not be the first

---

[1] *Ib.*, iii. p. 540. This trilogy, found in Article I. (*potentia, sapientia, bonitas*), and also in Calvin (*Institutes*, I. v. 3), appears to go back to *Wisdom*, vii. 24 ff.
[2] *Ib.*, i. pp. 314-6.   [3] *Ib.*, p. 313.

principle of all things. Wherefore we see no very great reason, but that in a rectified and qualified sense this may pass for true theology; that Love is the supreme Deity and original of all things; namely, if by it be meant eternal, self-originated, intellectual Love, or essential and substantial goodness, that having an infinite overflowing fulness and fecundity dispenses itself uninvidiously, according to the best wisdom, sweetly governs all, without any force or violence . . ., and reconciles the whole world into harmony.'[1]

We pass to Cudworth's view of the world. He agrees with Descartes that it is a world of extended matter and motion, but he proceeds to show that it exhibits also a species of motion other than that which occurs when a portion of matter changes its place. He conceives this after analogy with the self-motion of will, where there is movement towards a chosen end. This motion distinguishes living things from lifeless matter. Mechanism, Cudworth holds, cannot account for all the facts. There is more than local motion in a physical organism, for it is more than the aggregate of its parts; and there is more than local motion in certain physiological actions, such as respiration and beating of the heart. The human organism, without conscious control, can sustain continuous and prolonged action in which interim actions occur in co-ordinated series, as in dancing and singing. There is the phenomenon of instinct in certain lower forms of life—'the bees in mellification, and in framing their combs and hexagonial cells, the spiders in spinning their webs, the birds in building their nests' —which, so far from suggesting sagacity on their part, shows 'that something may act artificially and for ends, without comprehending the reason of what it doth. . . .'[2] And so for extension and thought, Cudworth substitutes extension, unconscious life, and conscious life. These three, he writes, are 'the first heads of being.'[3]

[1] *Ib.*, pp. 178-9.   [2] *Ib.*, p. 243.   [3] *Ib.*, p. 245.

On the strength of this and kindred evidence, Cudworth argues for a world-soul, or plastic nature, by whose agency material atoms are woven into one harmonious system. Though mighty in working, it is the lowest form of life, God's drudge, directing passive material towards ends which express His will. Alternative to this lesser providence —chance being excluded as an explanation of apparent rational control—there is only the absurd hypothesis 'that God himself doth all immediately, and, as it were with his own hands, form the body of every gnat and fly, insect and mite. . . .'[1] Two other points in favour of plastic nature are noted. In the first place, untoward phenomena, as John Smith also thinks,[2] may be put down to its 'errors and bungles,' the material upon which it works being 'inept and contumacious';[3] and, in the second place, a loop-hole is secured for God's intervention, when the interest of the good calls for 'a higher providence.'[4] Plastic nature is God's surrogate, making meaningless matter significant of His goodness, transforming the dull earth into a convenient dwelling-place for man and beast. The world-soul helps us to see how the world is very good.

Cudworth does not appear to attribute special cosmic function to the Holy Spirit; nor does he make any suggestion of a developing universe. When he speaks of a 'slow and gradual process, that is in the generations of things,'[5] and of 'the evolution of the world,'[6] he is thinking of growth *within* the whole. Matter, life, sentiency, and cogitation are levels of being, and an array of terms is employed to denote their distinctness: for example, a higher cannot be 'produced' or 'generated' by a lower, nor can it 'spring out of,' or 'result' or 'emerge' from a lower. The terms 'result' and 'emerge' seem to be used synonymously, and there is no hint that an emergent level, as

[1] *Ib.*, p. 218.   [2] *A Short Discourse on Atheism.*
[3] Harrison, i. p. 223.   [4] *Ib.*, p. 224.
[5] *Ib.*, p. 223.   [6] *Ib.*, iii. p. 477.

contrasted with a resultant, possesses new qualities not found in the factors which occasioned it.[1]

Our author praises Descartes for having rehabilitated atomism: 'we can never sufficiently applaud that ancient atomical philosophy, so successfully revived of late by Cartesius, in that it shows distinctly what matter is, and what it can amount unto, namely, nothing else but what may be produced from mere magnitude, figure, site, local motion, and rest. . . .'[2] He holds that material things act upon a knowing subject, and that knowledge begins with sensation. 'And there is in all sensation, without dispute, first, a passion in the body of the sentient, which bodily passion is nothing else but local motion impressed upon the nerves from the objects without, and thence propagated and communicated to the brain, where all sensation is made.'[3] Sensation is not passive, 'a body's bare reaction or resistance to that motion of another body,' but active, 'a cogitation, recognition, or vital perception and consciousness of these motions or passions of the body.'[4] It is action on the part of a body-soul complex, and the soul's function in the partnership is to experience 'a compassion with its own body';[5] and if it should occur without recurrence of the appropriate stimulus, it is called a 'phantasm.'[6] Colours, sounds, smells, and the like, are commonly attributed to things, but, strictly speaking, they belong to embodied souls:[7] 'so that they do in a manner mock us, when we conceive of them as things really existing without us, being nothing but our own shadows, and the vital passive energies of our own souls. Though it was not the intention of God or

---

[1] *Cf.* i. p. xlvi: ' . . . it being as certain to us, as any thing in all geometry, that cogitation and understanding can never possibly result out of magnitudes, figures, sites, and local motions (which is all that ourselves can allow to body) however compounded together. Nor indeed in that other way of qualities, is it better conceivable, how they should emerge out of hot and cold, moist and dry, thick and thin; . . .'
[2] *Ib.*, iii. p. 646.   [3] *Ib.*, p. 557.   [4] *Ib.*, p. 558.
[5] *Ib.*, p. 560.   [6] *Ib.*, p. 574.   [7] *Ib.*, p. 560.

nature to abuse us herein, but a most wise contrivance thus to beautify and adorn the visible and material world, to add lustre or embellishment to it, that it might have charms, relishes, and allurements in it, to gratify our appetites; whereas otherwise really in itself, the whole corporeal world in its naked hue, is nothing else but a heap of dust or atoms, of several figures and magnitudes, variously agitated up and down; so that these things, which we look upon as such real things without us, are not properly the modifications of bodies themselves, but several modifications, passions, and affections of our own souls.'[1]

Another step is taken when qualities of sensation are distinguished. Sounds are not colours, and smells are not tastes: 'wherefore that which judges of all the senses and their several objects, cannot be itself any sense, but something of a superior nature.'[2] Those who 'maintain the human soul itself to be but a mere blank, or white sheet of paper, that hath nothing at all in it, but what was scribbled upon it by the objects of sense,' are mistaken. 'For hereby, as they plainly make knowledge and understanding to be, in its own nature, junior to sense, and the very creature of sensibles; so do they also imply the rational soul, and mind itself, to be as well generated as the sensitive, wherein it is virtually contained; or to be nothing but a higher modification of matter, agreeably to that Leviathan doctrine, that men differ no otherwise from brute animals, than only in their organization, and the use of speech or words.'[3] But sensation is not the same thing as knowledge: the former 'lies flat and grovelling in the individuals,' the latter can 'rise up or ascend to an abstract universal notion.'[4]

In this epistemological process a sense-datum is, as it were, a question, and the intellectual essence signified is the answer: there is junior sensory invitation, and there is senior intelligent grasp. 'Sense is but a slight and superficial perception of the outside and accidentals of a corporeal

[1] *Ib.*, p. 644. [2] *Ib.*, p. 555. [3] *Ib.*, p. 438. [4] *Ib.*, p. 564.

substance, it doth not penetrate into the profundity or inward essence of it'; [1] and 'knowledge is not a knock or thrust from without, but it consisteth in the awakening and exciting of the inward active powers of the mind.'[2] Reason projects its interpretation upon assemblies of atoms, and names them objects; and to it belongs the task of conceiving an external world by weaving a conceptual scheme which will explain its meaning and purpose. 'Just in the same manner nature doth as it were talk to us in the outward objects of sense, and import various sentiments, ideas, phantasms, and cogitations, not by stamping or impressing them passively upon the soul from without, but only by certain local motions from them, as it were dumb signs made in the brain; it having been first constituted and appointed by nature's law, that such local motions shall signify such sensible ideas and phantasms, though there be no similitude at all betwixt them; for what similitude can there be betwixt any local motions and the senses of pain or hunger, and the like, as there is no similitude betwixt many words and sounds, and the thoughts which they signify.'[3] Cudworth would protest, no doubt, that he is not resorting to a *deus ex machina* at this point; for he holds that human reason is no pelican wandering in the wilderness, but a living image of God, and a partaker in the essences of the Divine Mind. Man thinks, within the limits of finitude, as God thinks. 'It is all one to affirm, that there are eternal rationes, essences of things, and verities necessarily existing, and to say that there is an infinite, omnipotent, and eternal Mind, necessarily existing, that always actually comprehendeth himself, the essences of all things, and their verities; or, rather, which is the rationes, essences, and verities of all things; for the rationes and essences of things are not dead things, like so many statues, images, or pictures hung up somewhere by themselves alone in the world: neither are truths mere sentences and propositions written down with

[1] *Ib.*, p. 565.   [2] *Ib.*, p. 566.   [3] *Ib.*, pp. 612-3.

ink upon a book, but they are living things, and nothing but modifications of mind or intellect; and therefore the first intellect is essentially and archetypally all rationes and verities, and all particular created intellects are but derivative participations of it, that are printed by it with the same ectypal signatures upon them.'[1]

The office of the material world is to awaken man's soul, his powers of sensation and reason. Things compete for his interest, and he must enjoy those only which he can weave into the moral and religious life. He must make them his servants by learning to master himself, which he will do by becoming a servant of God. Cudworth says in *A Treatise of Freewill* that there is 'an ever bubbling fountain in the centre of the soul, an elater or spring of motion, both a *primum* and *perpetuum mobile* in us, the first wheel that sets all the other wheels in motion, and an everlasting and incessant mover.'[2] And more particularly, that 'the soul of man hath in it $\mu άντευμα\ τὶ$, a certain vaticination, presage, scent, and odor of one *summum bonum*, one supreme highest good transcending all others, without which they will be all ineffectual as to complete happiness, and signify nothing, a certain philosopher's stone that can turn all into gold.'[3] He goes on to say that man's desire for good is of 'necessary nature,' and compares its constancy with conservation of motion in the Cartesian extended world. But this desire is one among many, and man must achieve internal harmony by exercising will. 'I say, therefore, that the $τὸ\ ἡγεμονικὸν$ in every man, and indeed that which is properly, we ourselves (we rather having those other things of necessary nature than being them), is the soul as comprehending itself, all its concerns and interests, its abilities and capacities, and holding itself, as it were, in its own hand, as it were redoubled upon itself, having a power of intending or exerting itself more or less, in consideration and deliberation . . . in order to self-improvement and the self-promoting of its

[1] *Ib.*, p. 626.   [2] P. 28.   [3] *Ib.*, p. 30.

own good, the fixing and conserving itself in the same.'[1] When this basic desire for good has been directed steadfastly towards an intelligible idea of the good, the good life is ensured; and immoral action occurs at precisely the same point as intellectual error, namely, in giving assent to an idea not clearly understood. But noble as free-will is, we must acknowledge humbly that it is a perfection of an imperfect being, and of a lower order than 'liberty as it is a state of pure perfection,'[2] *alias*, 'a communicated Divine perfection or participation of the Divine nature,'[3] which consists in habitual delight in the practice of goodness.

Nature's 'invitations' and the soul's 'inward and active anticipations'[4] are the requisites for living the good life. When we understand the world in the light of our native concepts, we can hear it whisper of God who made it, and who reveals through it our kinship with Himself. When we understand what the world has to offer, our blind groping after apparent goods yields place to a concentrated search for the supreme good which contradicts every competitor; and desire for value is transformed into knowledge of God. But in the realm of the eternal to know is to have, and to have is to be.

[1] *Ib.*, p. 36.   [2] *Ib.*, p. 63.   [3] *Ib.*, p. 65.
[4] Harrison, iii. p. 599.

V
HENRY MORE

I staied some time at Cambridge and was much delighted with Dr. More's conversation. There was a sweet simplicity in his whole manner that charmed me. I shall never forget one saying of his with relation to the disputes then on foot concerning Church government and ritualls, he said none of these things were so good as to make men good, nor so bad as to make men bad, but might be either good or bad according to the hands in which they fell.

BURNET.

CHAPTER V

HENRY MORE [1]

A FAVOURITE Biblical text with the Cambridge Platonists, it has often been pointed out, is '*The spirit of man is the candle of the Lord*'; [2] but probably we shall discern best the spirit that was Henry More by reference to a passage in the *Epistle to the Romans*—'*for the invisible things of him from the creation of the world are clearly seen, being understood by the things that are made, . . .*' [3] This text provides as serviceable a key to his mind as does another in the *Epistle to the Hebrews* to the mind of John Smith—'*for he that cometh to God must believe that he is, . . .*' [4] It is not suggested that More's approach to God is less immediate than Smith's, only that he prefers to see Him in nature, where He discovers Himself, and even to linger and listen while she sings silently to her Creator's praise. 'For it is manifest,' he writes, 'that this Lamp of God that burneth in us, is fed and nourished from external Objects.' [5] Nature, like Holy

---

[1] 1614–87.   [2] *Prov.* xx. 27.
[3] i. 20. Cf. *Divine Dialogues, Containing sundry Disquisitions & Instructions Concerning the Attributes and Providence of God*, London, 1668, *Preface*, where the deistic tendency of Descartes's mechanistic theory is deprecated: 'It is as confessed a Principle with him, that Matter alone with such a degree of Motion as is supposed now in the Universe will produce all the Phaenomena of the World, Sun, Moon, and Stars, Air, Water, Earth, Plants, Animals, and the Bodies of Men, in such order and organization as they are found. Which Principle in his Philosophy certainly must prove a very inept Interpreter of Rom. i. 19, 20, where the externall Power and Godhead is said clearly to be seen by the things that are made; insomuch that the Gentiles become thereby unexcusable.'
[4] xi. 6.
[5] *An Explanation of the Grand Mystery of Godliness*, 1660, p. 408.

Scripture, is in its own way a book of revelation, and he who runs may read. And by way of showing how reasonable it is that Christianity, although intended for all men, should be mysterious, he discloses how he himself could respond to the still small voice of nature whispering of eternal things. 'That a due measure of Obscurity makes a Mystery the more venerable, is a Truth suggested to us by several observations. How Shades and Silence affect our very Senses, every one can witness who is not of so course a contexture of Body that onely gross and fierce Objects can move him. But he whose Senses are more passive and delicate, can with pleasure relate how he is affected when he enters into some shady and invious Wood or Grove, the thickness of whose Trees and redoubled Shadows stops his sight and hopes of ever passing through all that growes on that Sacred ground; but what he sees, he approves of as delightful, and conceives a peculiar pleasure in that confused divination or obscure representation of things there, where his Eyes cannot reach, nor his Feet approach. The Silence also of the place encreases the solemness thereof, in which (as Plutarch saies well) there is something profound and mysterious.'[1] More's mysticism preserves a sound proportion, and he never lets his heart run away with his head, or for that matter with his body either; and he rebukes all Enthusiasts, who imagine that a man's union with God is of one kind with the manner of the union between the Divine and the human in the Person of Christ. Divinity in man, he says, is *Forma assistens*; Divinity in Christ is *Forma informans*.[2] Nature and human nature have each their own values; and in the historical order real values are being wrought out. Consequently, it is a perversion of Christianity to concentrate our attention upon the Christ of experience, and to neglect the Jesus of history; and if we seek to attain to the divine life that lies open to us, we shall hold fast to 'the Truth and Necessity of both Christ within

[1] *Ib.*, p. 453.   [2] *Ib.*, p. 14.

and Christ without.'[1] As we shall see in the sequel, right conduct performed amid the changing situations of this work-a-day world issues forth, when our highest spiritual principle and our animal propensities have become attuned; and it is folly to suppose that true peace comes by attempting to pass our time in aloofness from the body. Of those who err after this fashion, More asks: 'what do they effect but a clear Day shining upon a barren Heath, that feeds neither Cow nor Horse? neither Sheep nor Shepherd is to be seen there, but only a vast silent Solitude, and one uniform parchedness and vacuity.'[2]

More's reluctant pen caught the infection of his own 'Scripturient Age'; and we may risk making the generalization that all he wrote was designed in order to portray and defend the truth of man's happiness as he found it in his own life. He was convinced that the stage upon which man's life is set supplies him with all the background that he needs for living a life which is properly divine. This means that More's interest is religious in the main, but not on that account detached from philosophical and ethical study. On the contrary, he would have it that being at peace with God is consistent with feeling at home in the world, as well as with being zealous for the good of all God's creatures, the humblest included with the most highly favoured. We see More led along the divine path by the hands of two guides; and if he beholds visions sometimes unperceived by his guides, he would assure us that, but for their help, he would not be walking where he walks. Religion accepts gladly the findings of a true philosophy and a true ethic, and thereby assures itself of its own veracity. Faith transcends reason not either by opposing it or submitting to it, but by asserting its own reasonableness. More's design, he tells us in a preface, 'is not to Theologize in Philosophy, but to

[1] *Ib.*, p. ix.
[2] *A Collection of Several Philosophical Writings of Dr. Henry More*, London, 1662, *Conjectura Cabbalistica*, p. 158.

draw an Exoterick Fence or exteriour Fortification about Theologie';[1] and he asserts that he will substantiate certain philosophical truths, in order that certain objectors will have no excuse for attacking the Christian religion.

As we read More's treatises, we soon become aware that he is not concerned primarily with the project of establishing a philosophical system that will stand four-square against the assaults of all possible disputants to its title: and we overhear him while he analyses and justifies his own experience of God. He is far from belittling reason, but he finds that it is not competent to set out in so many propositions the exact bearings of his soul's relationship to God. The knowledge of God which has come to him cannot be expressed in a clear and distinct idea. He will disclose as much as he can understand, and having done this, he will confess that the remainder is indescribable. And the cause of this enforced reticence is not far to seek: the man is writing of something more elusive than an idea, deeper than a feeling, less effortful than an act of will, more patient than desire—of God's life manifested in his own. For the guidance of others, he will try to explain that human nature has all the requisites for making an ascent to this divine life, because He who is Himself Divine descends and draws it to Himself.

What contribution, in More's view, can we credit to reason in the movement which is man's ascent? A first reply, though but a partial one, is that reason, in the strength of its own natural light, explains to a man the meaning of his experience, and shows him that he must rule his life after certain self-evident principles, intellectual and moral. A further reply is that reason, working upon certain materials of its own providing as well as upon other materials presented by the external world, is able to demonstrate two truths which condition the possibility of there being a divine life open to man, namely, the existence of God and the immortality of the soul. Reason's business in the venture, in the first

[1] *Ib.*, p. vi.

place, is to construct a philosophy round these two pivots, God and man; and, very conveniently, the business has been already very well done. Plato wrote aforetime on behalf of the soul, and Descartes has even now been honouring God and the soul by putting the material universe in its own proper mechanical place; though, for that matter, it must be conceded that on this problem Plato and Descartes between them have said nothing but what can be read out of Moses by a discerning mind. But can reason be trusted? More's answer is interesting, because it shows how closely he allies reason with faith. He says that there is no trusting reason, unless there is at the same time a disposition to trust in the good God. 'But when I speak of demonstrating there is a God, I would not be suspected of so much vanity and ostentation, as to be thought I mean to bring no Arguments but such as are so convictive, that a mans Understanding shall be forced to confess that it is impossible to be otherwise than I have concluded. For, for mine own part, I am prone to believe that there is nothing at all to be so demonstrated. For it is possible that Mathematical evidence it self may be but a constant undiscoverable Delusion, which our nature is necessarily and perpetually obnoxious unto, and that either fatally or fortuitously there has been in the world time out of minde such a Being as we call Man, whose essentiall Property it is to be then most of all mistaken, when he conceives a thing most evidently true. And why may not this be as well as any thing else, if you will have all things fatall or casuall without a God? For there can be no curb to this wilde conceit, but by supposing that we our selves exist from some higher Principle that is absolutely Good and Wise, which is all one as to acknowledge That there is a God.'[1] And there is yet another condition to be observed, if indeed it be not a practical deduction from the first; for he who would essay to demonstrate the existence of the perfect Being, must evince in his conscience and manner

[1] *A Collection . . . An Antidote against Atheism*, p. 10.

of life that he strives after perfection in his motives and conduct.

It will be unnecessary to review More's proofs for the existence of God, because he merely repeats the arguments of those who have gone before; though it is important to note that he regards the proofs advanced as being his own peculiar and individual property, because reason itself, whose fruits they are, is as much his as anybody else's. 'For I borrowed them not from Books,' he avers in the *Preface* to *An Antidote against Atheism*, 'but fetch'd them from the very nature of the thing it self, and indelible Ideas of the Soul of Man.' The argument from the innate idea of God, that is to say, from the innate vigour of the mind, is exploited, in spite of Cudworth's hesitations as to its validity; the argument from conscience is marshalled too, with the addendum that a God, who shall apportion happiness in accordance with virtue in the next world if not in this, is clearly demanded; the evident providential ordering of the world, animals not being forgotten, is stressed; and —since he has to deal with 'the obstinate and refractory Atheist'—well-attested 'historical,' though miraculous, occurrences, amongst them included the doings of the Pied Piper of Hamelin,[1] are brought forward 'for the proving that there are Spirits.'[2]

In view of More's expressed approval of Descartes's work —an approval which subsequently he came to modify[3]—it

---

[1] *Ib.*, p. 100.
[2] *Ib.*, p. 142: 'For assuredly that Saying is not more true in Politicks, No Bishop, no King; then this in Metaphysicks, No Spirit, No God.'
[3] Cf. *Divine Dialogues*, p. 47: 'Cuphophron ("A zealous, but Airie-minded Platonist and Cartesian, or Mechanist")—Well, be the future Fate of things what it will, I doubt not but Cartesius will be admired to all posterity. Bathynous ("The Deeply-thoughtfull or profoundly-thinking man")—Undoubtedly, O Cuphophron; for he will appear to men a person of the most eminent wit and folly that ever yet trode the stage of this Earth.'
For an account of More's attitude towards Descartes, see P. R. Anderson, *Science in Defence of Liberal Religion*, 1933.

is important to observe that he qualifies his acceptance of the intellectual approach to God. He does not claim to entertain clear and distinct ideas of either God or man. Indeed he holds that we cannot isolate in thought substance from its attributes, and say that we know it independently of them. 'The Subject, or naked Essence or Substance of a thing, is utterly unconceivable to any of our Faculties': [1] so runs one of his axioms. And it follows, therefore, that while we cannot know God in substance, we can know Him in His attributes, which are 'as conspicuous as the Attributes of any Subject or Substance whatever: From which a man may easily define Him thus; God is a Spirit Eternal, Infinite in Essence and Goodness, Omniscient, Omnipotent, and of himself necessarily Existent.' [2] And More goes on to argue that 'the Notion of a Spirit is as naturally conceivable as the Notion of a Body'; [3] because we can at least be clear about their respectively distinctive properties, namely, the penetrability and indivisibility of spirit, and the impenetrability and divisibility of matter. And surely it is as easy to understand that spirit is penetrable, as it is that matter is impenetrable?

Our author's position, then, regarding reason is that, when inquiry into matters of the highest moment is being undertaken, that is to say, into those pertaining to God and the soul, reason must be sympathetically disposed, if satisfactory results are to be reached. A successful philosopher is that one who has pinned his faith to God's goodness, and has had experience of that goodness in the course of his own life. He has attained to a state of mind which More calls 'Divine Sagacity,' which is 'ever antecedaneous to that Reason which in Theories of greatest importance approves it self afterwards, upon the exactest examination, to be most solid and perfect everyway, and is truly that wisdom which is peculiarly styled the Gift of God, and hardly competible

---

[1] *A Collection* . . . *The Immortality of the Soul*, p. 19.
[2] *Ib.*, p. 23.   [3] *Ib.*, p. 41.

to any but persons of a pure and unspotted mind.'[1] But the situation in which a man finds himself in the Christian era is not as simple as this description of his enlightenment implies; for it has been modified by God, and from God's side. Amidst all the changing problems that confront him, there remains constant his own search for God; but whereas God was disposed in former times to give merely an answer, He has been now abundantly good, and revealed Himself in an Incarnation. Instead of moving towards man, He has come and tabernacled with him. Reason has been supplied with additional material to work upon and with further truths to explore; and Revelation calls, too, for a more intense faith and deeper purity of life in the seeker. More has been given, and more is being required.

So it comes about that we have a treatise under the paradoxical title, *An Explanation of the Grand Mystery of Godliness*; and the key to it is that since Revelation provides new fields for the exercise of reason, it will claim in return greater ventures from faith. God disclosed Himself in His Son in order to advance the very end for which He gave him being, namely, the divine life; and More is careful to show the bearing of the mysteries of the Ascended Lord and the Holy Spirit upon his attainment of this end.[2] Christianity is a rational religion, and owes its superiority over other religions to the fact that it can put forward a strong apologetic: 'and therefore he that takes away the use of Reason in Religion, undermines Christianity, and laies it as low as the basest Superstition that ever appeared in the World.'[3] We may be assured 'that God, who made our

---

[1] *Ib., The Preface general*, p. ix.
[2] *An Explanation*, p. 471: 'For whatever it (*i.e.* the old Mosaical Covenant) can suggest from without, the Spirit of God whispers to them from within, or indeed that living Form of all holiness and righteousnesse, the Image of Christ recovered in them, guides them as easily and as naturally to, as our external Senses guide our Natural man in this outward and visible world.'
[3] *Ib.*, p. 528.

Faculties, will never offer any thing to us to believe, that upon close debate does plainly contradict them.'[1] And it is reason, informed by the good, which in the last resort will accept or reject any truth that purports to be revealed by God: 'but I grant that it is still this Light within us, that judges and concludes after the perusal of either the Volumes of Nature or of Divine Revelation.'[2] On the other hand, if reason should become arrogant, and demand a fool-proof system of theology innocent of all mystery, it will have to be reminded that it asks for the impossible. Several considerations combine to show that the Christian Revelation does well in proclaiming mysteries. In the first place, we are apt to grow tired of what is wholly familiar, whereas 'perpetual expectation continues respect.'[3] Then, again, if we could soar up into the clear empyrean, where all is known, to what purpose could we devote our powers of contemplation and enjoyment? 'Wherefore that the Mind of man may be worthily employ'd and taken up with a kind of Spiritual husbandry, God has not made the Scriptures like an artificial Garden, wherein the Walks are plain and regular, the Plants sorted and set in order, the Fruits ripe, and the Flowers blown, and all things fully exposed to our view; but rather like an uncultivated field, where indeed we have the ground and hidden seeds of all precious things, but nothing can be brought to any great beauty, order, fulness or maturity, without our own industry; nor indeed with it, unless the dew of His grace descend upon it, without whose blessing the Spiritual Culture will thrive as little as the labour of the husbandman without showers of rain.'[4] Besides, since what is easily got is little valued, the Divine wisdom permits 'every man to carry home wares proportionable to the price he would pay in the open market for them.'[5] And, finally, those who claim that all revealed truth should be entirely void of mystery may fairly be pressed to justify

[1] *Ib.*, p. 455.   [2] *Ib.*, p. 409.   [3] *Ib.*, p. 454.
[4] *Ib.*, p. 4.   [5] *Ib.*, p. 3.

their assumption. Are they confident that such evinced curiosity is born of humble devotion, and not of pride?

But if those who 'contend for such an absolute plainness and clearness in all points of Religion, shew more of clownishness and indiscretion then of wit and judgement,'[1] their opposites, who pretend that true faith is divorced from reason, are in worse plight. More dreads Enthusiasm in every form, and attributes it to the work of imagination uncontrolled by reason, the ultimate cause being melancholy, which is a pathological condition of soul and body.[2] He says that if Christianity should ever come to nothing, the victor will prove to be Enthusiasm. And liberal as he is, he holds that the State ought not to tolerate sects 'that profess they believe against the Christian Faith from the illumination of such a Spirit as they can give no account of, viz. such as does not illuminate their Reason, whereby their doctrine may be accountable and intelligible to others, but only heat

---

[1] *Ib.*, p. 454.
[2] Hume's account of Enthusiasm is complete. 'But the Mind of Man is also subject to an unaccountable Elevation and Presumption, proceeding from prosperous Success, from luxuriant Health, from strong Spirits, or from a bold and confident Disposition. In such a State of Mind, the Imagination swells with great, but confus'd Conceptions, to which no sublunary Beauties or Enjoyments can correspond. Every thing mortal and perishable vanishes as unworthy of Attention. And a full Range is given to the Fancy in the invisible Regions or World of Spirits, where the Soul is at Liberty to indulge itself in every Imagination, that may best suit its present Taste and Disposition. Hence arise Raptures, Transports, and surprizing Flights of Fancy; and Confidence and Presumption still increasing, these Raptures, being altogether unaccountable, and seeming quite beyond the Reach of our ordinary Faculties, are attributed to the immediate Inspiration of that Divine Being who is the Object of Devotion. In a little Time, the inspir'd Person comes to regard himself as the chief Favourite of the Divinity; and when this Frenzy once takes Place, which is the Summit of Enthusiasm, every Whimsy is consecrated: Human Reason, and even Morality are rejected as fallacious Guides: And the Fanatick Madman delivers himself over, blindly, and without Reserve, to the supposed Illapses of the Spirit, and to Inspirations from above. Hope, Pride, Presumption, a warm Imagination, along with Ignorance, are, therefore, the true Sources of Enthusiasm' (*Essay—Of Superstition and Enthusiasm*).

them and make them furious against the Christian Church.'[1]
If a man should believe himself inspired by the Spirit, when
he is in fact moved by his own fancy, the way to convince
him of his mistake is to induce him to undergo rational
self-examination. 'To be inspired is, to be moved in an
extraordinary manner by the power or Spirit of God to act,
speak, or think what is holy, just and true.'[2] The acid test
of the Spirit's guidance is to inquire whether we are moved
to think and to act after the pattern of the Incarnate Life.
On this matter More is in agreement with what Cudworth
lays down in a sermon [3] where he warns against the delusions
of false fervency in worship: 'For the true demonstration
of God's Holy Spirit is no where to be looked for, but in
life and action, or in such earnest and affectionate breathings
after a further participation of the divine image, as are
accompanied with zeal and unfeigned endeavours to attain
it: this is the true praying in the Holy Ghost, though there
be no extemporaneous effusion of words.'

But Christianity was not destined to be undermined by
Enthusiasm. Before long it was to be attacked in the name
of reason. The issue at the end of the century turned out
to be this: if Christianity is a rational religion, grounded in
reason and appealing to reason, why need it be encumbered
by mysteries? If God has revealed truth hitherto unknown,
why should it not be as clear and distinct as truth known
without His aid? Locke had come forward to clip the wings
of the Platonists' reason. He decided that reason henceforth must be content to traffic in whatever ideas could be
come at by sensation and reflection. Truth, he said, in
effect, consists in propositions which express agreement
between these ideas. It may also, however, he continued,

[1] *Ib.*, p. 527. In denouncing Enthusiasts, More included the Quakers,
chiefly because, as he supposed, they denied the historic Incarnation;
but, on fuller acquaintance with their beliefs, he revised his opinion
of them.
[2] *A Collection . . . Enthusiasmus Triumphatus*, p. 2.
[3] Included in Jebb's *Piety without Asceticism*.

be revealed by God, in which case truth comprises a number of propositions derived immediately from Him, and to be found in Scripture. The assent, called faith, which we give to this truth, follows upon rational proof that God is the Author of it.[1] Reason must be satisfied also that truth of revelation does no violence to truth of nature.[2] Locke himself, of course, is satisfied on both these counts. But in this way of explaining things, philosophy has lost its fervour, and religion has begun to lose its soul. When Whichcote preached and wrote for reason's sake, he was defending the spiritual principle in man which goes out to close with living truth, to love it, and to live by it and for it; and when Smith reasoned, he was trying to make clear to himself the character of the Being for whom his soul was athirst, and the manner of the divine life that may taste Him. Smith's 'inward taste and relish of the Divinity,'[3] and More's 'divine sagacity,' have disappeared in Locke's reason, which, in religious matters, is become a mere judge of evidence. Locke was aware of the dangers of Enthusiasm, and it may be that his cooler temperament made him look askance, as More did not, at any alliance between reason and 'affection.'[4] He tells us, to be sure, that no rational being cares to be told that he does not love the truth, but he adds that

[1] *Essay*, IV. xix. 4: 'Reason is natural revelation, whereby the eternal Father of light, and Fountain of all knowledge, communicates to mankind that portion of truth which he has laid within the reach of their natural faculties. Revelation is natural reason enlarged by a new set of discoveries communicated by God immediately, which reason vouches the truth of by the testimony and proofs it gives that they come from God.'

[2] *Ib.*, 14: 'God, when he makes the prophet, does not unmake the man; he leaves all his faculties in their natural state, to enable him to judge of his inspirations, whether they be of divine original or no.'

[3] *Select Discourses*, p. 435.

[4] *Essay*, IV. xix. 16: 'Where reason or scripture is express for any opinion or action, we may receive it as of divine authority; but it is not the strength of our own persuasions which can by itself give it that stamp. The bent of our own minds may favour it as much as we please; that may show it to be a fondling of our own, but will by no means prove it to be an offspring of heaven, and of divine original.'

going beyond the evidence betokens love for something else.¹

Christianity has made appeal unto reason, and unto reason it shall go. So Toland writes his *Christianity Not Mysterious* (1696), and shows that 'what is once reveal'd we must as well understand as any other Matter in the World, Revelation being only of use to enform us, whilst the Evidence of its Subject perswades us.'

Toland's book was answered one year after publication by Peter Browne, a worthy disciple of Locke, who, if he does not succeed in raising the discussion from the level of a debate about so many propositions in a logical exercise into the warmer realm of personal relationship with God, where More easily moved, has some useful points to make about the character of this intelligible mystery which is Christianity, and about the manner of our comprehending it. He agrees with Toland that it is true to affirm, 'I can give no Assent without clear and distinct Idea's'; but refuses to conclude that, therefore, 'I must have a clear and distinct Idea of every thing I give my Assent to.' ² With Locke, he will proceed from the known to the unknown; with Locke, he is convinced of the certainty of the evidence for the truth of Christianity; and with Locke, he sees that certain Christian truths are 'above reason.' How then, in Browne's view, are these truths entertained by reason? He proceeds to make use of a very honourable conception to which Locke had given a cautious blessing. The latter had proposed that, in cases where sensory evidence is not forthcoming as a basis for knowledge, conclusions may sometimes be reached by the analogical method: for 'a wary reasoning from analogy leads us often into the discovery of truths and useful productions, which would otherwise lie concealed.' ³

---

¹ *Ib.*, 1.
² *A Letter in Answer to a Book Entituled Christianity not Mysterious*, London, 1703, 3rd ed., p. 27.
³ *Essay*, IV. xvi. 12.

It is scientific pursuits which he has primarily in mind; but he allows himself to write after a fashion that would have gratified St. Thomas himself, whose treatment of the analogical knowledge of God is worked out with thoroughness and insight. 'Observing,' Locke says, 'such gradual and gentle descents downwards in those parts of the creation that are beneath men, the rule of analogy may make it probable that it is so also in things above us and our observation; and that there are several ranks of intelligent beings, excelling us in several degrees of perfection, ascending upwards towards the infinite perfection of the Creator, by gentle steps and differences, that are every one at no great distance from the next to it.' Browne boldly adopts the Thomistic position,[1] and argues for an analogical knowledge of God and of things pertaining to the unseen world, hoping in this way to retain mystery in Christianity without sacrificing its rational character. God, he avers, in disclosing truths which man's unassisted reason could not discover, instead of giving him new faculties, chose the only other alternative, and translated the new truths into old and familiar terms. Our ideas of God and of His attributes, therefore, are not 'proper and immediate,' but 'improper' and 'mediate'; and we think of His omnipresence, for example, in terms of 'continued extension.'[2] A Christian mystery has two parts, the clearly and distinctly knowable part, commended to reason, and based upon ideas of sensation and reflection; and the incomprehensible part, appropriate to faith, and based upon the authority of God. 'As to this latter part of it, it is wholly exempted from the disquisition of Reason, and Faith alone can reach it, for our Reason fails us where we have no Idea's.'[3] Reason and

[1] *Cf.* R. L. Patterson, *The Conception of God in the Philosophy of Aquinas*, Ch. vii.
[2] *A Letter*, p. 37.
[3] *Ib.*, p. 45. Browne says that Enthusiasts and 'Votaries to strictest Reason and Evidence' both proceed from the same erroneous assumption, that what is fit to be called knowledge must answer to the test of immedi-

faith, in this view, become clearly and distinctly divorced; and faith, having been assured by reason that its venture will fare well, sets sail for the unfathomable waters of unsearchable truth. Faith is far from being a means for appropriating further knowledge, and is allotted the fruitless task of confessing that revealed truth cannot be known. Browne will have it that the Pauline phrase, '*for we know in part*,' [1] refers not to reason's clear grasp of what lies within a given segment, the remainder of the circle remaining hidden, but to a clear analogy lying outside a complete circle of incomprehensible truth. The meaning of the phrase is, he thinks, that 'the whole is reveal'd to us under the resemblance of some things in this World, whereof we have clear and distinct Idea's.' [2] But Locke's conception of reason and of faith is not More's: the latter holds, with Clement of Alexandria, that reason and faith interpenetrate. Browne's faith, like his reason, avails but to register impersonal assent to propositions; he does not entertain the idea that both may express the man. It was left to Berkeley

---

acy. 'Upon this very Mistake it is, that on one side Men will not stoop so Low as Reason; and that on the other, they will not venture to rise Above it.' (*The Procedure, Extent, and Limits of Human Understanding*, London, 1728, p. 50.)

[1] 1 *Cor.* xiii. 9.

[2] *A Letter*, p. 40. Thirty-one years later, Browne criticizes William King for his use of the analogical principle. In the latter's sermon, *Divine Predestination and Fore-knowledge consistent with the Freedom of Man's Will*, analogy is confused with *metaphor*: 'in pursuance of this oversight, he expressly asserts Love, and Anger, Wisdom, and Goodness, and Knowledge, and Foreknowledge, and all the other Divine Attributes to be spoke of God as improperly as Eyes or Ears.' Sceptics favour his assertion that 'the best Representations we can make of God are infinitely short of TRUTH,' whereas he really means that 'they signify more valuable Perfections and infinitely superior to what they are in us' (*The Procedure*, pp. 14, 15, 17). King's point is that we represent God's attributes as displayed in His works after analogy with human causation in producing similar effects: thus Divine Foreknowledge signifies that God 'can never be at a loss what to do in any Event'; and Divine Predestination that 'all things depend as much on God, as if he had settled them according to a certain Scheme and design . . . without regard had to any other consideration besides that of his own meer Will and Pleasure.'

among others to withstand this presentation of Christianity propounded in an age of reason; and he confutes it, as More would have approved, by pointing to man's experience of God. He concludes his treatise, *The Principles of Human Knowledge*, with a disparagement of barren speculations, and confesses that he will have laboured to no purpose, if he has not succeeded in inspiring his reader with 'a pious sense of the Presence of God.'[1]

The short volume entitled *Enchiridion Ethicum* (1666)[2] makes a more considerable contribution to More's theory of the good life than might have been hoped for by a student whose interest was barely sustained throughout the argument of some of his larger works. In this single effort he offers what is in effect a formal treatise on morals, including some discussion on the ideas of right and good; a psychological analysis of the emotional life, with a description of

[1] *Cf.* A. A. Luce: 'It is instructive to place side by side a title-page of Browne's and one of Berkeley's. On the title-page of his book, "The Procedure, Extent and Limits of Human Understanding," Browne has set the text, "As the heavens are higher than the earth, so are My ways higher than your ways, and My thoughts than your thoughts." Berkeley on the title-page of his "The Theory of Vision Vindicated and Explained," as if in answer to Browne, has set the text, "In Him we live and move and have our being."' (From a sermon on *The Right Rev. George Berkeley, D.D.*, published in *The Church of Ireland Gazette*, Sept. 28, 1934.)

A. A. Luce, *Berkeley and Malebranche*, p. 122: 'The technical distinction between immediate and mediate is a good servant but a bad master. When dealing with a process like knowing, especially the knowing of an Immense Object, where no clean cut between knowledge of His existence and knowledge of His nature is practicable, a man of Berkeley's stamp, hating jargon, loving fact, will not oppose too strictly mediacy and immediacy. Our knowledge of God, in fact, is immediate, in that we are in God and that immediate facts not representative ideas are the ground of our assurance. Our knowledge of God, in fact, is mediate, because we are not God but men; reflection on our part is required and we must "open the eye of the mind."'

[2] Quotations are taken from the translation by Edward Southwell— *An Account of Virtue: or, Dr. Henry More's Abridgment of Morals, Put Into English*, London, 1690—published by The Facsimile Text Society, New York, 1930. Cf. *Biographical Note* therein by Sterling P. Lamprecht.

its function in the completed whole which man strives to become; and some lessons in moral theology, such as Jebb might well have included in his *Piety without Asceticism* alongside the sermons taken from Cudworth. If he leans upon Aristotle for the general plan of his ethical theory, and borrows from Descartes in his treatment of the passions, he is careful, by his emphasis on meditation, prayer and worship, to set the goal of endeavour where the Christian mystics have always placed it. And true to his own school, he reminds us that he will not deal merely with moral principles and rules: for though it is helpful to be clear about these essentials, they are known best in experience. 'Vital goods,' he writes, 'are by our Life and Senses to be judged of, and enjoyed.'

The first words of the hand-book are these—'Ethicks are defined to be the Art of Living well and Happily.' The *well* involves some discussion of morality in the strict sense, that is to say, of such topics as virtue, and its relation to right reason, will, and the passions; while the *happily* refers to the fruit of the virtuous life, and calls for an appraisal of the good, and for some guidance as to how it may be reached in a world where things are often contrary to the desert of virtue. The first chapters elucidate these two cross-sections of the good life, and two further definitions are proposed. 'Virtue is an intellectual Power of the Soul, by which it over-rules the animal Impressions or bodily Passions; so as in every Action it easily pursues what is absolutely and simply the best'; and 'Happiness is that pleasure which the mind takes in from a Sense of Virtue, and a Conscience of Well-doing; and of conforming in all things to the Rules of both.' We are being led, evidently, to conceive that the level of life to which good conduct pertains, involving, as it does, control of motives which originate in the animal level, is interlocked ideally with the highest level to which we can attain, and where life and happiness are one and the same. The moral life is the only means of approach to the enjoyable life; and the enjoyable life finds inevitable expression in the moral life. A complete life is given to good works, because it has in view the goodness rather than the works; and a genuine enthusiast will remember that plain duties lie at hand.

More accepts the treatment of the passions advanced by Descartes; and it must be confessed that, even when allowance had been made for modifications introduced, the critical pupil hardly escapes from painting his own form of the ideal life in hedonist hues. He learned from Descartes that the soul is passive in a general sense when it is the object of an action, be the action within the soul or outside it; but that, properly speaking, a passion is an emotion, *e.g.* love or sadness, and is accompanied by a heightening or depressing of physical power. A passion is related only to the soul, just as sensations, which are passions in the general sense, are related to objects in the outer world, *e.g.* the sound of a bell, or to movements in the body, *e.g.* those associated with hunger. A passion, in the restricted sense indicated, is paralleled by certain occurrences in the body with which the soul is united, and it could not be experienced if the soul were not united with a body: and, in passages which read like descriptions of the interaction theory of the relation between soul and body, Descartes tries to show how a passion can be caused by the 'animal spirits,' which are, apparently, particles of rarefied matter of the same stuff as the blood. A passion is always, sometimes more and sometimes less, a confused state of the soul, incapable of precise analysis, though potent, owing to its influence upon the animal spirits, to initiate action terminating within or without the body. The passions are enmeshed in a teleological system, their function being to further ends conducive primarily to the good of the body, and secondarily to the good of the soul.[1] They appear also

---

[1] S. V. Keeling, *Descartes*, p. 151: 'Now any set of movements which constitutes the physiological counterpart of a sensation or an emotion

in the rôle of motives, to which the will may or may not give assent; though the will does not initiate action that can rightly be called moral, unless it accepts or refuses in the light of clear and distinct knowledge of what is good. The will's 'proper arms,' when in conflict with the passions, says Descartes, 'consists of the firm and determinate judgments respecting the knowledge of good and evil, in pursuance of which it has resolved to conduct the actions of its life'; [1] and 'because these passions can only bring us to any kind of action by the intervention of the desire which they excite, it is this desire particularly which we should be careful to regulate, and it is in this that the principal use of morality consists.' [2]

In a struggle between known good, entertained by reason, and imaginary good, sustained by passion, the will can undermine the force of passion, either by inhibiting the movements associated by nature or habit with the passion in the case, or by rationalizing the situation, with a view to rendering the action suggested by the passion unattractive, or, best of all, by prosecuting the intelligently known good: and when the third alternative obtains, the soul experiences a peculiar passion of its own making, distinguished from all other passions as an intellectual passion. For example, there is a 'joy that is purely intellectual, and which comes into the soul by the action of the soul alone, and which we may call an agreeable emotion excited in it, in which the enjoyment consists which it has in the good which its understanding represents to it as its own.' [3] Descartes holds

gives rise to "reactions," in the sense that it continues into, or incites, a further set of movements within, and sometimes also without, the stimulated body. In this the mechanism of emotion is able to effect all that volition can secure, or is in the habit of securing.'

[1] *The Philosophical Works of Descartes*, translated by E. S. Haldane and G. R. T. Ross, vol. i. p. 354 (*The Passions of the Soul*).

[2] *Ib.*, p. 395.

[3] *Ib.*, p. 372. *Cf.* S. V. Keeling, p. 181 n.: 'And similarly, for each of the primary emotions, there are two forms, one due to the self's immanent activity, another due to its body's transeunt activity, both being, however,

that 'our good and our harm depend mainly on the interior emotions which are only excited in the soul by the soul itself, in which respect they differ from its passions, which always depend on some movement of the spirits.'[1]

The upshot of this analysis of the affective life is that a virtuous man is one who pursues the goods to which his passions point—provided that he has examined and approved them, and enjoys the satisfaction of knowing that he has pursued. So 'in order that our soul may thus have something with which to be content, it has no need but to follow exactly after virtue. For whoever has lived in such a way that his conscience cannot reproach him for ever having failed to perform those things which he has judged to be the best (which is what I here call following after virtue) receives from this a satisfaction which is so powerful in rendering him happy that the most violent efforts of the passions never have sufficient power to disturb the tranquillity of his soul.'[2] Descartes would have the good life depend upon good motives; and the only motive which can be approved is one which bears evident testimony to its excellence, and is known intellectually. But it seems that enjoyment of a contented state of mind, which living in accordance with the known good yields, is the good proposed for man's chief end.[3] The virtuous man is happy, because he is satisfied that he has lived virtuously. He does not find happiness in choosing and doing what his considered judgment demands, but in a conscientious review of his past life. So while Descartes is in line with the moral intuitionists who hold that the good is known by reason, he is in line also with those hedonists who claim that the

---

states of the self and not of its body: *e.g.* states of "intellectual" love, joy, sadness, and desire; and states of "physical" love, joy, sadness, and desire (passions).'

[1] *Ib.*, p. 398.   [2] *Ib.*, p. 399.
[3] A. Boyce Gibson, *The Philosophy of Descartes*, p. 361 : 'Now Descartes places virtue in the direction of motive, and indicates that man's true good is a condition of mind depending on that direction of motive.'

good lies in the state of mind which is virtue's reward. He seems to say that it pertains to the intellect to see the good; to the will to desire and effect it; and to the passions, those of the intellect as free-born, and those of the body as bond-servants, to enjoy it.

We find that More takes over the six primary passions (in the restricted sense of the term) enumerated by 'the renowned Philosopher Des Cartes,' viz., 'Admiration, Love, Hatred, Cupidity, Joy, and Grief'; and that he follows him also in distinguishing the first, which is lacking in value tone, from the remaining five, which register some sense of approval or disapproval. Admiration is 'the very first passion,' because 'it strains up Attention beyond its wonted pitch . . . before we comprehend whether such Object will prove grateful or ungrateful to us.' He points out that he is at liberty to reduce these six passions to three, by eliminating cupidity (desire), joy, and grief, because they are derivatives from love and hatred; and by this simplification he counts himself successful in re-establishing the classical trichotomy of rational, irascible and concupiscible elements in the soul. He puts forward his own definition of passion: 'Passion then is a vehement Sensation of the Soul, which refers especially to the Soul it self, and is accompanied with an unwonted motion of the Spirits.' But it ought to be noted that he does not attribute the cause of passion to the action of the animal spirits: 'for in external Objects, which agitate the Sense or Imagination, it is the Soul moves the Spirits, and not the Spirits the Soul.' He refuses to discuss the problem of the 'Natural Causes' of passion, 'which lie abstruse and remote,' on the ground that this belongs to the field of 'Natural Philosophy'; and he goes on to ridicule the theory that the soul is 'fast penn'd up in a certain glandulous part of the Brain, called the Conarion,' from within which, as from a citadel, it wages moral combat against the animal spirits, 'even as it were some Pigmy that with a Feather or a Twig were employed in beating of the Winds.'[1] He disentangles the two primary passions, love and hatred, from the physiological system to which Descartes had attached them, and refers them entirely to the soul, and more particularly to the plastic soul, which is akin to the 'universal Plastic Principle,' or 'the Spirit of Nature.' The moral struggle, then, is between the intellectual and plastic parts of the soul, between two levels within one life; and when victory goes to the worthy side, the vanquished foe becomes enduring friend. More says that 'from such Conflict and such Victory, it is plain, there is a Certain Government or Empire acknowledged to be in the Soul; and that the intellectual part hath something which it doth teach and instruct, as a Father doth his Son; or which it breeds and trains up, as in a lower instance, a Huntsman doth his Dogs.'

More goes on to deal with the three passions, under which all others rank as derivative 'species'; and to each of the three he attaches a particular virtue. 'Thus Prudence stands in balance to Admiration; Sincerity to Concupiscence, and Patience to Fury.' But before we consider his

[1] Cf. *Divine Dialogues, The Publisher to The Reader*: '. . . Gal. 5, 17, where that Enmity and conflict betwixt the Flesh and the Spirit is mentioned, . . . what light the Cartesian Philosophy will contribute for the more plainly understanding this so important Mystery, may easily be conjectured from the 47th Article of his Treatise of the Passions, where the Combate betwixt the superiour and inferiour part of the Soul, the Flesh and the Spirit, as they are termed in Scripture and Divinity, is at last resolved into the ridiculous Noddings and Joggings of a small glandulous Button in the midst of the Brain encountred by the animal Spirits rudely flurting against it. This little sprunt Champion, called the Conarion, (or Nux pinea) within which the Soul is entirely cooped up, acts the part of the Spirit, as the animal Spirits of the Flesh. And thus by the Soul thus ingarrison'd in this Pine-kernell, and bearing herself against the Arietations or Jurrings of the Spirits in the Ventricles of the Brain, must that solemn Combat be performed, which the holy Apostle calls the War betwixt the Law of our Members and the Law of our Minde. . . . Besides, if this Conflict be not a Combat betwixt two contrarie Lives seated in the Soul her self, but this that opposes the Soul be merely the Spirits in such an Organized body (as Cartesius expressly affirms;) the Souls of the wicked and of the godly in the other state are equally freed from the importunities of Sin.'

account of the primary virtues, it will be advisable to delay for a moment over the nature of the passions whose material they are. More holds that passions in general are good, because they dispose us towards things that are good for us, and withdraw us from things that are harmful. He substantiates this view by falling back upon plastic nature, which is God's living and unconscious instrument for furthering His purpose. 'Hence it appears, that all the animal Instincts and Impulses do belong to the Reign of Nature, and are but imperfect Shadows of the Divine Wisdom and Goodness, which vouchsafes as in this manner to glimmer in the dark.' But human nature transcends mere nature, and man's good is intelligently discerned as well as passionately enjoyed. Passion in itself is 'blind.' It can at best move us to procure 'particular' goods; but it cannot secure 'universal' good, that is, the good which we hope to find in all the varied circumstances of life. To reason falls the task of discovering the best way to act in complicated circumstances; and it is because we are rational, that circumstances are complicated. The passions are to be directed as reason sees fit; and they must not be exterminated. The way of reason is not the way proposed by either Enthusiasts or Stoics.

Let not passion's incompetence tempt us to decry its value: for blind though it be, it often acts as surrogate for reason's rectoral insight; and we sometimes rate things 'that are laudable and just according as we find our passions excited by them.' Since God's goodness is reflected continually through all the grades of creation, we are entitled to say that 'there is something also, little less than Divine, which presides in the Animal Law'; and unless reason should intervene to divert us from a course of action charted out by passion, we are justified in allowing ourselves to be carried whither it bears us. It may even be a moral obligation to do what passion proposes. 'Wherefore seeing such Propensities are antecedent to all Choice and Deliberation, 'tis manifest they are from Nature and from God; and that therefore whatever they dictate as Good and Just, is really Good and Just: and we are bound to embrace and prosecute the same, not only towards our selves, but towards others; I mean as far as may without injury to a third.'

What is virtue, of which passions may be 'images'? Virtue has to do not only with the goods of life, but also with the best in life; and virtue, looking to the best, suppresses the passions in order to set them free: for the best adjusts inferior values in its own service. Love, for example—and anticipating More's conclusion—is the supreme value: but it is all the richer for being expressed in the passions; and, contrariwise, the passions are enriched, when they have become rooted and organized in love. The definitions of the primary virtues are constructed in relation to the primary passions on the one hand, and to reason on the other; and though these virtues are not ends in themselves, they are not mere means, for it is through them that passion and reason grow together and form a truly happy life.

The simplest way to discover virtue's place in the harmonious life is to begin by quoting More's definitions of prudence, sincerity, and patience, recalling that early in the *Enchiridion* he has drawn attention to the robust character of virtue, which, he says, signifies the same thing as fortitude. 'Prudence therefore is a Virtue, by which the Soul has such Dominion over the Passions properly so called, as well as over all sorts of corporeal Impressions, that the mind can receive no Impediment thereby, in rightly observing, and successfully judging of what is absolutely and simply the best.' 'Sincerity is a Virtue of the Soul, by which the Will is intirely and sincerely carried on to that which the Mind judgeth to be absolutely and simply the best.' 'Patience is a Vertue of the Soul, whereby 'tis enabled, for the sake of that which is simply and absolutely the best, to undergo all things; even that which, to the animal Nature, is totally harsh and ungrateful.'

These definitions seem to leave small scope for the passions, whose good functions More has so cogently approved; and in the virtuous life they might appear actually to be hindrances. The truth of the matter is that a particular good is always a possible enemy of the best; and that lest it should prevail, the best takes up virtue for armour. The best cannot be discerned when passion confuses judgment; the best cannot be willed when will is divided against itself; and the best cannot be attained when competing goods go unsacrificed. When we extract More's teaching from his artificially complete psychological trichotomy, we see that virtue's concern is with the purification of thought and desire and the stabilization of motive. Intellect is no motive to action, and passion may be a bad one. It is not only knowledge of the best, but affection for it that counts. Intellect is as ineffective as passion is blind; and virtue unites them in happy fellowship.

This brings us to a point where More's break with Descartes is complete; for he is not satisfied to identify the best with the peace that comes of a life well lived. He recognizes the importance of virtue's merited reward; and of the 'internal Joy' that follows upon cultivation of sincerity he writes that 'this is the state of that Peace, which is so constant and ineffable, that no Cares, no Crosses, or so much as Jealousies, can distract it.' But for a spirit of resignation, as such, he has no use. His counsel is not to contentment, but to contention. He would show that a virtuous man must be released from the enjoyment of his own virtue, and set free to love God and his neighbour: the true serenity of mind, he holds, 'hath no other Motions than those of Benignity and Beneficence.'

What More has in mind is a sentiment for the good, that is, a mental system in which emotions, instincts and impulses, as perfectly as may be, are organized by the idea of the good. Particular virtues, such as justice and bravery, are the binding links of the system, restraining or liberating, as is fitting on each occasion, the whole set of affective and impulsive tendencies. When passions emerge in a properly organized life, virtues emerge to deal with them. Everything happens, ideally, within a life quick to interpret and to use every experience in terms of one dominating interest. More is so anxious to delimit his vision of the ideal life, that he assigns it to the care of a special faculty, known as 'the Boniform Faculty';[1] and an examination of what he has to say about it shows that he is thinking of a perfect alliance between a cleansed intellect and a cleansed will: it marks the stage at which we learn to know and to desire the solitary best. 'It is plain,' he writes, 'that supreme Happiness is not barely to be placed in the Intellect; but her proper Seat must be called the Boniform Faculty of the Soul: namely, a Faculty of that divine Composition, and supernatural Texture, as enables us to distinguish not only what is simply and absolutely the best, but to relish it, and to have pleasure in that alone.' And although the ideal life is so highly exalted, it is truly catholic: for, with his usual care for the plain man, More objects when Aristotle 'placeth Happiness in Contemplation . . . since it would be confined to a few speculative Men and Philosophers, and so shut out the Bulk of Mankind, who could never be partakers thereof.' If we identify happiness with a passion, be it ever so intellectual a passion, we rob it of its vigour, and our joy will be reserved and tame. 'I beg leave,' he says, 'to call it rather by the Name of Intellectual Love': and, again, 'this Love is not more a Passion than is Intellection it self.'

The world in which More finds himself is a panorama of

---

[1] W. R. Inge, *The Platonic Tradition in English Religious Thought*, p. 57: 'He holds the mystical doctrine that there is a faculty in the soul, which he calls Divine Sagacity, whereby the truth may be known by intuition. Divine Sagacity is evidently much the same as the Neoplatonic *Nous*. . . . The "boniform faculty" of which he sometimes speaks cannot easily be distinguished from the Divine Sagacity just mentioned. It is that organ for the apprehension of truth, which, as Plotinus thinks, "all possess, but only a few use."'

God's love; and he finds that the only reasonable course is to accept God's principle for his own. He feels that his experience is shot through with providence; and overcome with blessings, he wants to bless God and man. He cannot find joy in meditating upon his own virtue. He will follow after virtue, because virtue points beyond itself to happiness, which is enjoyment of God. Of intellectual love he says: "'Tis by this the Soul relisheth what is simply the best; thither it tends, and in that alone it has its Joy and Triumph. Hence we are instructed how to set God before our eyes; to love him above all; to adhere to him as the supremest Good; to consider him as the Perfection of all Reason, of all Beauty, of all Love; how all was made by his Power, and that all is upheld by his Providence. Hence also is the Soul taught how to affect and admire the Creation, and all the Parcels of it; as they share in that Divine Perfection and Beneficence, which is dispersed through the whole Mass: So that if any of these Parcels appear defective or discompos'd, the Soul compassionates and brings help, strenuously endeavouring, as it is able, to restore every thing to that state of Felicity, which God and nature intended for it. In short, it turns all its Faculties to make good Men happy; and all its Care and Discipline to make bad Men good.'

In picturing the ideal life in this lofty strain, More does not forget the plain man's capacity and the tender-foot's misgivings: for besides helping us to see how the moral life is completed in the divine life, More shows us how to mount the lowest rungs of the ladder. Cudworth deals, in the main, with eternal and immutable ideas of morality; but More knows that they have to be applied in complex cases. Confronted by the paradox that none save the good can know the good, he points out that 'Right Reason' is a satisfactory substitute for the boniform faculty. Right reason, like Mercury, is God's interpreter. By its aid a man can do what is right, even though he may not see what is good. A true Platonist cannot be expected to let the good escape altogether from his sight; and for More the sight, though not the taste, of the good is an inalienable privilege of intellect. 'The heighth of Virtue is this, constantly to pursue that which to Right Reason seems best.' More has justified passion as 'a sort of confused Muttering, or Whisper of a Divine Law: but indeed the Voice of it is more clear and audible in the intellectual State'; and all who obey the heavenly voice shall in time enjoy the heavenly love. No less than twenty-three moral maxims are set down. One tells us to pursue the 'most perfect Good with the greatest zeal, and lesser Goods with a zeal proportionately less.' Evidently, a ready way of finding out whether our love for anything is too strong or too weak is to compare it with the measure of our love for something judged by right reason to be of greater worth. Included in the list is the golden rule, with this qualification—'so far forth as it may be done without prejudice to a Third.' The introduction of a third party's interest is to secure, presumably, that right reason will decide without undue influence.

More had already dealt with the good life from the standpoint of religion in *An Explanation of The Grand Mystery of Godliness.* In this work he shows that the divine life includes two lesser lives, the rational and the animal. Each of the three has its own centre of reference; and their distinguishing principles respectively are, 'an Obediential Faith in God,' right reason, and self-love, the last being understood in an a-moral sense. The intermediate level has open to it the alternatives, either of serving its inferior, or of sublimating itself under its superior: the highest level is secured, when interest is devoted singly to God.

To the animal life More assigns the working of physical mechanisms and their psychological counterparts; and he holds that these are correlated and guided by self-love, 'which though it sound odiously (as it ought to do taken in the worst sense) among men, yet it is a right and requisite

Property of life in every brute Animal.'[1] From self-love many 'pure and innocuous' 'Branches' grow, to wit, the animal passions; and, prophetic of Mr. A. F. Shand's treatment of the emotional systems, the four instances listed first are, anger, fear, sorrow, and joy.[2] Under the head of animal passion falls natural affection; the tendency to form groups for the sake of mutual benefit and protection, as exemplified in 'the Commonwealth of Bees'; and even 'such Vertues . . . as Political Justice, Temperance, Fortitude or Courage, a sense of Friendship, Fame, or Glory.'[3] And yet Richard Ward records that Hobbes is reputed to have said, 'That if his own Philosophy was not True, he knew of none that he should sooner like than More's of Cambridge'! More stops short of bestowing a religious sense upon animals, though he allows that the amazement betrayed by them in face of certain occurrences in nature is a shadow of our own feeling of veneration. And he suggests that if man's divination of the *numinous* is not associated with his reason, it will breed idolatry. 'That (men) sought out a First Cause on Whom the Order, Oeconomy, and Government of the world should depend, proceeded from the Sagacity of the Superior Faculties of their Souls; but that they so vainly pitched upon the Sun and Moon, proceeded from the brutish admiration and dull astonishment of the Animal Senses in them. . . . Otherwise Transportation of minde and Wonderment at the more noble Objects in the world is so far from having any harm in it, that it is an usual Property of the Philo-

---

[1] *An Explanation of the Grand Mystery of Godliness*, 1660, p. 46. *Cf.* J. Laird, *Hobbes*, p. 274: 'More strongly deprecated "the more refined exercises of a sort of theological Hobbianism" (Ward's *Life*, p. 14), but it is not at all clear that he was entitled to do so. Ethics, he held, was the art of attaining beatitude. This beatitude was the delight appropriate to a rational "boniform faculty"; and a sweetly superior suspicion of selfishness pervaded his theory. Indeed, he said emphatically (25), that the only intelligible sense of "good" was good to oneself.'
[2] *The Foundations of Character*, p. 38.
[3] *An Explanation*, p. 48.

sophical and Religious Complexion, and has its great pleasure and use.'[1]

The brief description of the middle life which follows is due to More's haste to get going on the mystery of the divine life; and the reader is suspicious that its value is being depressed in favour of its superior. We are reminded of Clement of Alexandria, who hardly credits pagan seekers after truth with all that they appropriated from the Logos in whose image they were made. At this point, nevertheless, More provides one of the most satisfactory descriptions of reason, as the Cambridge Platonists understand it, to be found in any writer of the school. '. . . a Power of Facultie of the Soul, whereby either from her Innate Ideas or Common Notions, or else from the assurance of her own Senses, or upon the Relation or Tradition of another, she unravels a further clew of Knowledge, enlarging her sphere of Intellectual light, by laying open to her self that close connexion and cohesion of the Conceptions she has of things, whereby inferring one thing from another she is able to deduce multifarious Conclusions as well for the pleasure of Speculation as the necessity of Practice.'[2] Among the branches of the rational root are to be found Natural Philosophy, Mathematics, Oratory, and 'an ability of discoursing and acting also after an exteriour way in matters of Religion.' More says that the moral tone of the middle life is 'such as that with which it is conjoined, whether Good or Bad, Divine or Animal.' In the latter event, a whole crop of undesirable characteristics sprout and grow, for example, 'crafty contrivances for the getting of Wealth,' 'merry wiles for the enjoyment of Pleasure,' and the spirit of eroticism generally, which impels to composing hymns or to theologizing abstractly about mere ideas.

The life of faith in God is of another temper; for here the soul enjoys something far transcending anything to which sensation, reflection, and its innate vigour can reach, some-

[1] *Ib.*, p. 50.   [2] *Ib.*, p. 51.

thing whose reality natural faculties may question, but cannot disprove. And the Christian Gospel is 'a kind of Engine,'[1] designed to raise man to this life. It is native to him to know that God is, and, in a measure, what He is; but he cannot know God, until He has come into his soul. Knowing God, in More's view, is not an intellectual, but a spiritual, act; and it involves a translation of the knower into a form of life in which he shares all that he can receive of God's own life. The new life bears three branches, humility, charity, and purity. 'These we call Divine Vertues,' More explains, 'not so much because they imitate in some things the Holy Attributes of the Eternal Deity, but because they are such as are proper to a Creature to whom God communicates his own nature so far forth as it is capable of receiving it.'[2] Humility is a disposition in which a man acknowledges his own poverty, and glorifies God for all that is good in human life, the apparent source notwithstanding; charity, or 'intellectual love,' is a disposition in which a man, 'enamoured of the Divine Perfections,' gives of himself to God and his neighbour, even as God has given of Himself to all; and purity is a disposition in which a man preserves a watchful eye against evidence of any motive likely to conflict with his settled devotion to the best.

The final word appears to be that culture of itself is not enough, and that a question-mark hovers over the value of every human interest. Even philosophy demands more than culture. The works of man's mind, as the works of his hands, do not satisfy his spirit. Satisfaction comes, when he engages in every undertaking for the sake of the one end that all things are designed to serve. Happiness is not had for the taking, but for the giving—in exchange for the soul. If it could be had without sacrifice, it would be the reward of selfishness. The religious attitude means devoting one's life to God, and it cannot reach a point of self-exhaustion, because the soul is renewed perpetually in His inexhaustible

[1] *Ib.*, p. 361.   [2] *Ib.*, p. 53.

life. Culture stands between the animal life and the divine life, between self-love and love.[1]

[1] *Ib.*, p. 54: 'But in being thus transformed into the Divine image of Intellectual Love our Mindes are not onely raised in holy Devotions towards God, but descend also in very full and free streams of dearest Affection to our fellow-Creatures, rejoycing in their good as if it were our own, and compassionating their misery as if it were our selves did suffer; and according to our best judgement and power endeavouring to promote the one and to remove the other.'

VI
RICHARD CUMBERLAND

Comes my old good friend, Mr. Richard Cumberland, to see me, being newly come to town, whom I have not seen almost, if not quite, these seven years. In his plain country-parson's dress. I could not spend much time with him, but prayed him to come with his brother, who was with him, to dine with me to-day; which he did do: and I had a great deal of his good company; and a most excellent person he is as any I know, and one that I am sorry should be lost and buried in a little country town, and would be glad to remove him thence; and the truth is, if he would accept of my sister's fortune, I should give £100 more with him than to a man able to settle her four times as much as, I fear, he is able to do. . . .

SAMUEL PEPYS.

CHAPTER VI

RICHARD CUMBERLAND

RICHARD CUMBERLAND [1] is not numbered among the Cambridge Platonists; for though he holds with them that man's good must be sought and found, in theory as well as in practice, by an examination of the actual situation which he occupies in 'the nature of things,' [2] his manner of approaching the great moral problem anticipates the new way of ideas soon to be proposed by Locke. In his *De Legibus naturae disquisitio philosophica*, published in 1672, he disclaims all intention of saying a word against any opinion that 'looks with a friendly Aspect upon Piety and Morality,' [3] whose joint cause the Platonists have upheld so well against Hobbes; but he feels that it is a rash thing 'to build the Doctrine of natural Religion and Morality' upon so questionable an hypothesis as that of innate ideas; and, what is more, he cannot suppose, 'without proof,' that the laws of nature have existed from eternity in the mind of God. The doctrine of innate ideas, he states, 'has been rejected by the generality of Philosophers'; and his expositor, James Tyrrell, writing two years after the publication of Locke's *Essay*, to which he can pay generous tribute,

---

[1] 1632–1718.
[2] The references following are to the English translation made by John Maxwell, and included in his *A Treatise of the Laws of Nature*, London, 1727. *Cf.* p. 191: 'The Nature of Things Does not only signify this Lower World, whereof we are a Part, but its Creator and Supreme Governor, God.'
[3] *Ib.*, p. 14.

observes that the said doctrine 'hath been exploded by all Philosophers,'[1] the Platonists only excepted.

Cumberland sets himself to account for the origin of our idea of benevolence, which is the chief idea in his well-rounded and somewhat circumscribed system of thought. He says that 'it is well known by the Experience of all Men, that those Ideas or Thoughts, which the Logicians call simple Apprehensions, are two ways excited in the Mind of Man; (1) By the immediate Presence and Operation of the Object upon the Mind; after which the Mind is conscious of its own Actions, and also of the Motions of the Imagination, or of the Ideas its Objects; and by Analogy to these, we judge the Minds of other rational Beings, God and Men. (2) By the Means of our external Senses, Nerves, and Membranes, in which manner we perceive other Men, and the rest of the Parts of this visible World. . . .'[2] It is by the first of these two ways of knowing, that is to say, by 'internal,' as opposed to 'external, sensation,' that we come upon our knowledge of benevolence. 'For what Benevolence is, and what are its Degrees, and consequently, what is any one's greatest Benevolence, we do not otherwise

---

[1] *A Brief Disquisition of the Laws of Nature according to the Principles laid down in the Rev. Dr. Cumberland's Latin Treatise*, 1692. Ed. 1701, Preface, p. xxv.

[2] The original reads (pp. 42-3): *Quandoquidem igitur omnium experientia notissimum est, duobus modis notiones seu Cogitationes, quae Apprehensiones simplices a Logicis dicuntur, in animo Hominis excitari;* (1) *Scilicet per immediatam praesentiam, & operationem objecti in mentem; quo modo suarum Actionum nec non motuum Imaginationis, seu phantasmatum sibi observantium mens est conscia; & ex analogia ad haec de mentibus aliorum Rationalium Dei, Hominumq; judicamus.* (2) *Mediante sensuum externorum, nervorum, membranarumq; ministerio, quo pacto alios Homines, reliquasq; Mundi hujus aspectabilis partes percipimus; statim patet Propositionis quam exhibui Terminos partim per internam, partim per externam sensationem innotescere.*

With Locke's caption, 'Brutes abstract not' (*Essay*, II. xi. 10), compare the following: *Brutis autem quae nec abstrahunt a singularibus, nec numerant, ut summas colligant (multo autem minus Naturam, qua Deus & homines conveniunt, percipiunt) harum notionum, neu competit* (*De Legibus*, V. viii).

understand, than by the Mind's reflecting upon itself; nor needs there any other help; for such is the Frame of the Mind, that it cannot but be thorowly sensible of its own Actions and Affections, as being most intimately united with it self.' In fact, we become aware of our benevolent activity, which is both voluntary and affective, in the same way as we become aware of our rational activity. The meaning which our author attaches to benevolence is easily entertained in mind, although, as he points out, theorizing about the notion may have no effect upon conduct. It is one thing to establish on rational grounds that benevolence is the ideal way of life, and another thing to be a benevolent man. Every one is sensible of having willed the good; and benevolence signifies willing the good with the whole heart as often as one is called upon to will, and willing it to the utmost limits of one's power. This word, benevolence, therefore is preferred by Cumberland for etymological reasons to the much misused word 'love': he says that benevolence 'implies an Act of our Will, join'd with its most general Object, and is never taken in a bad Sense.'[1] Benevolence, he would have us understand, is ideally characteristic of the will, be the will human or Divine; it belongs to the nature of things; it is a law of nature, *the* law of nature, 'which directs our voluntary Actions, about chusing Good and refusing Evil.'[2] The following is proposed as 'the foundation of all Nature's Laws': 'The greatest Benevolence of every rational Agent towards all, forms the happiest State of every, and of all the Benevolent, as far as is in their Power; and is necessarily requisite to the happiest State which they can attain, and therefore the common Good is the supreme Law.'[3]

[1] *A Treatise*, p. 42.   [2] *Ib.*, p. 39.
[3] *Ib.*, p. 41. The original reads: *Benevolentia maxima singulorum agentium Rationalium erga omnes statum constituit singulorum, omniumq; Benevolorum, quantum fieri ab ipsis potest, foelicissimum ; & ad statum eorum, quem possunt assequi, foelicissimum necessario requiritur ; ac proinde, commune bonum erit suprema lex* (*De Legibus*, I. iv.).

It is unnecessary to pursue the argument by which Cumberland tries to establish the whole truth of this law; but a few points taken here and there will suggest that his own view of the good life does not differ materially from the Platonism which he does not care to accept. The conception of universal benevolence which he so ably outlines may be said to draw its vitality from Platonism, and even from revealed religion of which it claims ostensibly to be independent. Our author's social philosophy, which sees humanity as an organism,[1] is too spiritual an entity to be the child of natural religion: it is reminiscent of the social aspect of the Kingdom of God as declared in the Gospels and of the Pauline doctrine of the Church as the body of Christ. It lacks the mark of that species of humanism which makes men no more than partakers reciprocally in good works, and emphasizes the truth that the ultimate source of human benevolence runs right up to God. Cumberland points out that an individual man's good cannot come, unless his environment, both material and spiritual, co-operates with him while he pursues it; and this means that each individual stands in the position of a receiver from an universal circle of men of good-will, and from God Himself, who, in His benevolence, has ordered the laws of motion, in accordance with which the material universe is directed, with a view to the good of the social whole. In the eyes of this natural philosopher, a man is a child of the heavenly Father, and more than a social animal —in fact, a member of a rational kingdom having but one solitary end, the good of the whole, which is necessarily

---

[1] *Ib.*, p. 60: '. . . the collective Body of all Mankind, as naturally subordinate to God their Governour.'

P. 99: The human mind 'is naturally fitted to become a Member of the greatest Society, consisting of all rational Beings with God at their head. . . .'

P. 202: 'For I consider God, and all Men, upon account of some resemblance in Reason, or an intelligent Nature, as represented under one Notion, which is extended to every particular by the word, All.'

inclusive of the good of all the parts. Here is the voice of Christian Platonism: 'But if (as is meet, and as is every where the Practice, even of the Vulgar;) we take care to solicit the Aid of the first Cause, to the Establishment of human Happiness, we shall find nothing in our selves more Divine, by which we may please the Deity, than that sincere and most extensive Love, (of which we have been hitherto discoursing,) which reaches even God himself, as the Head and Father of rational Beings, and all other rational Agents, as his Children, more like to himself than the rest of his Creatures are; and, in consequence, the most dear to him: "For we are his offspring," is the saying of Aratus the Cicilian.' [1]

Again, when we inquire into Cumberland's view of the mind of a man arrived at years of discretion, we shall not find that it has lost much for having been spoiled of innate ideas. The twin mental activities are understanding and willing; for instead of remaining inert in the midst of a world of objects, a man explores the relations which they bear to one another and to himself, and in consequence chooses that which appears to be good and refuses that which appears to be evil. We learn that 'the innate Activity of the divine Nature of the Mind, permits it not to be perfectly idle; nor can it do any thing else than (as occasion offers) understand, chuse, refuse, and determine certain Motions of the Body, in order to obtain what it has chosen.' [2] And we are informed that 'every one come to maturity, in proportion to the natural vigor of his Mind, is by the same Nature spontaneously carry'd on to such Operations, at once with the greatest pleasure, and with absolute necessity.' [3] And this 'natural Impulse' finds unimpeded expression, when the will performs that which the understanding has rightly judged to be the most comprehensive good attainable in a given case.[4] But the understanding itself, in making a true judgment that such and such an end is

[1] *Ib.*, p. 55.   [2] *Ib.*, pp. 98-9.   [3] *Ib.*, p. 98.   [4] *Ib.*, p. 173.

good, is only repeating a lesson learnt from observing the necessary connections which, in the nature of things, obtain between the happiness consequent upon certain types of action and the misery consequent upon others. The sanctions of rewards and punishments attaching to all possible actions constitute the weightiest evidence that the Deity advances for the objectivity of the moral law; and it is as natural for a rational being to know the rules of good living, as it is for him to add the digits.[1] Like a good Platonist, Cumberland counsels us to scan the glass of Providence, wherein the pattern of the good life is clearly seen by the eye of man.

Cumberland's teaching on God will in all probability encourage a reader of the *De Legibus* to return thanks for all the blessings of this life; but it is hardly to be hoped that the few ideas on this matter which are repeated often in its pages will arouse his spirit of devotion. There is, apparently, little to be said about Him who is the cause of our creation and preservation, because He transcends the limits of our understanding; but the wonder is that a God, who has admitted us into a fellowship of general benevolence with Himself, has not seen fit in addition to draw aside the veil of analogy and grant us the joy of His presence. Cumberland's aim, as against Hobbes, is to vindicate man's aptness for fellowship, and he sees that a fellowship of universal dimensions requires a Divine partner for its president; and yet he makes no effort to deal with the spiritual relationships necessary to establish and to maintain it. He takes us to God, first cause and prime mover, by way of our experience of the things around us and within us: the external world—that domain where the Royal Society is busily engaged in discovering laws of motion—is full of things which conduce to the preservation of our minds and bodies; and our own internal world of the soul is happy when it has chosen to act benevolently.

[1] *Ib.*, p. 97.

'For we come not at the Knowledge of God,' he writes, 'by immediate Intuition of his Perfections, but from his effects first known by Sense and Experience; nor can we safely ascribe to him Attributes, which from other Considerations we do not sufficiently comprehend.'[1] And the joy of the Divine life, which corresponds by analogy to the happiness of our own moral life, depends upon Divine goodness in alliance with Divine power. 'Certainly Power, how great soever it may be imagin'd, if it be consider'd without Wisdom and Justice, has in it no more of Happiness or Majesty, than what is to be found in a Mass of Lead of infinite Weight.'[2] And lest an objector should contend that men cannot logically be called upon to exercise benevolence towards a God whose happiness, *ex hypothesi*, is incapable of increase, Cumberland describes the one great end before them as 'Piety towards God, and Charity towards Men,'[3] and as 'the Honour of God join'd with the Happiness of Men';[4] and he advances the following acute reason why it is that God, who lacks nothing, can ask for our love: 'For, as it is certain, that to desire to be belov'd, implies no Imperfection in Man; in God, it is so far from carrying any Suspicion of Imperfection, that, on the contrary, it is an Argument of the Benignity of his Nature, because Men arrive at their greatest Perfection, by loving him. . . .'[5]

The outstanding contribution made by Cumberland to

---

[1] *Ib.*, p. 15.   [2] *Ib.*, p. 222.   [3] *Ib.*, p. 49.   [4] *Ib.*, p. 248.
[5] *Ib.*, p. 17. James Tyrrell's gloss on Cumberland at this point reinforces the latter's teaching: 'That altho God, the Head of this intellectual System, be indeed incapable of any Addition to his infinite Happiness and Perfection, yet the whole System (in as much as it includes all finite rational Beings) is capable of improvement in these its finite parts, which Improvement God cannot only desire, but ever did and will promote, both by his own Power, as also by that of all subordinate voluntary Agents, whereby God's essential Goodness becomes manifest to us: and the Good of the whole System may reasonably be judged as grateful or pleasing to God the head thereof, altho it can add nothing to himself' (*A Brief Disquisition*, p. xxxi).

ethical theory is that all, who will be at pains to read the meaning of the scheme of things to which we belong, may see that a lone man is as fictitious a thing as solitary happiness, and that the arrival of the completely happy man awaits the consummation of a perfected humanity. Bentham's ideal, 'the greatest happiness of the greatest number,' would have seemed to him far too small an end to be the greatest good: 'the greatest possible Happiness of all'[1] is the only end, he argues, comprehensive enough to employ the talents of every individual man; and it is the only standard fit to make each man live consistently with every other man and with himself. It has, moreover, a religious sanction: for God wills the good of all men. Cumberland would not have agreed with Butler, who thought that benevolence directed towards mankind is 'an object too general, and very much out of our view,'[2] and who preferred the simple maxim that counsels love of neighbour: Cumberland holds that the two, the wider love and the narrower, are not inconsistent, even if the latter is the more intense; and that the practice of benevolence in every direction is the best way of promoting it in the minds of those who do not practise it. For all his faith in human nature, he is not so optimistic as to imagine that our most sincere endeavours after the best will always bring the happiness we seek for others and for ourselves: for sometimes we err in our analysis of situations, and sometimes there are causes unknown to us working contrary to our purpose. But when our plans miscarry, we are happy if we are in a position to assure ourselves that we acted as we ought. 'This only can be inferr'd from those Evils, which sometimes happen to the Followers of Virtue, That all degrees of Happiness cannot always be obtain'd by our whole Power, even when perfectly regulated by the best Moral Precepts. It is, however, certain, That by obeying them we shall do every thing that is in our Power, to procure that Happiness of Life, which

[1] *Ib.*, p. 238.   [2] *Sermon*, XII.

is all that Morality, or practical right Reason undertakes to perform.'[1] And Butler's dictum, that 'to Us, probability is the very guide of life,'[2] is foreshadowed in this sentiment: 'For such is the condition of human Life, that we must lay out almost our whole Labour, our Expence often, nay expose Life it-self to Danger, for the Hope of such Things, as conduce to the Preservation or Happiness of our-selves, or of others, altho' that Hope be probable only, not certain; even in Affairs of Peace, such as Agriculture, Merchandize, etc., much more in the Chance of War.'[3]

[1] *A Treatise*, pp. 244-5. [2] *The Analogy, Introduction.*
[3] *A Treatise*, p. 187.

VII
NATHANAEL CULVERWEL

But it pleased God, having first melted him with His love, and then chastised him, though somewhat sharply, to take him to Himself; from the contemplation of the light of Nature, to the enjoyment of one supernatural, that φῶς ἀπρόσιτον—light inaccessible, which none can see and live, and to translate him from snuffing a candle here to be made partaker of the inheritance of the saints in light.

DILLINGHAM.

CHAPTER VII

NATHANAEL CULVERWEL

NATHANAEL CULVERWEL,[1] by reason of his judicious mind, can sit comfortably astride the old learning and the new; and his gift for astute criticism of other men's systems ensures for him a place among synthetical thinkers, and removes him from among the eclectics who form the camp-followers of philosophy's pioneers. Cumberland, according to Professor Laird, is 'rather a Cambridge Zenonian or Ciceronian than a Cambridge Platonist'; [2] and if a corresponding niche is sought for Culverwel, he may fairly, and not forgetting the freedom with which he treats St. Thomas, be called a Christian Aristotelian. He impresses us as being one who reverences antiquity as sincerely as he admires the modern mind and its search after fresh truth, both speculative and practical; but the ideal representative of the latter is Bacon, 'that great advancer of learning,'[3] and not Descartes, who 'resolves all his assurance into thinking that he thinks.'[4]

To an objector who should urge that putting new wine into old bottles is fraught with inevitable disaster to the bottles, Culverwel in all probability would reply that it is misleading to think of the traditional scheme of philosophical theology as being outworn. For beneath the old and familiar syllogisms of the schools, reason has been at work;

---

[1] Died 1650 or 1651.   [2] *Hobbes*, p. 275.
[3] *An Elegant And Learned Discourse of the Light of Nature, with Several Other Treatises*, London, 1652. The references to the *Discourse* are to the edition by John Brown, Edinburgh, 1857. P. 210.
[4] *Ib.*, p. 203.

and in all past ages it has borne measure of witness to the truth. The fact is, Culverwel says, that Aristotle has been vilified by the men who have hailed him as 'a pope in philosophy,' and looked upon his work as 'the irreversible decrees of learning'; whereas he is rightly honoured by those who imitate his critical attitude to traditional systems: 'for he scorned to enslave and captivate his thoughts to the judgment of any whatsoever.'[1] And 'it is against the mind and meaning of antiquity to stop the progress of religion and reason.'[2] But those who hearken to reason's voice speaking within them will hear her confess that she is not an all-competent guide along the way of life. 'Reason, when awakened, feels her own wounds, hears her own jarrings, sees the dimness of her own sight.'[3] And so it is entirely reasonable for reason to turn for guidance to the lesser light of faith; and St. Thomas did well to relate reason and faith as he did. 'For it is (God) that set up these two great luminaries in every heavenly soul,—the sun to rule the day, and the moon to rule the night; and though there be some kind of creatures that will bark at this lesser light, and others so severely critical, as that they make mountains of those spots and freckles which they see in her face; yet others know how to be thankful for her weaker beams, and will follow the least light of God's setting up, though it is but "the candle of the Lord."'[4]

The judgment of William Dillingham is sound, when he says that Culverwel 'abhorred the very thought of advancing the power of Nature into the throne of free grace, or by the light of Nature in the least measure to eclipse that of faith';[5] for throughout the *Discourse*, and the eight shorter essays appended to it, he continues to insist that mere nature of itself is both unable to explain itself, and also ineffective to develop its latent powers to the full, and that it awaits, therefore, the illuminating and vitalizing touch of the super-

---

[1] *Ib.*, p. 209.   [2] *Ib.*, p. 213.   [3] *Ib.*, p. 20.
[4] *Ib.*, p. 18.   [5] *To the Reader.*

natural. The burden of his message is the fact of the dependence of creature upon Creator. The first lesson in philosophy as well as in religion is that apart from God all is vanity, and that the true riches will be discovered to none save to those who have discovered and confessed their own poverty. And Culverwel succeeds in driving his lesson well home, without appearing in the least degree to depress human nature into the depths of total depravity. It is the folly, incompetence and sin on the part of a being possessed of so many and great gifts that sets the problem and points to the whereabouts of the answer. That man, who promises so well, should fall so inevitably, gives a hint that fulfilment is conditioned and made possible by a Power above. Culverwel's epigram, that 'all men are born Pelagians,'[1] as we shall see in the sequel, has to be interpreted more widely than in a moral sense; for intellectually, aesthetically and emotionally, to say nothing of spiritually, man is dependent upon the grace of God; and nature, in all its works, tends to behave like Narcissus. The Stoics are singled out as the supreme examples of secular humanism, because 'they fix their happiness in . . . the things in their own compass and sphere,'[2] and contend for 'a domestick Plerophory.'[3] 'Yet Nature has not such a fountain of perfection in itself, but that it may very well draw from another.'[4] 'Inferior creatures may, and do move within the compass of their natures, and yet they reach that end which was propounded and assigned to their being; but such was the special and peculiar love of God, which He manifested to a rational nature, as that it must be advanced above itself by a "supernatural aid," before it can be blest with so great a perfection as to arrive to the full end of its being.'[5]

The full end of man's being is *beatitudo*, the vision of God; and this spiritual gift is given only to glorified souls,

[1] *Discourse*, p. 263.　　[2] *Ib.*, p. 261.　　[3] *The White Stone*, p. 161.
[4] *Discourse*, p. 264.　　[5] *Ib.*, p. 268.

to whom also God gives the ability wherewith to enjoy Him. For since each degree of happiness consists in 'that harmonious conformity and correspondency that a faculty hath with its object,'[1] and 'the more rational and spiritual any being is, the larger capacity it has of pleasure,'[2] it follows that 'the nearer anything comes to mental joy, the purer and choicer it is':[3] and 'the soul by the enjoyment of God comes near the pleasure of God himself,' which 'is with Him that infinite satisfaction which He takes in His own essence, and in His own operations.'[4] But Culverwel is so anxious to maintain the dependence of the glorified soul, that he goes on to say that lest it should be 'too much oppressed with the weight of glory,'[5] God 'creates and prepares' for it 'such a supernatural disposition in an intellectual eye, by which it is clarified and fortified, and rightly prepared for beholding the Divine essence.'[6] Besides, the vision is not a comprehensive one, 'for a finite being will never be able fully to grasp an infinite essence,'[7] and consequently there will be in the future life 'degrees of happiness.'[7] And, finally, the vision is reserved strictly for disembodied souls, no exceptions being allowed, as by St. Thomas, in the cases of Moses and St. Paul. God, Culverwel explains, in his *Spiritual Opticks*, communicated His mind 'in a clearer way'[8] to Moses than to Jeremiah, to whom He spoke in the riddles of an almond tree and a seething-pot; and, as for St. Paul, 'whose soul was always mounting towards that third Heaven, whither he had once been rapt, and had there heard words that neither could nor might be uttered ... we finde him here[9] granting the imperfection of his knowledge, ... and encouraging himself with the consideration of the full and clear Vision, which we shall have of him hereafter, when we shall see God face to face in glory.'[10]

---

[1] *Ib.*, p. 240. [2] *Ib.*, p. 248. [3] *Ib.*, p. 249. [4] *Ib.*, p. 251.
[5] *Ib.*, p. 275. [6] *Ib.*, p. 274. [7] *Ib.*, p. 276. [8] P. 184.
[9] 1 *Cor.* xiii. 12. [10] *Spiritual Opticks*, p. 177.

Our author, we learn, has no sympathy with those who teach that the *summum bonum* can be attained by the method of securing a harmonious adjustment of the basic instincts. 'The harmonious composing of natural faculties, the tuning of those spheres will never make up a heaven fit for a soul to dwell in.'¹ Experience ought to teach a more sobering lesson. 'If men do but enquire, and look a little to the ebbings and flowings of their own spirits, to the waxing and waining of their own performances: surely they will presumably acknowledge, that they can't fetch a Plerophory out of these.'²

Until the time when the vision shall come, nature is directed by reason, which is drawn out chiefly by God's general providences in the created order; and by faith also, which is evoked in addition by His special providence in the Christian revelation, which includes the Incarnation, the Scriptures, and the experience vouchsafed by the Holy Spirit.³ And it is the life of faith, working in harmony with reason, which prepares for the life of the world to come, and the vision of God which will come with it. Yet again, man's dependence upon God is emphasized. 'God hath chosen this way of faith that He may stain the pride and glory of man, that He may pose his intellectuals, that God may maintain in man great apprehensions of Himself, of His own incomprehensibleness, of His own truth, of His

¹ *Discourse*, p. 264.   ² *The White Stone*, p. 125.
³ In *Spiritual Opticks : or a Glasse Discovering the weaknesse and imperfection of a Christians knowledge in this life*, five glasses in which we see darkly (1 *Cor*. xiii. 12) are enumerated: *in speculo mundi ; in speculo scientiarum* ('there is no greater vicinity then between truth and goodnesse; and heaven is full of knowledge, as it is of holinesse; and it is brimfull of both'); *in speculo verbi* ('All truths belonging to the Essence of a Christian, are plain and perspicuous: and there is an assisting Spirit, which though they perhaps may scoffe at, and some others may unjustly pretend to, yet without doubt it shall lead God's people into all truth'); *in speculo providentiae* ('Providence is very mysterious, and there is no readier way to Atheisme then to question it when we cannot give a sufficient account of it'); and *in speculo fidei* (Faith 'dies in the mount too like Moses').

own revelations, as that He may keep a creature in a posture of dependency so as to give up his understanding, so as to be disposed and regulated by Him.'[1]

Now faith, which schools us while we live here in the body in preparation for the state proper to vision, is itself reared upon reason, whose task is, primarily, to grapple with the visible and tangible environment in which we have our place. And in the last resort, reason is reducible to that living and conscious activity which deals with experience in the light of certain 'common notions' and principles, both intellectual and practical, derived therefrom. But the experience in and through which the rational leaven works itself is at bottom of the sensory order; and, but for contact with this, reason with its common notions would not exist. Plato, therefore, in Culverwel's interpretation, wrongly held that all knowledge is already latent in the newly born soul, waiting for release at the touch of the sensory button; and Origen's speculations on the soul's pre-existence would lead one to think that he 'had scarce read *Genesis*';[2] whereas Aristotle 'did not antedate his own knowledge, nor remember the several postures of his soul, and the famous exploits of his mind before he was born; but plainly professed that his understanding came naked into the world.'[3] 'Yet the Platonists in this were commendable, that they looked upon the spirit of a man as "the candle of the Lord," though they were deceived in the time when it was lighted.'[4] If the doctrine of innate ideas were true, 'the great doctor of the Gentiles' would not have written that 'the invisible things of him from the creation of the world are clearly seen, being understood by the things that are made.'[5] Culverwel apparently thinks that man's dependence will be all the more evident, if his most excellent gift of reason stands beholden to his body and to his material environment for his first lessons in theology. And he has

[1] *Discourse*, p. 236. [2] *Ib.*, p. 123. [3] *Ib.*, pp. 124-5.
[4] *Ib.*, p. 132. [5] *Rom.* i. 20.

no illusions as to the tedium which accompanies the mental processes involved in attaining to a philosophy: 'the mind having such gradual and climbing accomplishments, doth strongly evince that the true rise of knowledge is from the observing and comparing of objects, and from thence extracting the quintessence of some such principles as are worthy of all acceptation; that have so much of certainty in them, that they are near to a tautology and identity; for this first principles are.' [1]

Culverwel makes no attempt to draw up 'a catalogue of all these truths,' [2] and the following must suffice for examples of common notions and derivative principles in the field of intellectual endeavour: 'The whole is greater than its part'; 'Nothing can be, and not be, at the same time'; [2] and 'Whatever is, necessarily is, when it is.' [3] For our purpose, however, the most important one is that denoted by 'the law of nature,' namely, the moral law; because Culverwel follows those who reserve the term 'law' for the principles to which rational agents are subjected, and he holds that nature, in all its sub-human levels of being, has been set by God under the direction of 'impetuous propensions.' In making this distinction, he is in agreement with Cumberland, who holds that man lies under the law of nature, and things lower than man under the laws of motion. No precise definition of the law of nature, such as Cumberland gives, is forthcoming, though the following passage from Grotius is referred to with approval: '*Jus naturale est dictatum rectae rationis, indicans actui alicui, ex ejus convenientia vel disconvenientia cum ipsa natura rationali, inesse moralem turpitudinem, aut necessitatem moralem, et consequenter ab auctore naturae ipso Deo, talem actum aut vetari aut praecipi.*' [4] Formally, what the moral law requires is that man ought to adapt himself to the nature of things, or that he ought to realize the potentialities of his nature.

[1] *Discourse*, pp. 126-7.   [2] *Ib.*, p. 126.   [3] *Ib.*, p. 177.
[4] *Ib.*, p. 67; *De Jure Belli et Pacis*, i. 10.

And this law becomes explicit in man's reason after due consideration of certain more concrete practical 'first and alphabetical notions'[1] such as these: 'we must seek good, and avoid evil'; 'we must seek happiness'; and 'do not do to others what you do not wish to have done to yourself.' But the moral law, as we have just described it, and these elementary hints which it gives of itself, will prove to be defective guides, until reason has succeeded in extending them out 'in some such precepts as do most intimately and intensely conduce to the welfare and advantage of an intellectual being':[2] and maxims forbidding lies, theft, and other specific evils, are deduced in strict logic from more general principles. 'Particulars,' Culverwel says, 'are nearer to existence and operation than universals, and in this respect do more immediately steer and direct the motions of such a being. The one is the bending of the bow, but the other is the shooting of the arrow.'[3]

At this point occurs yet another instance of our author's teaching that man's is a dependent essence; for he will not allow to him the dignity of playing the rôle of his own lawgiver. That, he explains, 'would make the very same being superior to itself, as it gives a law, and inferior to itself, as it must obey it';[4] and obligation has no meaning apart from God to whom man stands in the relation of a child for whose happiness or well-being the moral law has been ordained. Reason has 'to warn the soul, in the name of its Creator, to fly from such irregularities as have an intrinsecal and implacable malice in them, and are prejudicial and destructive to its nature, but to comply with, and embrace all such acts and objects as have a native comeliness and amiableness, and are to the heightening and ennobling of its being.'[5]

Finally, we turn to Culverwel's treatment of a problem having special claims upon the attention of an age which

[1] *Discourse*, p. 81.   [2] *Ib.*, p. 84.   [3] *Ib.*, p. 85.
[4] *Ib.*, p. 74.   [5] *Ib.*, p. 99.

has aspired to establish new systems in place of old, the problem of certainty, and more particularly, in its religious form, the problem of assurance. After all that has been said of Culverwel's thought hitherto, we are prepared to find that we can be certain of the truth of our common notions, which are, so to speak, their own guarantees, and of our experience, in so far as it is saturated with them. Our knowledge must be self-evident, if it is true. Nor are we unprepared to learn that a measure of certainty obtains also in the sensory field; for sensation, though often misleading, sometimes stands as evidence for making an oath, and 'mathematical demonstrations choose to present themselves to the sense, and thus become ocular and visible.'[1] This is explained by the fact that 'it is the same soul that moves both in the sense and in the understanding.'[1] The mistake made by Descartes is that, having failed to refer to the touchstone of his common notions the propositions which he had under review, he could lay hold upon no other criterion of certainty save that of the 'reflecting and reduplicating'[2] of his own thinking. Culverwel's point seems to be that Descartes posed to himself the problem of certainty after he had shut off the 'I think' from all contributions offered by sensation, and denuded it even of all the formal principles by which thinking is carried on; and that, bereft of such content, the 'I think' had no resource left but to lapse into itself *ad infinitum.* And this procedure, Culverwel holds, leads to scepticism.

Men desire greatly to achieve certainty in their religious life, and since, in Culverwel's view, the formal truths of Christianity cannot be discovered from out of reason's natural wealth of common notions,[3] but are appropriated, on the contrary, by faith, it is imperative that men should know that they are not being misled by the projections of their own fancies. The problem, as Culverwel sees it, is a double one: How can we be certain, for example, both

[1] *Ib.*, p. 201.   [2] *Ib.*, p. 203.   [3] *Ib.*, p. 223.

of the truth of the proposition that Jesus Christ is God's Incarnate Son, and also of the fact that God reveals Him so to be? And his answer to the double question is, in brief, that the Spirit of God so assures us; and that any one of the truths peculiar to Christianity is appreciated as true, when it is known to be the express utterance of God. His meaning becomes clearer, when we recall his treatment of the meaning of moral obligation. Certain moral truths are discovered, he says, by reason, and when they are seen to be the expression of God's will for us, they become raised to the rank of law and therefore oblige us; so, in similar fashion, when religious truths are seen to be the revelation of God's mind and purpose, they elicit an assent on our part which is called faith. Our concern is not simply with the external evidence for Christian truth; but with the relation of this evidence to Christian truth; and Culverwel holds that the relation itself is of God's doing, and that, furthermore, our acceptance of the relation is of God's doing also. He points out that a miracle is impotent as evidence, until he who is witness of it discerns in it the hand of God.[1] 'Now this is the voice of reason, that God can, and that none but God can, assure you of His own mind; for if He should reveal His mind by a creature, there will still be some tremblings and waverings in the soul, unless He does withal satisfy a soul that such a creature does communicate His mind truly and really as it is, so that ultimately the certainty is resolved into the voice of God and not into the courtesy of a creature. This Holy Spirit of God creates in the soul a grace answerable to these transcendent objects; you cannot but know the name of it—it is called Faith, "a supernatural form of faith," as Mirandola the younger styles it, which closes and complies with every word that drops from the voice or pen of a

---

[1] *Ib.*, p. 228. Miracles are 'very suitably and proportionably subservient to faith, they being above natural power, as revealed truths are above natural understanding.'

Deity, and which facilitates the soul to assent to revealed truths; so as that, with a heavenly inclination, with a delightful propension, it moves to them as to a centre.'[1]

Culverwel deals with another phase of the problem of certainty in the religious life in *The White Stone*; for men who are already persuaded that God has in reality spoken His mind in Christ will desire further to be assured that their response to His revelation betokens such a spiritual condition as will not fail to win His acceptance. Here again, certainty depends, in the last resort, upon the influence of the Holy Spirit, who helps the soul to bear witness that its faith is genuine. And it turns out that increasing closeness to God involves both increasing dependence upon His grace, and also increasing consciousness of that dependence. It is the most faithful souls that are aware most acutely of their need for God. But apart from the Divine contribution to man's sense of assurance, there remains its psychology, on which our author has some interesting things to say. He defines assurance as 'a reflex act of the soule, by which a Christian clearly sees, that he is for the present in the state of grace, and so an heire apparent to glory.'[2] 'It is the most secret and retir'd operation; the soule withdrawes and bids the body farewell, and even here becomes an *anima separata*: it retires into its Closet, and bolts its sense up, where none can peep in, none can evesdrop it.' And the object of this withdrawal is to discover how the soul appears before God, and not to discover what it knows before itself. 'Those truths which I do clearly and evidently know, I also know that I know them. And that which I strongly believe, I know that I believe it.'[3] Admittedly, this act of introspection is 'fleeting and desultory' and 'quickly vanishes';[4] and 'none can so anatomize his own Spirit . . . so as every veine and nerve and muscle shall be obvious and apparent to his eye; but what does this hinder, but

[1] *Ib.*, pp. 228-9. [2] *The White Stone*, p. 102.
[3] *Ib.*, p. 107. [4] *Ib.*, p. 103.

that the general frame and bent of the Spirit, the byas and inclination of the soule may be clearly known?'[1] It is, therefore, upon the whole self [2] that this act of judgment is turned, and the question is as to its dominant tendency. When this tendency is set towards God, it is the movement known as faith; and a man can be as assured of its existence as he can of his own. Weakness of faith spells lack of assurance; and assurance is but 'the highest degree of faith.'[3]

[1] *Ib.*, p. 110. [2] *Ib.*, p. 104. [3] *Ib.*, p. 106.

VIII
GEORGE RUST

The Author was a Person with whom I had the Honour and Happiness of a very particular acquaintance; a man he was of a clear Mind, a deep Judgment and searching Wit: greatly learned in all the best sorts of Knowledge, old and new, a thoughtful and diligent Enquirer, of a free Understanding, and vast Capacity, join'd with singular Modesty, and unusual Sweetness of Temper, which made him the Darling of all that knew him: He was a Person of great Piety and Generosity; a hearty Lover of God and Men: An excellent Preacher, a wise Governour, a profound Philosopher, a quick, forcible, and close Reasoner, and above all, a true and exemplary Christian. In short, he was one who had all the Qualifications of a Primitive Bishop, and of an extraordinary Man.

JOSEPH GLANVIL.

CHAPTER VIII

GEORGE RUST [1]

GEORGE RUST, protégé of Taylor, and disciple of More, says Joseph Glanvil, 'had too great a Soul for the trifles of that Age, and saw clearly the nakedness of Phrases and Phansyes; He out-grew the pretended Orthodoxy of those days, and addicted himself to the Primitive Learning and Theology, in which he even then became a great Master.' [2] His literary remains include no *magnum opus*; and it is from a few academic sermons, funeral orations, and slender monograms, that we learn of his robust and exploring mind. 'God and a Man's own soul' [3] were for him the things first and foremost to be known; because true knowledge of them yields the only satisfying meaning of human life, which is properly human knowledge in action. And, since knowledge of our own souls involves knowledge of the spiritual relation we bear to God, it must be deeper, richer, and fuller, than the sense of the verbal propositions in which we try to convey it to another, and more compelling than the arguments by which we attempt to convince a sceptic of its truth. Ultimately, the sum of all knowledge is comprised in the truth that God is love, 'which is witnessed to us by Divine Revelation, by Creation and Providence, by the inward sense and experience of every good Man, and by the Nature of Reasoning it self.' [4]

---

[1] Died 1670.
[2] Glanvil's introductory letter to Rust's *A Discourse of Truth*, London, 1677.
[3] *The Remains of that Reverend and learned Prelate, Dr. George Rust, Late Lord Bishop of Dromore, in the Kingdom of Ireland. Collected and Published by Henry Hallywell.* London, 1686, p. 21.
[4] *Ib.*, p. 14.

In a sermon preached on the text, '*The spirit of man is the candle of the Lord, searching all the inward parts of the belly*,' [1] Rust undertakes to inquire into the character of the human soul; and his treatment, from a psychological point of view, is as clear as any to be found in the writings of his school. Rejecting all interpretations which identify the candle either with any single faculty, or with any form of supernatural grace, he prefers to identify it with the entire soul; because he holds that the soul is an organism, and that its 'parts,' being psychic powers, are functions of one whole. Thus he ridicules those who suggest that will and understanding are 'two Faculties both really distinct from the Soul and themselves,' as though will could be *potentia caeca*, ignorant of the good of its end, and as though it and other powers were 'clapt upon the soul' from without.[2] His own interpretation of the soul's 'parts,' denying, as it does, both to functions and to content alike, all possibility of complete isolation, explains satisfactorily the seriousness of sin. For viewing the 'parts' vertically, so to speak, as Plotinus does, in so many tiers, each differing from the other in an ascending or descending scale of values, Rust says that 'whatever aberrations we make from the laws of intellectual life, the ill effect of them is not confined to that chief and *principal part* of our Soul wherein that *life* is seated, but descends from thence and spreads its impure contagion through all the *Seats* of inferiour life, by reason of that close continuity which is in all the parts of the Soul.' [3]

Our author affirms categorically that the candle is truth; and since reason, the faculty for appropriating it, is no mere addendum to an irrational soul, but the leaven which spiritualizes and orders the whole, he intends us to understand that 'the Soul of Man . . . is so far the Candle of the Lord, as it is identified with Truth.' [4] But, we inquire, how does

---

[1] *Prov.* xx. 27.   [2] *Remains*, pp. 41-2.
[3] *A Letter of Resolution Concerning Origen and the chief of his Opinions*, London, 1661, p. 50.   [4] *Remains*, p. 23.

man's reason come to identify itself with truth? or, how is the candle lighted? and, further, what is truth itself? or, what does the candle reveal? In reply to the first question, Rust bids us throw our native light upon our souls. Introspective analysis shows, he says, that there are four different, interacting, interlocking, and complementary faculties. These are natural instinct, inward sense, outward sense, and reason, or discourse. 'The first is the Faculty that is conform'd to common Notions or Principles of immediate Truth, and the Natures and Essences of Things: . . . By the second we are able to feel and take notice of our own Actions, or receive Impressions from the Divine Mind, and to be irradiated with the Divine Light. The third is the Faculty whereby we are fitted to converse with the outward World, and to take notice of the Things that be and are done by us. By the fourth, making use of inward, outward and divine Sense, we do prove, convince, confute, raise Inferences, Deductions, &c. All which trains of Reasoning are onely so far true, as they follow upon Common Notions and Principles of Indemonstrable Light.'[1] This list, borrowed evidently from Lord Herbert of Cherbury,[2] professes to be complete; and we observe that the second faculty, 'inward sense,' leaves the way open for immediate contact with God. Rust sets God free to speak to man directly, as well as indirectly through a sacramental universe, and in the once-delivered historic revelation in Christ. Earlier in the sermon, he says that 'inward sense' 'is capable of being touched and affected by the Influences, Illapses and Descensions of God upon it, and of being irradiated and enlightned by the first Mind and Intellect.'[3]

When a man searches within himself, he finds that his soul is a living organism engaged in commerce with an environment which touches it sometimes through, and sometimes independently of, his body. He finds that, besides being sensitive to this environment in its two orders,

[1] *Ib.*, pp. 42-3.   [2] *De Veritate.*   [3] *Remains*, p. 40.

intellectual and material, he is equipped to receive it and to read off its meaning. He hears a deep within answering to a deep without. And with his recognition of a kinship between the harmony saturating environment and the harmony in his own soul, truth emerges. This candle of the Lord is a principle of self-reflection. So Rust can say that it is 'as it were a Candle lighted and set up by God, to search into and take notice of all the secrets that are inwombed in Man, his Thoughts, Desires, Affections, &c.'[1]

Then comes the second question, namely, What is truth? 'Pilate's question,' says Rust, 'hath always been the Great Inquiry of the World; but especially in these days of ours, when to doubt of all things begins to be a Principle in Divinity as well as in Philosophy.' And he proceeds in a series of oratorical flashes, worthy of Jeremy Taylor himself, to pillory all who treat truth as if it were merely the private possession of individuals, and as variable as their whims; and he suggests, as he moves in his flight, that intolerance is by no means the least evil arising from this narrow view. 'Should we go abroad in the World, and ask as many as we meet, *What is Truth?* we should find it a changeable and uncertain Notion, which every one cloaths his own Apprehensions with. Truth is in every Sect and Party, though they speak Inconsistencies among themselves, and Contradictions to one another. Truth is the Turkish Alcoran, the Jewish Talmud, the Papists Councils, the Protestants Catechisms and Models of Divinity; each of these in their proper place and region. Truth is a various uncertain Thing, changes with the Air and Climate: 'tis Mahomet at Constantinople, the Pope at Rome, Luther at Witemberg, Calvin at Geneva, Arminius at Oldwater, Socinus at Cracow; and each of these are sound and orthodox in the Circuit of their own Reign and Dominion. . . . And we know in our days into what new shapes this *Proteus* hath transform'd it self. Truth, 'tis worm-eaten Antiquity, an infallible

[1] *Ib.*, p. 23.

Chair, the strongest Lungs, the longest Sword, the most Voices. Truth is confident Ignorance, assisted with heady and turbulent Zeal, and backt with merciless Persecution of all Gainsayers. 'Tis presumptuous Incogitancy, accompanied with rigid and uncharitable Censures of all dissenting Judgments. 'Tis a Confession of Faith with an Anathema at the foot of every Article. 'Tis that which confutes Opinions and answers Arguments by branding them with Names of Reproach and Scandal. 'Tis a standard Measure in the hands of some particular Sect, to which all Mens understanding must be even'd and squar'd. 'Tis a State Mould committed to the keeping of some Party that is in greatest favour; whereinto all Opinions are cast; and those that are beyond its Capacity are rejected as Dross. In a word, Truth is a piece of Education, Interest, Humour, Fancy and Temper: 'tis that we are born to, suck in with our Mothers Milk, learn with our A B C . . . Once more; Truth is a piece of temper and complexion, 'tis light in a coloured glass, diversified according to the dispositions of Men; 'tis the several tinctures of Mens passions and affections; 'tis Cruelty in rigid and severe; 'tis fond Indulgence in soft and effeminate Natures; 'tis that which best gratifies a Man's lusts and corruptions.'[1] But, he concludes, the best

[1] *Ib.*, pp. 43-6. In *A Sermon Preached at New-Town The 23 of Octob. 1663 At the Funeral of the Right Honourable Hugh Earl of Mount-Alexander* . . . Dublin, 1664, he gives his reasons for his allegiance to the Church of England: ' . . . I have considered the Confessions, and Creeds, and terms of Communion propounded by the several Churches of Christendom, and I may truly say, with an indifferency of judgement, and when I had no other interest but that of truth; and after all, I can make this sincere profession, that I should sooner choose to be of the Communion of the Church of *England,* than any Church that I know of in the Christian world; for though it requires conformity in some things of external worship, yet they are, to speak the least of them, so harmless and innocent, so undetermin'd by any Law of God, and so much in the disposition of lawful Authority, that it is a wonder to me, that wise and sober men should ever raise any controversie about them: But in matters of opinion, where the minde and understanding is concern'd, which it is not in a mans own power to command, and can be subject to no other dictates, and impositions, but those of infallible

representation of truth is that it is 'the Life and Nature of the second Hypostasis in the Deity,' and he devotes many pages to a discussion on the subject of 'ideas' and their 'eternal and immutable relations.'[1] His theory turns out to be the same as Cudworth's, namely, that we know the truth by participating in the Divine mind. In the main, his argument is that, if there are not permanent relations prevailing between permanent terms, there is no truth to be known. Can any premisses taken at random, he asks, be made to prove any conclusion whatever? and, can any means serve a given end—lying, for example, the glory of God?

Truth, however, does not have the last word in a thorough-going interpretation of life; and, if we should hesitate to agree with Rust that this is the case, he would show us that the truth which we take to be ultimate is really a richer thing than the naked eternal and immutable ideas in the mind of God. We have not gone as far as we can go in our explanation of things, if we halt in contemplation before a stationary intellectual panorama of our living experience. It remains to give a reason why the truth is given for our learning, and why we are alive to enjoy it. So primacy of place goes to goodness over truth. God created the world, because He is good; and in creating, He communicates His goodness in varying degrees throughout the whole creation; and the same Divine motive is invoked in order to account for the Incarnation which was 'to teach us that the Power of God is always tempered with Goodness.'[2] Within 'the compass of Immensity'[3] God's goodness is at work, and everything that has life enjoys it in its own due measure. 'Infinite Goodness is the pregnant Womb from whence we

revelation, the Church of *England* does here allow so fair a latitude, that a sober, and ingenuous spirit can hardly desire a greater, I am sure he will no where else find nere so much.' [1] *Remains*, p. 23.

[2] *Ib.*, p. 3. In *Concerning Origen* (p. 15), Rust interprets that Father's view of the *idiomata* in the Trinity thus: 'They are these, *Original goodness*, or first *Plenitude* of Life and Being, All-comprehensive *Wisdom* or *Reason*, and *Demiurgal Love*.' [3] *Remains*, p. 6.

have our Birth and Off-spring. . . . It gives Being unto every Beast of the Field, and Bird of Heaven, and Fish of the Sea, and to every thing else, even to the most Contemptible Worm that creeps on the face of the Earth, that they may all enjoy that Life and Happiness which is proper to their Natures.'[1] Happiness, therefore, is not a special prerogative of man, but belongs to all living things, and characterizes even the mode of the Divine life itself. Supreme happiness is enjoyed alone by the Supreme Being, and our appropriate measure of happiness comes as we live in accordance with the highest principle of our nature. We are to live to give, as God lives and gives. In the sermon preached at the funeral of Jeremy Taylor, Rust says that 'the Happiness that belongs to a Rational and intellectual Being, can never be attain'd but in a way of holiness and conformity unto the Divine Will: for, such a temper and disposition of mind is necessary unto Happiness, not by virtue of any arbitrarious constitution of Heaven; but, the eternal Laws of Righteousness, and immutable respects of things, do require and exact it.'[2] Like Whichcote, our author believes that the good life is found outside the soul, before it is found within; and he contrasts the true love, which is an expansive venture, with a false 'Fond Self-love,' which welcomes God's love 'from that respect it hath to a Man's self.'[3] So it is 'the greatest happiness in the World, to be used as an Instrument to doe good to others.'[4]

[1] *Ib.*, p. 6.
[2] *A Funeral Sermon Preached at the Obsequies Of the Right Reverend Father in God, Jeremy, Lord Bishop of Down* . . ., London, 1668, p. 15.
Cf. Kant, who holds that ' whereas happiness, while it is pleasant to the possessor of it, is not of itself absolutely and in all respects good, but always presupposes morally right behaviour as its condition.' (*Practical Reason*, T. K. Abbott's Edition, p. 206.)
[3] *Remains*, p. 13. Hallywell says that 'nothing is more contrary to the free and universaliz'd Spirit of a Christian than this φιλαυτία Self-love, this narrow and contracted Nature, which acts as it were in a particular Sphere, and is wholly unconcerned for the rest of God's creation.' (*Remains, Preface*.) [4] *Ib.*, p. 8.

But the full measure of happiness is reserved until we pass to the future life, when there will be scope for the full exercise of our spiritual powers. The happiness we experience here is seldom free from some alloy; and even though we were able to make ourselves happy—which is not the case—there are always attendant circumstances, over which we have no control, to mar our joy. 'This life it is begun in a Cry, and it ends in a Groan; and he that lives most happily, his life is checker'd with black and white, and his dayes are not all Sun-shine, but some are cloudy and gloomy, and there is a Worm at the root of all his joy, that soon eats out the sap and heart of it; and the goard in whose shade he now so much pleases himself, by to-morrow will be wither'd and gone.'[1] It is true that, in the face of misfortune, a really conscientious man can always console himself with the assurance that he has followed the light whither it led him, and that he acted the truth as he saw it; but his contentment, considered in itself, is not happiness. In the true sense of the word, Rust explains, a man is happy, when his conscience assures him that he has been living on God's side in the moral struggle; and happiness so understood, as the concomitant of living conscientiously before God, is valued as an anticipation of a happiness to be completed in heaven. 'The pleasure of Vertue and Religion, especially while we are yet in the pursuit and prosecution of it, is the assurance that it gives of the care and protection of heaven, and that God will favour and reward it; without which hope, the satisfaction in a naked and unregarded vertue would not be considerable; and to say that the present pleasure that this hope administers is reward enough, is a piece of mockery, that does not become the Majesty and goodness of God in a matter of so great concernment.'[2]

Rust's whole attitude is a protest against demanding an interpretation of life from a man after you have cut him

---

[1] *A Funeral Sermon*, p. 5.
[2] *A Sermon Preached at New-Town*, p. 22.

adrift from his moorings. He believes that no problem whatever can be solved, unless there are rational principles to guide and correct the student; and that a man cannot investigate the problems which pertain to his own soul, without finding, in the course of his introspection, that there are certain canons of truth. This means that he has been taken out of himself, and become spectator of his soul from a higher ground upon which he stands comfortably and at home. And all his knowledge, in so far as it is true, is a sharing in what God knows in completeness. As with the intellectual, so with the moral and religious life: for here, too, is partnership with the Divine life. The wrong way is to set about making demands on God and neighbour; the happy way is to get outside oneself, or rather, to yield oneself up to the possession of Love. Our author says that 'the inward experience of every good Man bears witness' to the fact that 'He is acted by a free and Universaliz'd Spirit, and an all-spreading and diffusive Love. He looks not on himself as a partial and determinate Being, but as a Part and Member of the Universe, and accordingly serves not his own particular Interest, but the Good and Welfare of the whole.'[1] And to the witness of 'inward sense and experience' that God is love, the voices of Creation, of Providence, and of Revelation lend their aid. This is the first principle. And of his teaching about it Rust affirms: 'I do not know that I have spoken any thing which, as to me, is not as clear and evident as common Notions, and of whose Truth I make no more doubt than I do of my own Existence, which the so much admired Monsieur hath made the first Principle of his Philosophy.'[2]

[1] *Remains*, p. 7.   [2] *Ib.*, p. 14.

IX
EDWARD STILLINGFLEET

So this set of men at Cambridge studied to assert and examine the principles of religion and morality, on clear grounds, and in a philosophical method. . . . The most eminent of those who were formed under those great men were Tillotson, Stillingfleet and Patrick.

BURNET.

CHAPTER IX

EDWARD STILLINGFLEET [1]

EDWARD STILLINGFLEET shares with the thinkers already dealt with in this study the common view that man's happiness, here as hereafter, consists in knowing God; but he attempts to vindicate it by appealing to a kind of evidence for which a mind of Whichcote's temper had little interest. We shall assure ourselves the better of our kinship with God, he thinks, if we include within our survey of religious experience some of the signal acts of God done in days remote from our own. The reasons known in the heart will then be justified by the voice of tradition, and religious philosophy will have claimed history for her ally. So we have in Stillingfleet the well-worn distinction between natural religion and revealed, and an emphasis laid upon God's progressive revelation to a people of His choice; and a primary place is assigned to Scripture, which is the written record of God's word.

He takes us back to the candle of the Lord as it was lighted first in Adam. In the *Origines Sacrae* (1662), we learn that 'Scripture-history' tells of a golden age when Adam, the ideal prototype of his posterity, had a 'clear and distinct' [2] knowledge of God, as well as a 'particular knowledge' of all the created things round about him of which he was able to make any use. It is obvious to reason, we are told, that this should be the case: because Adam could neither obey nor

[1] 1635–99.
[2] *Works*, vol. ii. p. 2. The title is—*Origines Sacrae : or A Rational Account of the Grounds of the Christian Faith, as to the Truth and Divine Authority of the Scriptures, and the Matters therein contain'd.*

commune with a God whom he did not know; nor could he exercise dominion over things that he did not understand. Had he remained true to the 'Light set up in his Understanding,' [1] the race would not have been obliged to grope in darkness. One of the major results of his fall has been uncertainty as to the goal of human life and the means of reaching it. The clear knowledge proper to paradise on earth has become exchanged for 'the operose deductions of Reason (the pleasant toyl of the Rational Faculties since the Fall),' [1] and in some cases for a condition of 'lazy ignorance' in which too many have been content to remain well pleased. By slow degrees the tradition of man's original happiness grew obscure, and the luckless race entered upon an age of 'corruption' such as Athanasius describes. The periods of colonization, to which were incidental intensive cultivation of the soil, 'traffick,' the emergence of the new rich, social factions within, and wars without, left little leisure for the pursuit of 'Arts or Sciences'; [2] and by the time that communities were established, men had all but lost memory of the primal deposit of truth which Adam knew. Corruption, moreover, had taken possession of the will as well as of reason, so that pagan philosophers 'could not certainly but strangely wonder, that a Principle indifferent to be carry'd either way, should be so almost fatally inclin'd to the worst of them.' [3]

This account of the fall and decline of man being accepted, it follows that the possibility of restoration will depend in part upon recovery of at least as full a measure of the knowledge of God as had been forfeited, and in part upon fulfilment of such conditions as God may see fit to impose upon an apostate. We have to reckon, Stillingfleet insists, with the problem of fallen man, and therefore with a being whose faculties are impotent to see the good and do the right. 'Had Man indeed remain'd without offending his Maker, he might still have stood in his favour upon the

[1] *Ib.*, p. 2.   [2] *Ib.*, p. 11.   [3] *Ib.*, p. 307.

general terms of Obedience due from the Creature to his Creator, and to all such particular Precepts which shou'd bear the impress of his Maker's will upon them; beside which, the whole Volume of the Creation, without, and his own Reason within wou'd have been sufficient Directors to him in the performance of his duty.' Hence the plan of restoration must lie with God; and, on purely rational grounds, we are led to see the reasonableness of revealed religion: 'a particular Revelation is now become necessary, that Mankind may thereby understand on what terms God will be pleas'd again, and by what means they may be restored into his favour.'[1]

In order that God's fresh disclosures should avail to win man's response, it must needs be that penal corruption shall not have passed beyond the point at which he would cease to remain a rational being; and so if man's light can grow dim, and yet more dim, it cannot be extinguished. At this stage of his exposition, Stillingfleet introduces the 'common notions,' and endeavours to show how they have been obscured by association with common errors; and also the twin truths, both either misused or wilfully denied, upon which natural religion is based, namely, the existence of God and the immortality of the soul. Three causes of intellectual and religious error are noted. The first of these is some form or other of prejudice, and is reminiscent of Bacon's four idols: 'there are few in the World that look after Truth with their own Eyes, most make use of Spectacles of others making, which makes them so seldom behold proper lineaments in the face of Truth; which the several tinctures from Education, Authority, Custom and Predisposition do exceedingly hinder men from discerning.'[2] The second occasion of error lies in failing to work out the legitimate implications of a given truth to the end, and erroneous views are semblances of truth: 'for the general knowledge of a Divine Nature, supposing men ignorant of

[1] *Ib.*, p. 228.   [2] *Ib.*, p. 5.

the true God, did only lay a foundation to erect his idolatrous Temples upon; and the Belief of the Soul's surviving the Body after death, without knowledge of the true way of attaining Happiness, did make men more eager of embracing those Rites and Ceremonies, which came with a pretence of shewing the way to a blessed Immortality.'[1] The third reason why men err lies in the difficulty of disengaging the original deposit of truth once and for all delivered to Adam from the succeeding layers of false traditions which conceal it: 'for tho' History be frequently called the Light of Truth, and the Herald of Times, yet that Light is so faint and dim, especially in Heathen Nations, as not to serve to discover the face of Truth from her counterfeit, Error; and that Herald so little skill'd, as not to be able to tell us which is of the elder House.'[2] But our author makes it clear that although the call of truth is heard by the intellect, any effectual reply will involve the motions of the heart. 'For so pleasing is the enquiry, and so satisfactory the finding of Truth after the search, that the relish of it doth far exceed the greatest Epicurism of Apicius, or the most costly entertainments of Cleopatra; there being no Gust so exquisite as that of the Mind, nor any Jewels to be compared with Truth.'[3] Accordingly, he deprecates the detached attitude of some who will admit the existence of God, and yet refuse His claims upon their lives: 'for it is very possible for men, meeting with such insuperable difficulties about the casual concourse of Atoms for the production of the World, or the eternal existence of Matter, to assert some Eternal Mind, as the first Cause of these things, which yet they may imbrace only as an Hypothesis in Philosophy to solve the Phaenomena of Nature with, but yet not to make this Eternal Mind the object of adoration.'[4]

[1] *Ib.*, pp. 5-6.   [2] *Ib.*, p. 9.   [3] *Ib.*, p. 4.
[4] *Ib.*, p. 7. Cf. *Ib.*, p. 245 : 'And thus I assert it to have been in the present case, in all those Politic Governours who at first brought the World into both Civil and Religious Societies, after they were grown

Common notions, then, being subject to corruption, it lay open to Providence to provide a true account of sacred history; and Stillingfleet goes on to justify Moses in his capacity as historian. His story is authentic: for, in the first place, Noah's father, Lamech, was contemporary with Adam for fifty-six years, and Noah himself was contemporary with his grandfather, Methuselah, for six hundred years, 'according to our most learned Primate of Armagh'; [1] and, in the second place, the veracity of his narrative stood unquestioned by his own people, whose failings it is at no pains to conceal. In his capacity as law-giver, Moses is again a faithful witness, because he attests his knowledge of God's will by means of miracle, which is the only credential proper to a direct revelation of universal import. 'Now what conviction there can be to any sober mind concerning Divine Authority in any person without such a Power of Miracles going along with him, when he is to deliver some new Doctrine to the World to be believ'd, I confess I cannot understand.' [2] Stillingfleet evidently takes this line regarding miracle, because, fearful of the subjectivism of 'croaking Enthusiasts,' [3] he is anxious to secure a rational ground for revelation. He cherishes the fact of 'immediate' [4] revelation, when God, as He sees fit, 'gives demonstrable evidence to the inward senses of the soul'; [5] but he holds that this is no evidence to an outsider that God has spoken. And he goes on to draw a useful distinction between the modes of Divine action employed in revealing truth hitherto unknown to man, and in illuminating the mind of a 'believer.' The first is an act of Divine inspiration, whereas the second,

Rude and Barbarous; for as it had been impossible to have brought them into Civil Societies, unless there had been suppos'd an inclination to Society in them, so it had been equally impossible to have brought them to embrace any particular way of Religion, unless there had been a natural propensity to Religion implanted in them, and founded in the general belief of the existence of a Deity.'

[1] *i.e.* James Ussher.   [2] *Works*, ii. p. 88.   [3] *Ib.*, p. 67.
[4] *Ib.*, p. 89.   [5] *Ib.*, p. 98.

'which is by enlightening the faculty,'[1] is an act of Divine grace. Moses, being authorized to convey 'an extraordinary Message' to the world at large, was therefore empowered to commend it by extraordinary means.

It would have been gratuitous folly on the part of Moses, considering the circumstances of his time, to have set about proving that there is a God; for, in addition to the testimony borne to that truth by his miracles, there was the phenomenon of God's voice heard at Mount Sinai, and, besides, the memory of His doings on the occasion of the Flood was still green. But at a later time, when true religion, having passed through an intermediate stage of polytheism, declined into atheism, it became imperative that some men at least should discuss the problem of His existence, because 'the order of the World seem'd to tell them there was really a God.'[2] And so ineradicable are common notions, that even the sceptical Epicurus could not abate the force of the moral argument; for 'there is an Elastical power in Conscience that will bear its self up notwithstanding the weight that is laid upon it.'

Stillingfleet treats the problem of God's existence under three heads. In the first place, he shows that the true idea of God is 'most consonant to Reason.' Of all our ideas, he says, once we have rescued it from spurious imitations, this one 'hath fewer entanglements,'[3] because it is the most removed from 'corporeal Phantasms.' An idea is neither a sensation nor an image, but 'the objective Being of a thing as it terminates the Understanding, and is the form of the act of Intellection.'[4] Considered only as an act of the mind, an idea is always true; but considered as a duplicate in mind of a corresponding existing thing, it may be false. The idea of a golden mountain, for example, when referred to the mind that thinks it, is true, but, when referred to the world of things, is false. 'And the proneness of the Understanding's error,' Stillingfleet writes, 'ariseth from the

[1] *Ib.*, p. 89.   [2] *Ib.*, p. 230.   [3] *Ib.*, p. 231.   [4] *Ib.*, p. 232.

different nature of those things which are represented to the Mind; for some of them are general and abstracted things, and do not at all suppose existence, as the nature of Truth, of a Being, of Cogitation; other Ideas depend upon Existence suppos'd, as the Idea of the Sun, which I apprehend in my Mind because I have seen it; but besides these, there are other Ideas in the Mind, which the Understanding forms within its self by its own power, as it is a Principle of Cogitation; such are those which are called *entia rationis*, and have no other Existence at all but only in the Understanding, as *Chimaera's, Centaures,* etc.'[1] The idea of 'an absolutely Perfect Being' comes under the first of these three classes, and before proceeding to prove that it is not a false idea, or that God exists, it is desirable to show that it is an idea natural to reason and within its power to frame. This our author does by pointing out that no sensation or phantasm can possibly occasion it; and that there is no single corporeal object to go partner with it. This idea is a 'pure act of Intellection.'[2] 'Corporeal Phantasms . . . alone hinder us from a distinct Conception of it.'[2] Ideas of the second class are accounted for by matter and motion, 'those two grand Principles of the Universe';[3] and ideas of the third class by 'a kind of African Copulation'[4] imposed by the mind upon the 'corporeal Phantasms of outward Beings.'[5] The idea of God cannot be 'fictitious';[6] because it does not comprise a number of memory-images: nevertheless, in process of arriving at it, the 'Plastic Power of the Understanding'[7] takes its cue from things in the external world. Here Stillingfleet, preferring the Platonic attitude, takes considerable liberty with his Cartesian exemplar. 'If any difficulty be made concerning the forming such a Notion in ones mind,' he says, 'let the Person who scruples it, only inquire of himself whether he judges all Beings in the World equal; whether a Mushroom hath in it all the perfections

[1] *Ib.,* p. 232. [2] *Ib.,* p. 235. [3] *Ib.,* p. 233. [4] *Ib.,* p. 232.
[5] *Ib.,* p. 233. [6] *Ib.,* p. 232. [7] *Ib.,* p. 233.

which Man hath?' His point is that the perfections which we include in the idea of God are the extensions of values which we have discovered in our experience of men and things. And if our several ideas of perfections, conditioned in this way, do come to us one by one, our idea of God, so far from being a mere term to denote the sum of them, represents the simplicity of their mutual harmony. 'So that from hence it appears that the consideration of the Perfections which are in the Creatures, is only an occasion given to the Mind to help it in its Idea of God, and not that the Idea it self depends upon those Perfections as the causes of it: as in the clearest Mathematical truths the Manner of demonstration may be necessary to help the Understanding to its clearer assent, tho' the things in themselves be undoubtedly true.'[1] It follows, on this reasoning, that while there is no such thing as a connate idea of God, 'in the Sense which connate Ideas are commonly understood,'[2] 'the Mind will form as settl'd and clear a notion of God, as of any thing which in the judgment of Epicurus, his infallible Senses did the most assure him of.'[3] And despite Stillingfleet's hesitation, in view of 'the unlimited power of the Understanding in conception,'[4] as to the impossibility of an imperfect being arriving at the idea of a perfect being in the event of there not being one in existence, he thinks it to be 'highly probable' that an idea so 'consonant to Reason' has been 'imprinted ... by that God whose Idea it is.'[5]

Having arrived at a 'clear and distinct' idea of God by a more devious path than the one that Descartes trod, our author proceeds to the second stage in his argument. He points out that the ideas of eternal and infinite matter and eternal and infinite space, entertained by atheists, are fraught with greater difficulty than the idea of an eternal and infinite rational Being; and, as for the hypothesis that the world as we know it originated from 'a fortuitous Concourse of

[1] *Ib.*, p. 235. [2] *Ib.*, p. 233. [3] *Ib.*, p. 234.
[4] *Ib.*, p. 235. [5] *Ib.*, p. 234.

Atoms,' he says that 'we must grind the Sun to Powder, and by a new way of Interment turn the Earth into Dust and Ashes, before we can so much as imagine how the World cou'd be fram'd.'[1] Moreover, he contends that those who maintain that it cannot be demonstrated that God exists will be obliged to admit that it cannot be demonstrated that the world has come from a fortuitous concourse of atoms. But—and this is the point—if demonstration means advancing 'such a sufficient proof . . . as the nature of the thing is capable of,'[2] then it can be demonstrated that God exists.

In the third and final stage of his argument, Stillingfleet commends three proofs for the existence of God, namely, the ontological proof, the proof from design, and the indirect proof that some existing things are of such a nature as to be 'inaccountable without a Deity.'[3] These proofs are prefaced by a repetition of the point he has only just made—that the nature of a problem determines the nature of the evidence to be employed in solving it. 'There is no demonstration in Euclide will serve to prove that there are such places as the Indies: we cannot prove the Earth is round by the judgment of sense; nor that the Soul is immortal by corporeal Phantasms. Every distinct kind of Being hath its peculiar way of probation; and therefore it ought not to be at all wondred at, if the supreme and infinite Being have his peculiar way of demonstrating himself to the minds of Men.'[4]

The ontological proof, in Stillingfleet's presentation, really begins where the argument from universal consent leaves off. The idea of God, he says, is entertained by all men in the same way as common notions are, and on that account

---

[1] *Ib.*, p. 238.   [2] *Ib.*, p. 240.   [3] *Ib.*, p. 242.
[4] *Ib.*, pp. 241-2. *Cf.* p. 68: 'Whoever yet undertook to bring matters of fact into Mathematical demonstrations, or thought he had ground to question the certainty of any thing that was not prov'd in a Mathematical way to him? who wou'd ever undertake that Archimedes was kill'd at Syracuse, by any of the Demonstrations he was then about? or that Euclide was the undoubted Author of the Geometry under his name?'

it must be the product of universal reason, and not of popular collaboration. 'A common and universal Effect must flow from some common and universal Cause,' and so it will follow that God has 'stamped an universal Character of Himself on the minds of Men.'[1] It is as futile to deny the universality of the idea, as to say 'that it is not natural for Men to have two legs, because some have been born with one';[2] and it is unreasonable to conclude that 'an indelible idea' in the mind of man is fictitious and otiose, when 'the Instincts of irrational Agents argue something real in them.'[3]

The ground thus prepared, Stillingfleet proceeds to say that the criterion of truth is 'clear and distinct perception';[4] that it is satisfied 'when upon the greatest consideration of the nature of a thing, there appears no ground or reason at all to doubt of it'; and that it applies only in matters where reason abstracts 'wholly from sensation.' The question is whether this criterion will allow us to include necessary existence in the idea of God, and Stillingfleet replies in the affirmative. For if it were true that existence is attributed to the idea of God 'merely on the Act of the Mind joyning together,'[5] it would be possible for the Mind to 'divide' one from the other, which it cannot do without destroying the idea. Their connection is, therefore, 'immutable.' Again, whereas all other clear and distinct ideas do not warrant more than presumption of possible existence, this idea alone requires necessary existence, because there is no conceivable hindrance to existence. Readers who may remain unsatisfied by the argument are bidden to refer to Descartes and Henry More, 'those judicious Authors, who have made it their peculiar business to manage it, and vindicate it from all objections.'[6] It 'falls in only here,' he adds, 'as an Evidence that God hath imprinted a Character of himself on the Minds of Men, seeing we have so

[1] Ib., p. 242.   [2] Ib., p. 247.   [3] Ib., p. 245.
[4] Ib., p. 250.   [5] Ib., p. 252.   [6] Ib., p. 253.

clear and distinct an Idea of such a Being, from whom, if we take away necessity of Existence, we destroy that Notion which our Minds have of an absolutely perfect Being.'

Finally, Stillingfleet essays to show that a spiritual substance, which man is, cannot be accounted for on the principles of matter and motion; and that we must refer it to God for origin. Man is spirit: because, first, he can correct errors associated with sense-perception by criticizing them in the light of clear and distinct ideas, and view clear and distinct ideas which are beyond the scope of sensation and imagination; and, second, he can 'retire' [1] into himself and from out of his memory recover things long since past —an impossible feat, if as Hobbes says, memory is nothing but 'decaying Motion.' [2] And so the Platonists, more rightly, though rashly, have made the human soul out to be a particle, not of matter, but 'of the Divine Nature it self, a little Deity in a Cottage, that stays here a-while, and returns to that upper Region whence it came.' This argument for the existence of a Spirit who presides over spiritual beings becomes enhanced, when we recall the miracles recorded in Scripture; for they cannot be explained, as Henry More and others have shown, by 'the Art of Judicial Astrology.' [3] 'Now then,' Stillingfleet concludes, 'it being an acknowledg'd Principle in Nature, That every thing continues in the course it is in, till something more powerful put it out, if then such things have been in the World, which have been real alterations in the course of Nature, as the Sun's standing still in the time of Joshua, then there must be something above Matter and Motion, and consequently that there is a God.' [4]

We pass on to review Stillingfleet's account of revealed religion. He likens it to a 'superstructure' [5] built upon what remained of the primal deposit of knowledge after the fall. It transcends, but does not outrage, reason. Its content is

[1] *Ib.*, p. 262.   [2] *Ib.*, p. 263.   [3] *Ib.*, p. 264.
[4] *Ib.*, p. 264.   [5] *Ib.*, p. 265.

stated briefly in 'the Creed,'[1] and comprises such mysteries as the following: the Trinity, the Incarnation, the hypostatic union, the satisfaction for sinners made by Christ, the Resurrection, and the influence of the Holy Spirit upon the soul of man.[2] We identify it rightly with Christianity; but we have to remember that God's act in Christ was prepared for since the days of Moses and before. 'For can any thing be more plain than the gradual progress of divine Revelation from the beginning of the World?'[3] We can trace 'by what steps *God* train'd up his Church till the fulness of time was come,'[4] and the first step, apparently, was that upon which Adam himself stood. 'That fair resemblance and portraicture of God himself, and his Will upon his Word (if I may so express it) had its Ground-work laid upon Man's first Apostacy in the Promise made *Gen.* iii. 15, whereon some further lines were drawn in the times of the Patriarchs, but it had its σκιαγραφία, it was shadowed out the most in the Typical and Ceremonial Law, but was never filled up to the life, nor had its perfect ζωογραφία, 'till the Son of God himself appeared unto the World.'[5]

How, we inquire, can we be certain that the separate propositions in which revealed truth is stated are true? They are, *ex hypothesi*, as beyond our comprehension as they are beyond our discovery; and we need to know how our criterion of clarity and distinction can be satisfied in the sphere of revelation. Stillingfleet tempers the keenness of this question by pointing out that even in the sphere of natural religion there obtains a clear and distinct idea of God incomprehensible; 'for if he be a Being infinite, he must be incomprehensible.'[6] It is true, no doubt, that our idea of a perfect being takes its rise in our natural insight into perfections; but this is the insight of an imperfect being: for 'the manner whereby we form our Conceptions of God, is, by taking away all the imperfections we find in

---

[1] *Ib.*, p. 149. [2] *Ib.*, pp. 112, 149, 152, 381. [3] *Ib.*, p. 131.
[4] *Ib.*, p. 377. [5] *Ib.*, p. 131. [6] *Ib.*, p. 147.

our selves, from the Conception we form of a Being absolutely perfect, and by adding Infinity to all the Perfections we find in our own Natures.'[1] This process argues for 'a vast distance' between the finite and the infinite mind. Moreover, on what grounds do we hold that God's plan shall conform to our way of thinking? We are no 'absolute Masters of Reason,' and we are unable to lay down all the conditions of a Divine revelation: it is enough that it should accord with our common notions. Let us beware of treating some philosophical theory 'as a System of infallible Rules collected from the natures of things.' 'Let the Principles we proceed by,' he continues, in the manner of Bacon, 'be first manifested to be collected from a most certain and universal inspection into the nature of all Beings, let the manner of the process be shewed how they were collected (lest they labour with the common Fault of Chymists, of establishing Hypostatical Principles from the Experiments of some particular Bodies, which others do as evidently refute) and lastly, let it be made appear that these Principles, thus collected, will serve indifferently for all Beings, spiritual as well as material, infinite as well as finite, and when this Task is exactly perform'd, we will make room for Reason to sit upon the Bench, and bring the Scripture as the prisoner to its Bar.'[2] How could principles derived empirically from a survey of natural phenomena serve to measure truths of a higher order? 'Now it cannot otherwise be conceiv'd but that these Theories or Principles formed from such a narrow inspection into the natures of things, must make strange work when we come to apply those things to them, which were never look'd at in the forming of them.'[3] On the substance of Divine revelation, we are, therefore, as Butler affirms on other grounds, 'in no sort judges beforehand.'[4]

[1] *Ib.*, p. 148.   [2] *Ib.*, p. 149.   [3] *Ib.*, p. 148.
[4] *The Analogy of Religion Natural and Revealed to the Constitution and Course of Nature*, II. iii. 3.

Seeing that revealed truth cannot, in the nature of the case, be self-evident, we must look elsewhere for proof that revelation is what it purports to be; and infallible testimony can come from no other quarter than from God Himself. The problem resolves itself, then, into one of establishing the fact of revelation; and evidence which will show beyond all doubt that God has actually declared new truths to man, and imposed further obligations upon him, is required. Stillingfleet finds in the miracles which accompanied the teaching of both Moses and Jesus Christ the sole and sufficient evidence that God disclosed His mind in their words and works. He holds that there are *à priori* grounds for thinking that revelation will be attested by miracle, and also by prophecy. 'The possibility of a power of Miracles cannot be question'd by any who assert a Deity and a Providence; for by the same Power that things were either at first produced, or are still conserv'd (which is equivalent to the other) the course of Nature may be alter'd, and things caus'd which are beyond the power of inferiour Causes: For tho' that be an immutable Law of Nature as to Physical Beings, that every thing remains in the course and order wherein it was set at the Creation; yet that only holds till the same power which set it in that order shall otherwise dispose of it.'[1] Events occurring in nature which are obviously 'above the reach of nature,'[2] and 'alter the whole series of things,' must originate in the will of Him from whom nature has origin. As Butler points out, miracles prove revelation, because revelation itself is miraculous.[3]

Stillingfleet makes two interesting points about the miracles of Christ, in order to show how appropriate they are to the message which He came to deliver. The first is that whereas the miracles of Moses were calculated to terrify the Israelites, and so to win them from idolatry, the miracles

---

[1] *Ib.*, p. 160. Butler says that 'a miracle, in its very notion, is relative to a course of Nature' (*Analogy*, II. ii. 6).
[2] *Ib.*, p. 86.   [3] *Analogy*, II. ii. 5.

of Christ betokened God's goodness. 'Those terrible Signs at Mount Sinai being very suitable to the severity and rigor of the Law: and the gracious Miracles of our Saviour to the sweetness and grace of the Gospel.'[1] His works and His words were all of a piece, and if we have good reason to accept the first, we are committed inevitably to the second. In Christ history and dogma meet. 'Thus it is in reference to the Doctrine of Christ,' our author writes; 'for, the truth of that is so interwoven with the truth of the story of Christ, that if the Relations concerning Christ be true, his Doctrine must needs be Divine and Infallible.'[2] The second point is that many of the miracles of Christ demonstrate that the goodness of God is strong to penetrate within the citadel of sin, and to conquer the hostile powers that hold man in chains. If God wins men from ignorance by appealing to their innate love of truth, He wins them too from sin by conquering the power of evil. Herein we have 'the highest Rational Evidence, that (Christ's) Power was of God, which tended so much to the destruction of the Kingdom of Satan.'[3]

But can we be certain that the Bible contains a true account of God's revelation? This is a question as to strength of evidence, and so 'moral certainty'[4] is all that we can hope to find. We may be certain, however, that a revelation which concerns all men must be universally accessible and easily intelligible;[5] and we may be certain too that no medium save a written one could escape corruption by mixture with fable and fancy. And if, as reason tells us, the fate of man's immortal soul depends upon the manner of his life, God's will for him 'must not be lock'd up in the Cabinet Council of Heaven, but must be so far declar'd and reveal'd, that he may be fully acquainted with those Terms which his Happiness depends upon.'[6] In point of fact, the words and works of Moses are attested by eye-witnesses, as well as by the continued persistence of the Jewish com-

[1] *Works*, ii. p. 162.   [2] *Ib.*, p. 180.   [3] *Ib.*, p. 166.
[4] *Ib.*, p. 69.   [5] *Ib.*, p. 67.   [6] *Ib.*, p. 228.

monwealth; and the words and works of Jesus Christ by eye-witnesses, as well as by the triumphs of His Church over paganism and sin: the Gospel made its way in face of opposition from the secular arm,[1] and the Apostles who preached it were ready to give their lives in its cause. If we reject all this as insufficient evidence, 'we must destroy all Historical Faith out of the World.' [2]

Stillingfleet's *apologia* for Christianity does not stop short with the arguments which he can adduce in order to commend it; for he writes warmly, and in the manner of all Christian Platonists, of an evidence in the heart which defies complete analysis. There is, he knows, a no-man's-land of the soul reserved for the action of the Spirit of God; and here a man can close with something too delectable for description. 'But altho' I assert that these rational evidences are sufficient arguments of the truth of the Doctrine they come to manifest; yet I would not be so understood, that I thereby resolve all Religion into a mere act of Reason and Knowledge, and that no more power is requir'd in the Understanding to believe the Gospel, than to believe a Mathematical Demonstration.' [3] So he deprecates the growing habit of reading other works to the neglect of Bible study, which, in God's providence, is a means for drawing us towards the things that belong to our eternal happiness.[4] Scripture is the 'Rule of Faith,' [5] which guides our thinking on holy things, and the 'Rule of Life,' [6] which governs our conduct. And if it does contain some truths beyond our comprehension, all that pertains to our salvation is therein 'deliver'd with the greatest evidence and perspicuity.' [7]

---

[1] *Ib.*, pp. 192, 201.   [2] *Ib.*, p. 69.   [3] *Ib.*, pp. 157-8.
[4] *Ib.*, The Epistle Dedicatory. *Cf.* The Hon. Robert Boyle, *Some Considerations Touching the Style Of the H. Scriptures* (1661), p. 113: 'Scarce any thing has given me a favourabler Character of Luther, than his Wish, that all his Books of Devotion were burnt, when he once perceiv'd that the Peoples fondnesse and Over-valuation of them produc'd a Neglect of the Study of the Bible.'
[5] *Ib.*, p. 220.   [6] *Ib.*, p. 386.   [7] *Ib.*, p. 382.

Stillingfleet is an ardent opponent of Hobbes, fully alive to the danger of an over-Platonized Christianity. In the *Origines Sacrae*, he shows that materialism is an unsatisfactory theory; and that the properties of reason which condition man's experience of God and the world, namely, the innate idea of God and the innate common notions, leave him open and disposed to accept God's disclosure of Himself in Christ. But he shows that the disclosure was made in terms of a human life, being evidenced by events which transcended the course of nature in which matter and motion ordinarily have coherence. If man is 'brutish,' he has become so of his own most grievous fault; and he is to be restored to manhood again, not by a self-made system of education, but by Divine enlightenment, which follows upon God's pardon, secured in the satisfaction for sin made by the Cross of Christ. The glowing eloquence which characterizes the following passage, descriptive of the Apostolic message, could hardly have been sustained by one that had not himself come under the spell which it breaks. 'That all Men shou'd be bound in order to their Salvation, to believe in one who was crucify'd at Hierusalem, was a strange Doctrine to the unbelieving World: but if the Apostles had but endeavour'd to have suited their Doctrine to the School of Plato, what rare Persons might they have been accounted among the Heathen Philosophers! Had they only in general terms discours'd of the Benignity of the Divine Nature, and the Manifestations of Divine Goodness in the World; and that, in order to the bringing of the Souls of Men to a nearer participation of the Divine Nature, the perfect Idea of true Goodness, and the express Image of the Person of God, and the resplendency of his Glory had veil'd himself in Humane Nature, and had every where scatter'd such beams of light and Goodness, as warm'd and invigorated the frozen Spirits of Men with higher sentiments of God and themselves, and raised them up above the feculency of this terrestrial Matter to breath in a fresher air, and converse with more noble objects, and by degrees to fit the Souls of Men for those more pure illapses of real Goodness, which might always satisfy the Soul's desires, and yet always keep them up 'till the Soul shou'd be sunning it self to all eternity under the immediate beams of Light and Love: And that after this Incarnate Deity had spread abroad the wings of his Love for a while upon this lower World, 'till by his gentle heat and incubation he had quickened the more pliable World to some degree of a Divine Life, he then retreated himself back again into the superiour World, and put off that veil by which he made himself known to those who are here confin'd to the prisons of their Bodies: Thus, I say, had the Apostles minded applause among the admired Philosophers of the Heathens, how easy had it been for them to have made some considerable additions to their highest speculations, and have left out any thing which might seem so mean and contemptible as the death of the Son of God! But this they were so far from, that the main thing which they preached to the World, was, the vanity of Humane Wisdome without Christ, and the necessity of all Mens believing in that Jesus who was crucify'd at Hierusalem.' [1]

Our next task is to inquire into Stillingfleet's estimate of philosophy, and in particular into his opinion of the value of Plato's contribution to the sum of our knowledge about God and man. What is the proper attitude of a believer in the Christian revelation, which is reasonable revelation, in that it is acceptable to reason and defensible by reason, but not rational revelation, as though embracing only truths comprehensible by reason, towards reason's own native conclusions concerning the chief problem that besets human endeavour? Stillingfleet's approach to philosophy is one of benevolent suspicion. He cannot afford to show himself too generous a judge, because in his eyes reason is corrupted, and must perforce, once its apologetic for revelation has been concluded, remain behind, while faith goes forward to

[1] *Ib.*, pp. 183-4.

enjoy the inheritance: he cannot say less, because, despite human apostacy, some traces of the indelible deposit of truth remain. He repeats a rumour circulated widely in the seventeenth century, and propagated in ancient Christian apologetic by Justin Martyr,[1] Clement of Alexandria,[2] Origen,[3] and Tertullian,[4] that the best Greek philosophers 'borrowed' from the Mosaic tradition;[5] and he is inclined to accept the opinion of Justin, himself a convert from Plato,[6] that the latter, in view of popular contempt for the Jews, and mindful of the lot meted out to Socrates, deemed it prudent to conceal the source of his inspiration.[7] So, whereas the sacred writings treat of sacred mysteries 'in a clear and perspicuous manner,'[8] and the Christian way of life can be envisaged readily by men of 'common capacities,'[9] Plato is 'ambiguous and uncertain in his Discourses of a Deity,'[10] and 'wrapt up and disguis'd his Notions in such a fabulous and ambiguous manner, that partly he might be less known from whence he had them, and that they might find better entertainment among the Greeks, than they were ever like to do in their plain and native dress.'[11] 'How doth he mince his excellent matter,' asks Stillingfleet, 'and plays as it were at Bo-peep with his Readers, sometimes appearing and then pulling in his Horns again?'[12] But we can make sense of Plato's obscure passages, if only we will treat them allegorically: for, seeing that Moses always said what he meant, it is reasonable 'to remove the Cabala from Moses to Plato.'[12] By this method of treatment, Plato's theory of the descent of pre-existent souls becomes the orthodox tradition of a historic fall, and his language in the *Phaedrus*[13] about the soul's wings moulting and fledging refers to our experience of the combat between reason and appetite.[14] The creation myth in the *Timaeus*, especially when read in

[1] *Apol.*, i. 59.   [2] *Str.*, i. 350.   [3] *Cont. Cel.*, iv. 39.
[4] *Apol.*, 47.   [5] *Works*, ii. p. 316.   [6] *Ib.*, p. 190.
[7] *Ib.*, p. 177; p. 324.   [8] *Ib.*, p. 382.   [9] *Ib.*, p. 207.
[10] *Ib.*, p. 8.   [11] *Ib.*, p. 316.   [12] *Ib.*, p. 174.
[13] 246 ff.   [14] *Works*, ii. p. 319.

the light thrown upon it by the *Sophist*,[1] appears to be in keeping with the Mosaic account, because God Himself created the chaotic matter out of which He formed our well-ordered universe.[2]

Plato's teaching about creation was indeed perverted by 'the latter Platonists,'[3] whom Stillingfleet, unlike his Platonist contemporaries, distinguishes critically from the master. They understood creation as an eternal process; a theory which, our author points out, makes the world as necessary to God as He is to the world. Some of them likened God's creative power to the perpetual light-giving power of the sun. 'True,' replies Stillingfleet, 'were God of the Nature of the Sun, it wou'd be so with him; or were the Sun of the Nature of God, it wou'd not be so with it. But there is this vast difference between them, that tho' God be essentially and necessarily Good, yet the communications of His goodness are the effects of his Will, and not merely of his Nature.' About another problem in origins, however, some of the 'more modern Philosophers,'[4] *e.g.* Hierocles, Porphyry, and Simplicius, knew more than Plato; because they taught that the source of sin lies in man's will, while he appears to be uncertain whether it is to be attributed to matter, or to 'some malignant Spirit in it.'[5] Students of Plotinus, Porphyrius, Iamblicus, and Hierocles will find that they 'write in a higher strain concerning many weighty and important Truths . . . than the most sublime of the ancient Philosophers had done'; but it is probable that they owed their inspiration not to Plato and Pythagoras, but to a Christian, namely, Ammonius of Alexandria, 'that great restorer of Philosophy,'[6] the teacher of Herennius, Origen, and Plotinus. 'It is an easy matter to conceive, what an excellent improvement might be made of the ancient Platonic Philosophy, by the advantage of the Scriptures, by one who was so well vers'd in both of them,

[1] 265 f.   [2] *Works*, ii. p. 269.   [3] *Ib.*, p. 275.
[4] *Ib.*, p. 315.   [5] *Ib.*, p. 313.   [6] *Ib.*, p. 315.

as Ammonius is suppos'd to have been; and how agreeable and becoming would that Philosophy seem, which had only its rise from Plato, but its height and improvement from those rich and truly Divine Truths which were inlaid with them?'[1]

Stillingfleet inclines to modify the 'borrowing' theory so as to bring it into line with his own view of an original revelation delivered to Adam. He suggests that Plato, and Pythagoras upon whom he leaned, may have come into contact with some of its derivatives in the course of their travels. As a matter of fact, the Phoenicians, Egyptians and Chaldeans were civilized at a time when the Greeks were unorganized and a people 'barbarous and rude.'[2] It was the 'home-bred' Greeks, like Aristotle, for example, who taught the eternity of matter, whereas the 'water' of Thales and the 'matter' of the *Timaeus* are obviously in keeping with the earth 'without form and void' of Moses.[3] Thus 'we find that Greece from its begining shin'd with a borrow'd Light; and saw not by an extramission of Rays of Knowledg from its self, but by an intromission of those representations of things which were receiv'd from other Nations.'[4] Her philosophy degenerated, because its exponents, instead of 'scraping and searching into the Natures of things,'[5] took to arguing about speculative questions, a pastime 'which help'd as much to the finding out of Truth, as the fighting of two Cocks on a Dung-hill doth to finding out the Jewel that lies there.' The first piece of deliberate syncretism took place probably when Philo 'began first to exercise his Wit on the Text of Moses, with Platonic Notions.'[6]

It turns out, then, that while Stillingfleet is free, like Clement and Origen, to adopt a fairly liberal attitude

---

[1] *Ib.*, p. 316.   [2] *Ib.*, p. 267.   [3] *Ib.*, p. 269.
[4] *Ib.*, p. 267. On p. 269, readers are referred to Boyle's *Sceptical Chymist* for experimental evidence that 'mixt Bodies . . . spring from no other material Principle than the Particles of fluid Matter.'
[5] *Ib.*, p. 270.   [6] *Ib.*, p. 268.

towards philosophy, which is, rightly understood, no more than a partial measure of revealed religion, sometimes more and sometimes less corrupted, he has some affinity with Tertullian, who, in some of his moods, can find nothing whatever that is wholesome in pagan literature. He does not go the length of demanding what Jerusalem has to do with Athens, but he is aware 'what tampering there was betimes, rather to bring Christianity down to Philosophy, than to make Philosophy truckle under the truth and simplicity of the Scriptures.'[1] He holds that if Christianity is to appeal with any hope of success to them that are without, it must be established on a rational basis; but that if it suffers itself to be completely rationalized, it must degenerate into philosophy. Over and above all the rational evidence that can be adduced in its support, it has its own 'Spiritual Evidence,'[2] which, to them that are within, is the most real and convincing. This peculiar evidence, the witness of religious experience, betrays itself in a region of the soul which philosophy is not equipped to explore; and in the lives of the Apostles we can observe the working of a spiritual power that goes with it. It occurs, as the best heathen philosophers knew, within a life lived in the Divine presence; but it is the prerogative of Christianity to show how God in Christ comes close to men and makes Himself known. Stillingfleet's strictures on the Epicurean philosophy, which sets God at a far and unqualified remove from man, anticipate the dangers imminent with the coming age of reason; and he, at least, cannot be accused of having prepared, even unwittingly, the way for deism. Epicurus went wrong, he points out, in combining an assertion of God's existence with a denial of His providence; for this position involves a virtual denial that God is good. He 'made Him sit as it were with his Elbows folded up in the Heavens, and taking no cognizance of Human actions.'[3] But surely if Epicurus took a delight in cultivating his own garden, God will delight

[1] *Ib.*, p. 317.   [2] *Ib.*, p. 158.   [3] *Ib.*, p. 297.

to order the world for His glory? 'Must so excellent a Nature as God's was, by his own acknowledgment, be presently tired with Business; when the more excellent any Nature is, the more active and vigorous it is, the more able to comprehend and dispatch Matters of Moment with the least disturbance to it self? Is it a pleasure to a Nurse to fill the Child with her Milk? Doth the Sun rejoice to help the World with his constant Light? And doth a Fountain murmur till it be deliver'd of its Streams, which may refresh the Ground? And is it no delight to the Divine Nature to behold the effects of his Goodness upon the World?'[1] So convinced is our author of the practical value of the doctrine of Divine immanence, that he will have nothing to do with the idea of a world-soul, defended by Cudworth and More; and he prefers, with Descartes, to speak of 'a continu'd Creation.' He dubs a world-soul 'a Man-midwife to Matter.'[2] 'But we had rather believe God himself,' he says, 'to be perpetually resident in the World, and that the Power which gives Life, and Being, and Motion to every thing in the World, is nothing else but his own Providence; especially since we have learnt from himself, that it is in him we live, and move, and have our being.' Once we begin to harbour the erroneous opinion that God does not concern Himself with our lives and fortunes, we are well on the way towards abandoning concern for Him. The doctrine of a remote God tends to weaken moral fibre. In common with Whichcote and Taylor, Stillingfleet finds the source of moral obligation in the *de facto* relation in which we stand towards God; and the significance of revelation for practical life is just this, that it makes us clear as to our dutiful place in God's scheme. 'Man's obligation to Obedience unto God, doth necessarily suppose his Original to be from him.'[3]

Stillingfleet attempts to strengthen his case for Divine immanence by pointing to our sense of the fitness of sanc-

---

[1] *Ib.*, pp. 298-9.   [2] *Ib.*, p. 300.   [3] *Ib.*, p. 66.

tions; and he says that human nature being what it is, we may expect that the claims of religion will not lack reference to our hopes and fears. Epicurus ought to have known that 'it is not Worth but Power, nor Speculation but Interest that rules the World.' [1] He is not thinking, of course, of Divine power and human interest after the fashion of Hobbes: the power is, like Whichcote's; the power of God who is essentially good; and the interest is, like Whichcote's, man's interest in 'eternal Happiness.' [2] 'For if Men ought not to have an Eye and respect to their own future Condition, nor serve God on the account of His Power to make our Souls miserable or happy, much less ought Men to serve God with any regard to his Providence, since the matters which Providence is employ'd about in this World, are of infinitely less moment, than those which concern our Future State.' [3] Rewards and punishments are 'the Sinews of Religion,' and 'were it not for those Magnetical hooks of Obedience and Eternal Interest, there are few would be drawn to a due Consideration of, much less a Delight in so Amiable and Excellent a Nature' [4] as God. Butler agrees, when he says that although we are obliged to love God, the Author of our being, 'and with whom we have a nearer and more constant intercourse, than we can have with any creature,' nevertheless, hope of reward and fear of punishment are 'absolutely necessary to be often recollected in such a world as this.' [5]

Stillingfleet writes sometimes as though he identified revelation with Scripture; but he has no doubt but that revelation consists in the Person of Christ. The Apostles, he says, 'never dreamt of any Divine Goodness which shou'd make Men happy without Christ: No, it was their design to persuade the World that all the communications of God's Goodness to the World were wholly in and thro' Jesus Christ.' [6] A philosopher's disadvantage is that he has

[1] *Ib.*, p. 297. [2] *Ib.*, p. 374; *cf.* p. 381. [3] *Ib.*, p. 298.
[4] *Ib.*, p. 297. [5] *Sermons, The Preface*, 44. [6] *Works*, ii. p. 184.

Edward Stillingfleet

not experienced the love of God in Christ. His standard of values is based upon experience of 'the promiscuous scatterings of good and evil in this Life,'[1] and he may 'in the general know what things are pleasing and acceptable to the Divine Nature, from those differences of Good and Evil which are unalterably fix'd in the things themselves';[2] but he can neither exorcise the evil which spoils his corrupted soul, nor find assurance of forgiveness. Christianity promises not these only, but also eternal bliss.

The following extract, which might have come from the pen of Whichcote, will show that Stillingfleet has vindicated in his own experience the religion which he sought to vindicate in history:

'For is it possible that the Soul of Man should ever enjoy its full and complete Happiness in this World, when nothing is able to make it happy, but what is most sutable to its Nature, able to fill up its large Capacity, and commensurate with its Duration? but in this life the matter of Mens greatest delight is strangely unsutable to the nature of our rational Beings, the measure of them too short for our vast Desires to stretch themselves upon, the Proportion too scant and narrow to run parallel with Immortality. It must be then only a Supreme, Infinite and Eternal Being, which by the free communications of his Bounty and Goodness can fix and satiate the Soul's Desires, and by the constant flowings forth of his own uninterrupted streams of Favor will always keep up Desire, and yet always satisfy it: One whose Goodness can only be felt by some transient touches here, whose Love can be seen but as thro' a lattice, whose constant presence may be rather wish'd for then enjoy'd, who hath reserv'd the full light and fruition of himself to that future state, when all these dark veils shall be done away, and the Soul shall be continually sunning her self under

[1] *Ib.*, p. 228. [2] *Ib.*, p. 375.

immediate beams of Light and Love. But how or in what way the Soul of Man in this degenerate condition should come to be partaker of so great a Happiness, by the enjoyment of that God our Natures are now at such a distance from, is the greatest and most important inquiry of Human Nature; and we continually see how successless and unsatisfactory the endeavors of those have been to themselves at last, who have sought for this Happiness in a way of their own finding out: The large volume of the Creation, wherein God hath describ'd so much of his Wisdom and Power, is yet too dark and obscure, too short and imperfect to set forth to us the way which leads to eternal Happiness. Unless then the same God who made Mens Souls at first, do shew them the way for their recovery; as they are in a degenerate, so they will be in a desperate condition: but the same Bounty and Goodness of God, which did at the first display it self in giving Being to Mens Souls, hath in a higher manner enlarged the Discovery of it self, by making known the way whereby we may be taken into his Grace and Favor again.'[1]

In 1697, thirty-four years after the publication of his *Origines Sacrae*, Stillingfleet had occasion to compose a lengthy defence of the doctrine of the Trinity. Tuckney's fear that freedom of thought, of the kind that Whichcote appeared to him to advocate, might give further scope to Socinians and others for spreading their nefarious opinions, was not without some justification; and now Stillingfleet feels himself obliged to combat their view of God. He attempts to do so on the three grounds of Scripture, antiquity, and reason; but it is with the third only that we are concerned, chiefly because of the light thrown by his discussion upon Descartes and Locke. He and his

[1] *Ib.*, p. 376.

opponents are agreed that their respective positions are determined by reason; but the reason upon which they rely, as he will show, is an arrogant faculty which is ignorant of its own self-imposed limitations.

The argument turns on the significance to be given to two terms, namely, 'substance' and 'person'; for the Socinians object to their use in what they call 'the new Creed, or Athanasian Religion.'[1] Stillingfleet makes the following quotation from one of their pamphlets: 'we deny the Articles of the new Christianity, or the Athanasian Religion, not because they are Mysteries, or because we do not comprehend them; but we deny them because we do comprehend them; we have a clear and distinct Perception, that they are not Mysteries, but Contradictions, Impossibilities, and pure Nonsense. We have our reason in vain, and all science and certainty would be destroy'd if we could not distinguish between Mysteries and Contradictions.'[2] Stillingfleet's case is that the Socinians have been led into this way of talking, because they have been captivated by the 'new way of Reason.'[3] And in these days, when there are those who deny the fact of revelation, it is regrettable, he thinks, that some who profess Christianity should commit themselves to an epistemological theory which, as he will show, precludes all attainment of certainty. Formerly, opponents of the faith were atheists; but now the fashion is deism: 'for Atheism is a rude unmannerly Word, and exposes Men to the Rabble, and makes Persons shun the company and avoid the Conversation and Dealing with such who are noted for it.'[4]

Many passages are quoted *verbatim* from the *Essay of Humane Understanding*,[5] and discussed with vigour and

---

[1] *Works*, vol. iii. p. 413. The title is *A Discourse in Vindication of the Doctrine of the Trinity : With an Answer to the late Socinian Objections against it from Scripture, Antiquity and Reason. And a Preface, Concerning the different Explications of the Trinity, and the Tendency of the present Socinian Controversie*.
[2] *Ib.*, p. 434.   [3] *Ib.*, p. 503.   [4] *Ib.*, p. 428.   [5] *Ib.*, p. 505.

clarity; but we shall content ourselves with reference to two points only, namely, the problem of substance, and the problem of certainty. Stillingfleet's thesis is that Locke cannot in logic advance beyond his own starting-point. If all ideas are derived from sensation or reflection, and reason is equipped merely to register and connect them one way or another, philosophy's task is soon ended.

How does Locke account for the general idea of substance? He says that 'it is by a Complication of many simple Ideas together: because not imagining how these simple Ideas can subsist by themselves, we accustom our selves to suppose some Substratum wherein they do subsist, and from which they do result, which therefore we call Substance.'[1] In reply to this statement, Stillingfleet proposes a dilemma: 'And is this all indeed, that is to be said for the being of Substance, that we accustom our selves to suppose a Substratum? Is that Custom grounded upon true Reason or not? If not, then Accidents or Modes, must subsist of themselves, and these simple Ideas need no Tortoise to support them: For Figures and Colours, &c. would do well enough of themselves, but for some Fancies Men have accustomed themselves to. If it be grounded on plain and evident Reason, then we must allow an Idea of Substance, which comes not in by Sensation or Reflection; and so we may be certain of some things which we have not by those Ideas.' Stillingfleet agrees that the idea of substance is not a simple idea of sensation or reflection; but he maintains that, instead of being supposed, it is *conceived*. And he gives good reason why 'the Mind doth form' the idea of substance: 'since it is a Repugnancy to our first Conceptions of things, that Modes or Accidents should subsist by themselves, and therefore the Rational Idea of Substance is one of the first, and most natural Ideas in our Minds.' This is all in keeping with what he has said before in the *Origines Sacrae*, where he shows that the

[1] *Ib.*, p. 504 (*Essay*, II. xxiii. 1).

idea of God ('a settl'd Notion'[1]) is a construction of the mind ('a pure act of Intellection'[2]), the component elements being, not phantasms, but the ideas of the perfections ('proceeding in its ordinary way of Intellection, to form a notion of such a Being, which hath Wisdom, Goodness and Power in it, without any limits and bounds at all');[3] and that the act of construction, so far from composing together ideas presented by sensation, or even by reflection, is itself the source of the ideas which it unites. The following passage from the *Origines Sacrae* dealing with the origin of our idea of God, written a generation before the appearance of the *Essay*, shows that the unity in substantial unity cannot be simply an *addendum* to attributes, but that it is in some manner constitutive. He writes that the 'Understanding in forming this Idea of God, doth not by distinct acts first collect one Perfection, and then another, and at last unite these together, but the simplicity and unity of all these Perfections is as necessarily conceiv'd as any of them. Granting then that the Understanding by the observing of several Perfections in the World, might be able to abstract these severally from each Being wherein they were, yet whence shou'd the Idea of the Unity and Inseparability come? The Mind may, it is true, knit some things together in fictitious Ideas . . .; but these several Perfections are so far from speaking repugnancy to each other, that the Unity and Inseparability of them is as necessary to the forming of this Idea, as any other Perfection whatsoever.'[4]

The upshot of this matter is, then, that substance is not 'an uncertain Supposition of we know not what,'[5] but it is 'essence';[6] and that we may have 'as clear and distinct a Conception of this in our Minds, as we can have from any such simple Ideas, as are convey'd by our Senses.'[7]

The second point concerns a criterion of certainty, and

[1] *Ib.*, vol. ii. p. 233.
[2] *Ib.*, p. 235.
[3] *Ib.*, p. 233.
[4] *Ib.*, p. 235.
[5] *Ib.*, vol. iii. p. 503 (*Essay*, I. iv. 18).
[6] *Ib.*, p. 504.
[7] *Ib.*, p. 505.

Stillingfleet introduces it in connection with some criticisms offered upon Locke's proofs for the existence of God. He professes admiration for two of these,[1] but objects that they are based upon 'Principles of true Reason,'[2] and not upon ideas; for surely a philosopher, who places his certainty in clear and distinct ideas, ought to have demonstrated the existence of God from an idea, either the idea of God, or the idea of the self? Stillingfleet professes himself not greatly taken with the ontological argument, on the ground that a clear and distinct idea of God is 'too weak to support so important a Truth';[3] but Locke, he thinks, is not free to dispense with it. Instead of adopting it, however, he justifies his rejection of it after a fashion which gives away his case. This argument, says Locke, 'is a doubtful thing from the different Make of Mens Tempers, and Application of their Thoughts.'[4] To which Stillingfleet makes reply: 'What can this mean, unless it be to let us know, that even clear and distinct Ideas may lose their Effect by the difference of Mens Tempers and Studies; so that besides Ideas in order to a right Judgment, a due Temper and Application of the Mind is required.'

The Socinians, in borrowing from Locke, were playing into the hands of the deists; but his teaching about the criterion of certainty cannot in its turn be regarded as a legitimate application of the principle adopted by Descartes. He was a 'Thinking Man,' and 'he endeavour'd to lay the Foundations of Certainty, as well as he could'; and he laid them, not in ideas, but in 'the Perception of the Acts of his Mind.' These acts were so clearly and distinctly perceived, that he was certain of his own existence. But, Stillingfleet protests—if we understand him correctly—in a brief and subtle paragraph which puzzled Locke himself,

---

[1] It is remarkable that he passes over Locke's affirmation that *Rom.* i. 20 contains 'as certain and clear a truth as can any where be delivered' (*Essay*, IV. x. 7).
[2] *Ib.*, p. 508.   [3] *Ib.*, p. 507.   [4] *Ib.*, p. 508 (*Essay, Ib.*).

that the certainty here does not lie in the clearness and distinctness of the perception taken by itself; because the matter perceived, namely, 'the Acts of the Mind,' presents plain evidence 'which is of that Nature, that the very Doubting of it proves it.'[1] We can be certain when we clearly and distinctly perceive in all cases 'where there is the like Degree of Evidence.' But there are no cases in addition to the one before us, where this evidence is forthcoming. A criterion of certainty which holds in the peculiar case of 'acts of the mind' cannot be applied 'to things without ourselves; of which we can have no other Perception, than what is caused by the Impressions of outward Objects'; and Descartes, therefore, was mistaken in thinking that clearness and distinctness of perception is a general criterion of certainty.

Locke, pious layman, was perplexed and pained by this episcopal criticism of his *Essay*, and attempted to clear himself in a lengthy letter which appeared three months later. He argues that his own account of the idea of substance has, in fact, been confirmed by his opponent; for the *Essay* had said that we must 'suppose' some common subject or support, 'because we cannot conceive how simple ideas of sensible qualities should subsist alone'; and now Stillingfleet writes that we must 'conceive' a substratum, 'because it is a repugnancy to our conceptions of things, that modes and accidents should subsist by themselves.'[2] He points out that this view of the origin of the idea of substance has nothing whatever to say to the being of substance, 'the being of things depending not on our ideas.'[3] He protests that the dilemma proposed by his adversary assumes quite wrongly that when sensation and reflection are set as the sole origins of ideas, all contribution towards knowledge from reason is thereby precluded. It is admitted

---

[1] *Ib.*, p. 507. *Cf.* p. 544 (*An Answer to Mr. Locke's Letter* ... 1697).
[2] *The Works of John Locke*, 1823, vol. iv. p. 13.
[3] *Ib.*, p. 18.

on both sides that simple ideas, such as 'red' and 'thinking,' are not independently existing ideas. 'Hence,' Locke argues, 'the mind perceives their necessary connexion with inherence or being supported; which being a relative idea superadded to the red colour in a cherry, or to thinking in a man, the mind frames the correlative idea of a support.' [1] But lest an onlooker should imagine that the final words in this quotation concede what Stillingfleet contended for when he wrote that 'Mind doth form' the idea of substance, it must be added that Locke continues impenitently that the 'general indetermined idea of something, is, by the abstraction of the mind, derived also from the simple ideas of sensation and reflection: and thus the mind, from the positive, simple ideas got by sensation or reflection, comes to the general idea of substance.' Then he makes the point that if the idea of substance is really as clear and distinct as a simple idea of sensation, then Stillingfleet will be bound to admit that an idea of a general substance or essence, *e.g.* of man, is as clear and distinct as the idea of the red colour of a cherry.[2]

Locke denies that the *Essay* places certainty in the clearness and distinctness of ideas; his contention is that certainty lies in our perception of agreement or disagreement between ideas. He will even admit that 'in some cases we may have certainty about obscure ideas,' as when, for example, we are certain that we are ourselves existing thinking substances: though, obviously, clearer and more distinct ideas 'contribute very much to our more clear and distinct reasoning and discoursing about them.' [3] That the *Essay* passed over the ontological proof does not imply that God's existence cannot be established from clear and distinct ideas other than the idea of God; and the author never said that 'we cannot have any certain knowledge of the existence of any thing, whereof we have not a clear, distinct, complex idea.' [4] And if the proof was passed over,

[1] *Ib.*, p. 21. [2] *Ib.*, p. 25. [3] *Ib.*, p. 42. [4] *Ib.*, p. 47.

the intention 'was not to deny that the idea of a most perfect being doth prove a God, but to blame those who take it for the only proof, and endeavour to invalidate all others.' [1] Since *belief* in God is 'the foundation of all religion and genuine morality,' any proof—even the ontological, which is 'not conclusive'—that will help to confirm this belief ought to be welcomed: and preference for one proof over another is largely a matter of temperament. To the suggestion that his criterion of certainty had been borrowed from Descartes, Locke returns a blunt denial. He acknowledges gladly his debt to that great master for his own 'first deliverance from the unintelligible way of talking of the philosophy in use in the schools'; but of the imperfections of the *Essay* he writes—'I must own to your lordship they were spun barely out of my own thoughts.' [2] And he protests that he cannot detect any difference between certainty by way of agreement or disagreement between ideas and certainty by way of reason. 'All that reason or the mind does, in reasoning or arguing, is to find out and observe that agreement or disagreement: and all that argument does is, by an intervening idea, to show it, where an immediate putting the ideas together will not do it.' [3]

Locke concludes that he must continue to rest content with 'the condemned way of ideas,' [4] seeing that his critic has failed to disclose a third source of ideas. But the bishop need not despair of him: because 'a mistaken philosopher' may be 'an orthodox Christian.' [5] The *Essay*, he says, was not written in order to strengthen either Socinian or Trinitarian: and it is as unreasonable for either of them to dispute its conclusions as it would be for the rival sides in the controversy about nature and grace to argue that the ideas of these things do not derive from sensation and reflection.

These remarks introduce the problem of the relation of revelation to reason; and, fortunately, Locke has dealt with

[1] *Ib.*, p. 53.   [2] *Ib.*, p. 48.   [3] *Ib.*, p. 62.
[4] *Ib.*, p. 93.   [5] *Ib.*, p. 68.

it in *The Reasonableness of Christianity, as Delivered in the Scriptures* (1695). What is Christianity; and why do we accept it? The reply given to these questions had already provoked criticism from another quarter before Stillingfleet penned his *Vindication*. But the final paragraph in the postscript to the first of the two letters written to Stillingfleet ought to be compared with the substance of the work written previously: it seems to propose revealed truth for acceptance by a mode of faith which is disengaged from reason and at the same time to register regret that revealed truth should be so exalted. The paragraph reads as follows: 'The holy scripture is to me, and always will be, the constant guide of my assent; and I shall always hearken to it, as containing infallible truth, relating to things of the highest concernment. And I wish I could say, there were no mysteries in it: I acknowledge there are to me, and I fear always will be. But where I want the evidence of things, there yet is ground enough for me to believe, because God has said it: and I shall presently condemn and quit any opinion of mine, as soon as I am shown that it is contrary to any revelation in the holy scripture. But I must confess to your lordship, that I do not perceive any such contrariety in any thing in my Essay of Human Understanding.' [1]

Convinced that the simple Gospel had been complicated and obscured by makers of systems and creeds, Locke tells us that he undertook to discover for himself what the original teaching of its Founder might be.[2] The method employed was strictly empirical: he read the *Gospels* and the *Acts* with the intention of making clear to his own mind what it was that Jesus and the apostles preached. Their teaching, he finds, is comprised in the proposition that Jesus is the Messiah, it being understood that the term 'Messiah' is

[1] *Ib.*, p. 96.
[2] *Ib.*, vol. vii. p. 102: 'But I cannot allow to them, or to any man, an authority to make a religion for me, or to alter that which God hath revealed.' *Cf.* Whichcote's aphorism (112): 'I will not make a Religion for God: nor suffer any to make a Religion for me.'

equivalent to Son of God.[1] 'This was the only Gospel-article of faith which was preached by them.'[2] He maintains that the proposition in question is acceptable to reason; but that, apart from the credence elicited by its content, the miracles of Jesus Christ are sufficient evidence that both He and His message are of God.[3] To one critic, unnamed, who objected that Hobbes also had identified Christianity with this solitary truth, Locke replies that he was unaware that the *Leviathan* had said so; and to another, John Edwards, who complained that in this, as in other matters, the *Reasonableness* was 'all over Socinianized,'[4] he instances a sermon by John Tillotson,[5] and also a work by Simon Patrick,[6] where the same alleged error was perpetrated. It must be acknowledged, he admits, that the Messiahship of Jesus is an 'abridgment'[7] of the Christian revelation, and the equivalent of the primitive *regula fidei* as outlined by Tertullian.[8] Acceptance of this single truth is sufficient to *make* a man a Christian, and to ensure his reception into the Church; but a convert will be obliged to search the Scrip-

[1] *Ib.*, vol. vii. p. 30.   [2] *Ib.*, p. 102.
[3] *Ib.*, pp. 134-5; 143. Cf. pp. 84-5: 'For though it be as easy to omnipotent power to do all things by an immediate over-ruling will, and so to make any instruments work, even contrary to their nature, in subserviency to his ends; yet his wisdom is not usually at the expense of miracles (if I may so say), but only in cases that require them, for the evidencing of some revelation or mission to be from him. . . . If it were not so, the course and evidence of things would be confounded, miracles would lose their name and force, and there could be no distinction between natural and supernatural.'
[4] *Ib.*, p. 162.   [5] *Ib.*, p. 172.   [6] *Ib.*, p. 179.
[7] *Ib.*, p. 276. Jeremy Taylor sets his minimum of belief within a context reminiscent of Ignatius of Antioch and Clement of Alexandria: 'If we acknowledge Christ to be our Lord, that is, our law-giver and our Saviour, to rescue us from our sins and their just consequents, we have all faith; and nothing else can be the foundation, but such articles which are the confession of these two truths, "Christ Jesus our Lord," "Christ Jesus our Saviour"; that by faith we be brought unto obedience and love, and by this love we be brought to Christ, and by Christ unto God; this is the whole complexion of the christian faith, the economy of our salvation' (*Works*, vi. 435).
[8] *Ib.*, p. 278.

tures, and to accept all truths therein revealed in so far as he can know them. 'He believes all that God has made necessary for him to believe, and assent to; and as for the rest of divine truths, there is nothing more required of him, but that he receive all the parts of divine revelation, with a docility and disposition prepared to embrace and assent to all truths coming from God; and submit his mind to whatsoever shall appear to him to bear that character.'[1] And since men's capacities for truth are as various as God's measures of enlightenment, 'almost every particular man in this sense has, or may have, a distinct catalogue of fundamentals, each whereof it is necessary for him explicitly to believe, now that he is a Christian';[2] and no man may fix the precise content of another's faith.[3] Are we to conclude, Locke inquires of Edwards, that 'the church of England disguises the faith of the Gospel,'[4] when, upon profession of the Apostles' Creed and without specific declaration of the 'satisfaction' made by Christ, she administers Baptism to those of riper years?

It is instructive to examine what Locke means by the faith which yields assent to the substance of Christian revelation. Genuine faith, he says, completes itself so inevitably in repentance, that the New Testament often employs the one for the other. He gives the identification a peculiar turn; and the quotation following reveals his own religious attitude, which is predominantly moralist, and even legalist. 'These two, faith and repentance, *i.e.* believing Jesus to be the Messiah, and a good life, are the indispensable conditions of the new covenant, to be performed by all those who would obtain eternal life.'[5] The significance of this passage will be clear, once we have read it in the light of his theory of natural religion, to which we now turn.

Christianity, says Locke, presupposes the fall of Adam;

[1] *Ib.*, p. 156. [2] *Ib.*, p. 232. [3] *Ib.*, p. 233.
[4] *Ib.*, p. 271. [5] *Ib.*, p. 105.

and we cannot understand what God intended that it should effect, unless we have understood the nature and condition of man to whom it was preached. Fortunately, we possess the Scriptures, 'a collection of writings, designed by God, for the instruction of the illiterate bulk of mankind, in the way to salvation'; [1] and from them we learn that Adam fell from a state of 'perfect righteousness,' or 'perfect obedience,' and merited the loss of 'bliss and immortality.' When the Bible says that God visited Adam with death, it means what it says, and no more: 'I must confess, by death here, I can understand nothing but a ceasing to be, the losing of all actions of life and sense.' [2] But the mortality in which Adam involved all his descendants is not penal; and the goodness of God forbids us to think that men are born 'under the necessity of sinning continually, and so multiplying the provocation.' We may not complain that eternal life is beyond our reach, continues Locke in a manner reminiscent of Calvin, because it is not ours by right; and, after all, it is better to enjoy mortal life with its attendant ills than not to live at all.[3] For explanation of the empirical fact of universal sin—'all have sinned' [4]—we have to look elsewhere than to Adam; and we find it in each man's own disobedience to God's commandment as known to his own reason. It is just as impossible for a moral philosopher to live up to the dictates of the moral law, as for a zealous Jew to satisfy his code; for both are condemned by 'the law of works.' [5] All men, therefore, do in fact incur penal death; and since, with complete cessation of human life, God's purpose would fail, He finds a way out. He substitutes 'the law of faith' for 'the law of works,' and reckons faith that Jesus is Messiah as the equivalent of perfect obedience to law. Immortal life is bestowed in return for obedience of assent to what God declares to be believed, seeing that obedience of behaviour in accordance with what

[1] *Ib.*, p. 5. [2] *Ib.*, p. 6. [3] *Ib.*, p. 8.
[4] *Rom.* viii. 23. [5] *Works*, vii. p. 13.

He demands to be done has failed. And faith does not release a believer from 'works': it supplies 'the defect of full obedience.'[1] This is, of course, a mistaken interpretation of St. Paul's antithesis between faith and works.[2] The apostle's idea of justifying faith is void of legalist associations: his teaching is that when human endeavour realizes that nothing whatever can be done to win salvation, God accepts the soul's confession of helplessness, and saves it by His own work in Christ and the Spirit. 'The law of faith then, in short,' writes Locke, 'is for every one to believe what God requires him to believe, as a condition of the covenant he makes with him: and not to doubt of the performance of his promises.'[3] It is little wonder that Edwards refers to the 'author of the new Christianity';[4] for Locke's concern about assent to propositions and obedience to laws marks him out for a sincere and pious moralist, who will always go by the book.[5] He has little to say about communion with God, saving that Christ directed attention to the inwardness of worship, and not to its externals. 'Praises and prayer, humbly offered up to the Deity, were the worship he now demanded; and in these every one was to look after his own heart, and to know that it was that alone which God had regard to, and accepted.'[6] But the account which he gives of repentance is strictly impersonal. 'Repentance is an hearty sorrow for our past misdeeds, and a sincere resolution and endeavour, to the utmost of our power, to conform all our actions to the law of God'; and 'a sincere obedience to the law of Christ, the remainder of our lives.'[7]

But Locke does not confuse revealed religion with natural,[8]

---

[1] *Ib.*, p. 14.   [2] *Rom.* iii. 27.
[3] *Works*, vii. p. 16.   [4] *Ib.*, p. 272.
[5] *Ib.*, p. 111 ff.; p. 125. *Cf.* p. 289: 'My Christianity, I confess, is contained in the written word of God. . . .'
[6] *Ib.*, p. 148. *Cf.* p. 129: 'This oblation of a heart, fixed with dependence on, and affection to him, is the most acceptable tribute we can pay him, the foundation of true devotion, and life of all religion.'
[7] *Ib.*, p. 105.   [8] *Ib.*, p. 5.

and he is firmly persuaded that men can enjoy immortality only by the gift of God through Christ. It is interesting to observe what he has to say about the place of reason in man's quest for God. Having rejected the doctrine of the total depravity of man, he accounts for reason's meagre success by falling back upon the Cartesian expedient of laying blame upon the passions and general sloth. God is sufficiently made manifest in His works; but the generality of men will not and do not think. 'Sense and lust blinded their minds in some, and a careless inadvertency in others, and fearful apprehensions in most . . . gave them up into the hands of their priests, to fill their heads with false notions of the Deity, and their worship with foolish rites, as they pleased: and what dread or craft once began, devotion soon made sacred, and religion immutable.'[1] If the few who came to know God had divulged their secret, the multitudes would not have hearkened. Socrates exposed polytheism, and we know his fate. 'Whatsoever Plato, and the soberest of the philosophers, thought of the nature and being of the one God, they were fain, in their outward professions and worship, to go with the herd, and keep to the religion established by law.'[2] Natural religion was anything but rational religion;[3] whereas Christianity is 'plain, simple, reasonable.'[4]

Reason had failed in morals too; and though a few men here and there were aware of what God demanded, the common tendency had been to cultivate religion as though it had no connection with morals.[5] 'Experience shows, that the knowledge of morality, by mere natural light (how agreeable soever it be to it) makes but a slow progress, and little advance in the world.'[6] Moral obligation can derive its authority from two sources only, from either reason or revelation.[7] But where is the philosopher who is recognized as an authority in the sphere of conduct? Certain individuals,

[1] *Ib.*, p. 135. [2] *Ib.*, p. 136. [3] *Ib.*, p. 139. [4] *Ib.*, p. 188.
[5] *Ib.*, p. 139. [6] *Ib.*, p. 140. [7] *Ib.*, p. 142.

no doubt, have delivered many worthy precepts; but if we hearken to Seneca, for example, in some points, why not in all?[1] Reason did not provide the world with 'a complete morality';[2] and it did not deduce 'all the parts' of morality 'by clear and evident demonstration.'[3] And in those communities where just laws prevail, we find too often that these have been grounded in 'convenience,'[4] and not in 'the law of nature.'[5] The final sanction of all law is 'a clear knowledge and acknowledgment of the law-maker,'[6] and this is provided in the Christian revelation.

Locke's regard for 'the eternal, immutable standard of right,'[7] to which, 'from the constitution of his very nature,'[8] man is bound, places him within the tradition which the Cambridge Platonists set themselves to conserve. But whereas they certainly treat the moral life as an integral part of the religious life, he appears to identify them. He seems to lay emphasis upon what reason may know of what God wills should be done, rather than upon the consequences for conduct of what reason may know of what God is. 'The same spark of the divine nature and knowledge in man, which, making him a man, showed him the law he was under, as a man; showed him also the way of atoning the merciful, kind, compassionate Author and Father of him and his being, when he had transgressed that law. He that made use of this candle of the Lord, so far as to find what was his duty, could not miss to find also the way to reconciliation and forgiveness, when he had failed of his duty: though, if he used not his reason this way, if he put out or neglected this light, he might, perhaps, see neither.'[9] The language and the thoughts are Whichcote's, but not the temper.

[1] *Ib.*, p. 141. [2] *Ib.*, p. 141. [3] *Ib.*, p. 142.
[4] *Ib.*, pp. 142, 144. [5] *Ib.*, p. 144. [6] *Ib.*, p. 144.
[7] *Ib.*, p. 133. [8] *Ib.*, p. 112. [9] *Ib.*, p. 133.

ADDITIONAL NOTES

I
JOHN CALVIN

WE do injustice to Calvin, no less than to Whichcote, if we fail to recognize that both men quenched their thirst at the waters that flow from the same spiritual rock; because, in rejecting the austere and extreme predestination doctrine of the reformer, Whichcote was but discarding an intellectual interpretation, based doubtless upon Scriptural models, of a religious experience common to both. In Calvin, Augustinian theology may suffer from hardening of the arteries; but the fervent heat of the Alexandrian tradition still continues to throb within it. And when Whichcote speaks of an empty soul made full by the good things of God in Christ, he is repeating a confession often uttered in the *Institutes*. 'Therefore it is prooved that they falsely, yea and wrongfully pretend the knowledge of Christ, although they can eloquently & roundly talke of the Gospel. For it is not a doctrine of tongue, but of life: and is not conceived as other learnings be, with onely understanding and memorie, but is then onely received when it possesseth the whole soule, and findeth a seate and place to hold it in the most inward affection of the hart.'[1]

It were an idle task to attempt to justify Calvin's view of the ways of God with men. God, he holds, willed, and therefore foresaw,[2] the fall of Adam, and in him the

---

[1] Thomas Norton, *The Institution of Christian Religion, written in Latine by M. John Calvine, Translated into English according to the Authors last edition*; . . ., London, 1611, III. vi. 4.

[2] *Ib.*, III. xxii. 1. *Cf.* III. xxi. 5: 'When we give foreknowledge to God, we meane that all things alway have beene and perpetually doe remaine under his eies, so that to his knowledge there is nothing to come

apostacy, ruin and corruption of his whole posterity; and God, he holds also, willed to restore in Christ from among the *corrupta massa* [1] a small number of souls [2] upon whom to bestow the gift of blessed immortality. 'Predestination we call the eternall decree of God, whereby he had it determined with himselfe what he willed to become of every man. For all are not created to like estate: but to some eternall life, and to some eternall damnation is foreappointed.' [3] 'For the first man fell, because the Lord so judged it to be expedient: why he so judged, is unknowen to us: yet it is certaine that he so judged for no other reason but because he saw that thereby the glory of his name should be worthily set forth.' [4] Scripture not having divulged His secret counsel in this matter, our pious course is to maintain a 'learned ignorance': [5] it is, indeed, a 'terrible decree'; [6] but we must be humble and content to rest in His will, for He acts, not arbitrarily, but after His own law.[7]

The consequences of Adam's fall can be summed up in two words, deprivation and depravation. Man is deprived henceforth of that measure of the knowledge of God and of His will, a supernatural gift,[8] which ought to have prepared him, had he heeded it, for enjoyment of the fuller knowledge of heaven,[9] termed *aeterna beatitudo*.[10] He is

or past, but all things are present, and so present that he doth not imagine onely by conceived formes (as those things are present to us, whereof our mind holdeth fast the remembrance) but he truly beholdeth and seeth them as set before him. And this foreknowledge extendeth to the whole compasse of the world and to all creatures.'

[1] *Ib.*, III. xxiii. 3.   [2] *Ib.*, III. xxi. 7.   [3] *Ib.*, III. xxi. 5.
[4] *Ib.*, III. xxiii. 8.   [5] *Ib.*, III. xxi. 2.
[6] *Ib.*, III. xxiii. 7: *Decretum quidem horribile, fateor.*
[7] *Ib.*, III. xxiii. 2: *qui sibi ipsi lex est.*
[8] *Ib.*, II. ii. 12.   [9] *Ib.*, IV. xvi. 19.
[10] *Ib.*, II. ii. 26. *Cf.* I. xv. 6: *Sicut autem absque controversia ad coelestis vitae meditationem conditus fuit homo, ita ejus notitiam animae fuisse insculptam certum est. Et sane praecipuo intelligentiae usu careret homo, si sua eum lateret felicitas: cujus perfectio est cum Deo conjunctum esse.*

depraved in each and every faculty [1]; in his reason, in his will, and in his appetites. His reason,[2] in spiritual things, is blind and dull,[3] feeble,[4] ignorant,[5] and given over to doubts,[6] deceits [7] and unprofitable speculations.[8] His will is perverse: for whereas, in the state of original righteousness,[9] will,[10] though 'pliable to either side,[11] was free to choose either good or evil, now, in the fallen state, it is both directed by blind reason and also subjected to the violence of the appetites.[12] His appetites [13] are all become intemperate,[14] inordinate, diseased,[15] evil and sinful.[16]

The reprobate, however, are men and not brutes, and the image of God in them is never completely defaced: witness, for instance, the natural man's desire for truth [17] and goodness,[18] and his conscience [19] with its obligations and condemnations. They retain even the seed of religion: [20] though it cannot bear any fruit, because their knowledge of God [21] is not 'pure and clear,' [22] but 'confused.' [23] But God gives to them all, to some more and to some less, certain degrees [24] of an inferior grace,[25] which are really

---

[1] *Ib.*, IV. xv. 10.
[2] *ratio; humana mens; communis sensus* (I. v. 3); *naturae lumen* (II. ii. 24).
[3] *Ib.*, II. ii. 19.   [4] *Ib.*, I. vi. 4.   [5] *Ib.*, II. ii. 12.
[6] *Ib.*, II. ii. 7.
[7] *Ib.*, II. ii. 25: *Tot obruitur hallucinationum formis nostra ratio, tot erroribus est obnoxia, in tot impedimenta impingit, tot angustiis irretitur, ut plurimum a certa directione absit.*
[8] *Ib.*, II. ii. 12.
[9] *justitia originalis* (IV. xv. 10); *integritas* (I. xv. 8).
[10] *liberum arbitrium.*
[11] *in utramque partem flexibilis erat ejus voluntas.*
[12] *Ib.*, II. ii. 12.
[13] *appetitiones; desideria* (II. ii. 24); *naturalis inclinatio* (II. ii. 26).
[14] *Ib.*, III. iii. 7.   [15] *Ib.*, II. ii. 24.   [16] *Ib.*, III. iii. 10.
[17] *Ib.*, II. ii. 12.   [18] *Ib.*, II. ii. 26.
[19] *Ib.*, II. viii. 1: *lex illa interior.*   [20] *Ib.*, I. v. 1.
[21] *insculptum* (I. ii. 3); *inscriptum* (I. iii. 1).
[22] *Ib.*, I. v. 15: *ad puram usque et liquidam Dei cognitionem.*
[23] *Ib.*, I. iv. 4: *confusa Dei notitia.*
[24] *Ib.*, II. iii. 4: *speciales Dei gratias.*
[25] *Ib.*, II. ii. 17: *generalem Dei gratiam.*

gifts of the Holy Spirit, and bestowed 'for the common benefite of mankinde,'[1] enabling them to attain to many of the good ends that lie within the confines of this mortal life. 'Neither is there cause,' Calvin explains, 'why any man should aske, what have the wicked to doe with Gods spirit, which are altogether estranged from God. For where it is said that the spirit of God dwelleth in the faithfull onely: that is to be understanded of the spirit of sanctification, by the which we are consecrate to God himselfe, to be his temples: yet doth he neverthelesse fill, moove, and quicken all things with the vertue of the same spirit, and that according to the propertie of every kinde which he hath given to it by law of creation.'[2] The whole range of the arts, 'both the liberall, and the handie crafts,'[3] is salvaged by this expedient: but no moral value can possibly accrue in the pursuit of them, because the reprobate, consumed by ambition and pride, cannot devote their works to the glory of God.[4]

It is important to recognize the character of the restrictions which Calvin places upon philosophy. In the first place, philosophy is an art of reason by nature blind to spiritual reality, but by grace possessed of partial and temporary vision. In the second place, it is an art of depraved man, necessarily perverted in its conclusions by the influence of perverted will and inordinate appetites. Divine illumination is good, but it need not be accompanied by the gift of sanctification, which re-creates an evil will. A soul is not quickened by having Baconian idols removed from view, or even by adopting Cartesian methodology, but by God's shattering of the prince of idols, self-love. So Calvin writes: 'I denie not that there be heere and there read in Philosophers, concerning God, many things well and aptlie spoken, but yet such as doe alway savour of a certaine giddie imagination. The Lord gave them in deede,

---

[1] *Ib.*, II. ii. 16: *in publicum generis humani bonum.*
[2] *Ib.*, II. ii. 16.   [3] *Ib.*, II. ii. 14.   [4] *Ib.*, II. ii. 13-16; I. v. 3-4.

as is above said, a little taste of his Godhead, that they should not pretend ignorance to colour their ungodlinesse: and many times he mooved them to speake many things, by confession whereof themselves might be convinced: But they so sawe the things that they sawe, that by such seeing they were not directed to the truth, much lesse did attaine unto it, like as a wayfaring man in the middest of the field, for a sudden moment, seeth farre and wide the glistering of lightning in the night time, but with such a quickly vanishing sight, that he is sooner covered againe with the darknesse of the night, than he can stirre his foote, so farre is it off that he can be brought into his way by such a helpe. Beside that, those small drops of trueth, wherewith as it were by chaunce, they sprinkle their bookes, with how many and how monstrous lies are they defiled? Finally, they never so much as smelled that assurednesse of Gods good will toward us, without which, mans wit must needs be filled with infinite confusion. Therefore mans reason neither approcheth, nor goeth toward, nor once directeth sight unto this truth, to understand who is the true God, or what he will be toward us.'[1]

Epicureans and Stoics are cited as illustrations of erroneous philosophers: the former 'dreame of an idle and slothfull God,'[2] and the latter disallow special providences, handing the course of the world over to fate.[3] The Stoics are no less ignorant in their ethical doctrines. When they bid us live 'according to nature,'[4] they show that they are unaware that human nature is fallen nature, and their teaching about free will is so much talk about a faculty which we do not possess.[5] The lengths to which they will go in curbing the emotional life is further evidence that they misunderstand God's ideal for man. 'You see how to beare the crosse patiently, is not to be altogether astonished, and without all feeling of sorrow: as the Stoickes in old

[1] *Ib.*, II. ii. 18.   [2] *Ib.*, I. xvi. 4.   [3] *Ib.*, I. xvi. 8.
[4] *Ib.*, III. vi. 3.   [5] *Ib.*, III. viii. 9.

time did foolishly describe a valiant harted man, to be such a one, as putting off all nature of man, was alike moved in prosperity and in adversitie, in sorrowfull and joyfull estate, yea such a one as like a stone was mooved with nothing: and what have they profited with this high wisedome? Forsooth they have painted out such an image of wisdome as never was found, and never can hereafter be among men: But rather while they coveted to have too exact and precise a patience, they have taken away all the use of patience out of mans life. And at this day also among Christians there are new Stoickes, that reckon it a fault not onely to grone and weepe, but also to be sad and carefull. . . . But we have nothing to do with that stonie Philosophie, which our master and Lord hath condemned not onely by his word but also by his example. For he mourned and wept both at his owne and other mens adversities.'[1] Finally, the doctrine that virtue is to be desired for its own sake is a child of pride,[2] and akin to the doctrine of justification by works.

Plato comes in for more generous treatment. He is 'the most religious and most sober'[3] of all philosophers. He is about the only one among them all to see that the soul of man is an immortal substance.[4] He teaches 'that the soveraigne good of the soule is the likenesse of God, when the soule having throughly conceived the knowledge of him is wholly transformed into him.'[5] He acknowledges 'the soveraigne good of man to be his conjoyning with God. But what maner of conjoyning that was, he could not perceive so much as with any small taste, and no marvell, sith he had never learned of the holy bond thereof.'[6] He says that 'the life of a Philosopher is a meditation of death, but we may more truely say, that the life of a Christian man is a perpetuall studie and exercise of mortifying the flesh, till it being utterly slaine, the Spirit of God get the dominion

---

[1] *Ib.*, III. viii. 9.   [2] *Ib.*, III. vii. 3.   [3] *Ib.*, I. v. 10.
[4] *Ib.*, I. xv. 6.   [5] *Ib.*, I. ii. 3.   [6] *Ib.*, III. xxv. 2.

in us.'[1] But he falls into the common error of assuming that the soul can of itself rule its own life for good: because, while under no illusion as to the strength of immoderate appetites, he imagines that reason and will, working in harmony, can prevail.[2] Besides, consistently with this error, he identifies sin with ignorance, a piece of rationalization soon exposed by the simple fact of consciousness of guilt.[3]

Calvin's finding is that in spiritual things reason is discredited, and that we must turn elsewhere for guidance, to Holy Scripture, in fact, wherein is contained[4] and published[5] God's word speaking all things necessary for salvation. 'Reade Demosthenes or Cicero, reade Plato, Aristotle, or any other of all that sort,' he exclaims: 'I grant they shall marvellously allure, delite, moove, and ravish thee. But if from them thou come to this holy reading of Scriptures, wilt thou or not, it shall so lively moove thy affections, it shall so pearce thy hart, it shall so settle within thy bones, that in comparison of the efficacie of this feeling, all that force of Rhetoricians and Philosophers shall in maner vanish away: so that it is easie to perceive that the Scriptures, which doe farre excell all gifts and graces of mans industrie: do in deede breath out a certaine divinitie.'[6] It does not fall to reason, either to prove that Scripture is Divine revelation,[7] or to interpret its meaning when accepted as such. He who reads it must know 'that the first degree of profiting in Gods schoole, is to forsake his owne wit.'[8] There are, however, several arguments which help towards establishing the authenticity of Scripture: for example, its internal harmony;[9] its extreme antiquity, outdating post-Mosaic religious literatures;[10] its occasional condemnations of its own heroes;[11] its miracles;[12] its age-long success in

[1] *Ib.*, III. iii. 20.   [2] *Ib.*, II. ii. 3.   [3] *Ib.*, II. ii. 22, 25.
[4] *Ib.*, IV. viii. 8.   [5] *Ib.*, I. ix. 12.   [6] *Ib.*, I. viii. 1.
[7] *Ib.*, I. viii. 5.   [8] *Ib.*, III. ii. 34.   [9] *Ib.*, I. viii. 1; II. xi.
[10] *Ib.*, I. viii. 3, 4.   [11] *Ib.*, I. viii. 4.   [12] *Ib.*, I. viii. 6.

securing credence from all sorts and conditions;[1] and its writers' own testimony borne often in martyrdom.[2] If St. Augustine has seemed to ground the authority of Scripture in that of the Church, it must be remembered that he was dealing with the Manichees, to whom the Holy Spirit had not given the self-authenticating assurance (*certitudo*) of His own authorship.[3] It is from His inspiration that Scripture derives its unity of material and purpose; for 'that whole bodie compacted of the Law, Prophecies, Psalmes and Histories, was the word of the Lord to the old people,'[4] and the Apostles, 'authentike secretaries of the holy Ghost,'[5] were faithful to that word, when they wrote of its fulfilment in Christ.[6] 'The successors' of the apostles, therefore, are obliged to preach exclusively that which is written in Scripture, and abridged in the Apostles' Creed.[7]

The elect alone are privileged to enjoy the distinctively supernatural gifts, such as repentance, reconciliation, illumination, sanctification, assurance,[8] perseverance, salvation, love for God and charity towards man: for theirs is an effectual calling.[9] God has willed it so; and He begins His good work in them by granting to them an initial gift of faith, whereby all other spiritual gifts are apprehended. It is a 'perfect definition' of faith to say 'that it is a stedfast and assured knowledge of Gods kindnes toward us, which being grounded upon the truth of the free promise in Christ, is both reveiled to our minds, and sealed in our

---

[1] *Ib.*, I. viii. 12. [2] *Ib.*, I. viii. 13. [3] *Ib.*, I. vii. 3.
[4] *Ib.*, IV. viii. 6. [5] *Ib.*, IV. viii. 9.
[6] *Ib.*, IV. viii. 8. *Cf.* I. vii. 4: 'But I answer, that the testimonie of the holy Ghost is better than all reason. For as onely God is a convenient witnesse of himselfe in his own word, so shall the same word never find credit in the harts of men, untill it be sealed up with the inward witnesse of the holy Ghost.' IV. xvii. 32: 'Neither ought this to seeme incredible, or not consonant to reason, because as the whole kingdome of Christ is spirituall, so whatsoever he doth with his Church, ought not to be reduced to the reason of this world.'
[7] *Ib.*, II. xvi. 18. [8] *Ib.*, III. xxi. 7: *certitudo*.
[9] *interior gratiae efficacia* (III. xxi. 7); *Interior igitur haec vocatio pignus est salutis quod fallere non potest* (III. xxiv. 2).

hearts by the holy Ghost.'[1] 'When in defining Faith we call it knowledge,' Calvin explains, 'we meane not thereby a comprehending, such as men use to have of those things that are subject to mans understanding. For it is so farre above it, that mans wit must goe beyond and surmount it selfe to come unto it, yea, and when it is come unto it, yet doth it not attaine that which it feeleth, but while it is perswaded of that which it conceiveth not, it understandeth more by the very assurednesse of perswasion, than if it did with mans owne capacitie throughly perceive any thing familiar to man.'[2]

The gift of perseverance enables God's elect to withstand all manner of temptation, and especially that which is occasioned by innate concupiscence; for Calvin conceives spiritual progress as the counterpart of the progressive destruction of sin. 'And this restoring is fulfilled not in one moment, or one day, or one yeare, but by continuall, yea and sometimes slow proceedings God taketh away the corruptions of the flesh in his elect, clenseth them from filthinesse, and consecrateth them for temples to himselfe, renuing all their senses to true purenesse, that they may exercise themselves all their life in Repentance, and know that this warre hath no end but in death.'[3] The elect must be prepared to encounter concupiscence, as long as they are in the body: and when St. Paul soliloquizes upon the struggle between flesh and spirit,[4] he is not expressing the experience of a reprobate mind.[5] Concupiscence, furthermore, is not merely sinful, but sin, and involves guilt, whatever St. Augustine may seem to say to the contrary, when he terms it 'infirmity': 'we account the very same for sinne, that man is tickled with any desire at all against the law of God, yea we affirme that the very corruption that ingendreth such desires in us, is sinne.'[6] 'Baptisme indeed promiseth us that our Pharao is drowned, and the mortifi-

[1] *Ib.*, III. ii. 7.   [2] *Ib.*, III. ii. 14.   [3] *Ib.*, III. iii. 9.
[4] *Rom.* vii. 7 ff.   [5] *Institutes*, II. ii. 27.   [6] *Ib.*, III. iii. 10.

cation of sinne: yet not so that it is no more, or may no more trouble us, but onely that it may not overcome us.'[1] The elect are entered upon a life of continual repentance; and their first cleansing in Baptism, no matter how long since begun, is the begining of continuous cleansing. 'Wherefore it is also no doubt but that all the godly throughout all their life long, so oft as they be vexed with knowledge in conscience of their owne sinnes, dare call backe themselves to the remembrance of Baptisme, that thereby they may confirme themselves in the affiance of that onely and continuall washing which we have in the blood of Christ.'[2] It is concupiscence, at least in its social reference, that the last of the Ten Commandments forbids: for whereas the preceding prohibitions of the second table are directed against specific acts, 'coveting' denotes the inordinate desires and imaginings out of which deliberate actions are born. One positive end of the eighth commandment is 'that men should studie to defend and further the commodities and profit of other':[3] but the positive end of the tenth is that 'the conceptions of our minde' be directed to 'the rule charitie.'[4]

Calvin writes his *Institutes* in order 'to comprehend in an abridgement the summe of the doctrine of the Gospel':[5] but he is insistent that the Gospel is not doctrine, but life—*non enim linguae est doctrina, sed vitae*,[6] that Christ is both light and life. Christ mediates between the Father and the

---

[1] *Ib.*, IV. xv. 11.   [2] *Ib.*, IV. xv. 4.   [3] *Ib.*, II. viii. 46.
[4] *Ib.*, II. viii. 49. *Cf.* John Prideaux, Συνειδησιλογία˙ or, *The Doctrine of Conscience, Framed according to the points of the Catechisme, in the Book of Common-Prayer*, London, 1656: 'The last commandment puts the ax to the root of the tree, and excepteth not against externall acts, with internall purposes, and assent: but the very motions of corrupted nature, that bubble up against Gods law. So that originall sin is here as it were knocked on the head, lest the cockatrice, not crushed in the egge, might prove a masterlesse serpent. The vertues here prescribed are a hearty submission to Gods command, without the least regret within, and a content with outward meanes, without grudging at others more happy condition' (pp. 111 f.).
[5] *Ib.*, III. xix. 1.   [6] *Ib.*, III. vii. 4.

elect: and the 'form'[1] of His Incarnate life, which is an ever-recurrent rhythm of life through death, is reproduced in them.[2] This new life is referred to each one of the Persons in the Trinity: for 'both of our cleansing and regeneration we obtaine and after a certaine maner distinctly perceive the cause in the Father, the matter in the Sonne, and the effect in the holy Ghost.'[3] It is described in terms of New Testament symbolism: the elect are grafted into the death and life of Christ,[4] and into the body of which He is Head;[5] they put on Christ, and grow together into Him;[6] they are adopted into the Father's family in His Son, their Brother;[7] they are partakers now of His substance,[8] *i.e.* of His righteousness, eternal life, innocence, etc., and ultimately of the Divine nature.[9]

We shall conclude this note on Calvin's system, as it bears upon the writers treated of in the preceding pages, by referring to his idea of humanism. We have noted that God gives good gifts to the reprobate, and that He gives better, and the best, gifts to His own elect: now we add that He is said to have created the world for the good of man, and to order it for the same end. 'We know that the world was made principally for mankindes sake':[10] 'God hath ordained all things for our guard and safetie';[11] and He punishes the wicked 'so far as he foreseeth to be expedient for preserving of the university of things.'[12] His providence, whether displayed in His 'works,' or felt in man, has been designed both to check *amor sui* and to evoke

---

[1] *Ib.*, III. vi. 3. [2] *Ib.*, III. viii. 1. [3] *Ib.*, IV. xv. 6.
[4] *Ib.*, III. iii. 20. [5] *Ib.*, III. vi. 3. [6] *Ib.*, III. xxiv. 5.
[7] *Ib.*, III. xx. 36.
[8] *participes substantiae ejus facti* (IV. xvii. 11).
[9] *ut consortes efficeremur divinae naturae* (III. xi. 10): ii. *Pet.* i. 4. St. Paul teaches 'that man was made of like forme to God, not by inflowing of his substance, but by grace and power of his spirit. For he saith, that in beholding the glory of Christ, we are transformed into the same image, as by the Spirit of God, which surely so worketh in us, that it maketh us not of one substance with God' (I. xv. 5): 2 *Cor.* iii. 18.
[10] *Ib.*, I. xvi. 6. [11] *Ib.*, I. xiv. 22. [12] *Ib.*, II. iii. 3.

gratitude and worship. Man is naturally a social being,[1] and lives under the rule that all Divine gifts are to be held on trust for the advancement of his neighbour's good.[2] And, remarkable to relate, Calvin includes among these gifts, man's capacity for progress in the cultural and manual arts. 'Neither have they onely a power or facilitie to learne, but also to devise in every arte some new thing, either to amplifie or make perfecter that which hath been learned of an other that went before, which thing, as it mooved Plato erroniouslie to teach, that such conceiving is nothing else but a calling to remembrance, so by good reason it ought to compell us to confesse, that the begining thereof is naturally planted in the wit of man.'[3] When the economic principle of division of labour is regarded in this light, the services exchanged among men bear the stamp of God's consecration.[4] God has, in fact, 'named all such kinds of life, vocations';[5] and it is quite wrong to suppose that a cloistered life is the best of lives for winning perfection, and so to 'take away the same from all the callings of God.'[6]

What, then, is the proper attitude towards this mortal life and the things thereof? It is that of a traveller[7] making his way to heaven, by God's guidance, through a strange country, where the roads, by His appointment, are strewn with good things and beset by evils; it is that of a saint, who does not dare either to despise the blessings of this life or to refuse its battles, lest he should forfeit God. In comparison with the life to come, this life is to be counted vain;[8] but, emphatically, since it is the life wherein fulness of life has to be won, it may not be hated.[9] And lest self-love should too easily divert the goods of earth to its own end, God has seen to it that they shall be assorted suitably with evils. 'That they should not with too much ease take pleasure in the benefits of Marriage, he either maketh them

---

[1] *Ib.*, II. ii. 13. [2] *Ib.*, III. vii. 5. [3] *Ib.*, II. ii. 14.
[4] *Ib.*, III. vii. 5. [5] *Ib.*, III. x. 6. [6] *Ib.*, IV. xiii. 11.
[7] *Ib.*, III. x. 1. [8] *Ib.*, III. ix. 4. [9] *Ib.*, III. ix. 3.

to be vexed with the frowardnesse of their wives, or plucketh them downe with ill children, or punisheth them with want of issue.'[1] Goods are classified as follows: necessities simply; necessities affording delight—'in herbes, trees, and fruites, beside diverse profitable uses, there is also a pleasantnesse of sight, and sweetnesse of smell'; and delights simply—in flowers, for example, 'shall it be unlawfull either for our eies to take the use of that beautie, or for our smelling to feele that sweetnesse of savour?'[2] Calvin, apparently, was much impressed by natural beauty; for he believes that it is a function of the Holy Spirit to preserve 'the beautie of the world,'[3] and avers that 'nothing can be devised more beautifull to behold'[4] than the stars and planets in their courses. All good things were ordained that God might be praised in them, which principle fixes their measure, and forbids such excesses as gluttony, drunkenness and conceit in dress. Intemperance will be guarded against by observing two Pauline rules. The first is 'that they which use this world, should be so minded as though they used it not';[5] and the second, that a contented mind is proof against all the chances of fortune, for 'he that hardly and unquietly beareth a private and base estate, will not abstaine from pride if he climbe to honours.'[6]

What advantage, then, hath philosophy? Little, either way, it would appear. The elect, on the one hand, need not turn to it for enlightenment, when they possess already a 'Christian philosophy'[7] in Scripture, and the grace of the Holy Spirit to certify to its truth. 'If this thought be of force with us, that the word of the Lord is the onely way, that may lead us to search whatsoever is lawfull to be learned of him, that it is the onely light, which may give us light to see whatsoever we ought to see of him: it shal

---

[1] *Ib.*, III. ix. 1.
[2] *Ib.*, III. x. 2.
[3] *Ib.*, I. xiii. 14.
[4] *Ib.*, I. xiv. 21; *cf.* I. v. 2.
[5] *Ib.*, III. x. 3: 1 *Cor.* vii. 3.
[6] *Ib.*, III. x. 5: *Phil.* iv. 12.
[7] *christiana philosophia* (III. vii. 1).

easilie hold backe and restraine us from all rashnesse.'¹ The reprobate, on the other hand, who may exercise the gift of philosophy by the grace of the Spirit, are not enlightened with such a measure of the knowledge of God as is sufficient for salvation, nor are they blest with that faith which conditions assurance. And though their outward conduct, because of grace given, is often admirable, their wills still remaining perverse, we are to say that they possess 'images of vertues,'² but not the real thing. 'Hereby we easily perceive that whatsoever man thinketh, purposeth or doth, before that he be reconciled to God by faith, is accursed, and not onely of no value to righteousnesse, but of certaine deserving to damnation.'³ And when theology tries to disregard the fact that reason is blind and will weak, it resorts to the shameful expedient of trying to square Scripture with philosophy.⁴

¹ *Ib.*, III. xxi. 2.   ² *Ib.*, III. xiv. 2.
³ *Ib.*, III. xiv. 4.   ⁴ *Ib.*, II. ii. 3.

II

LANCELOT ANDREWES

ON

THE CANDLE OF THE LORD

As the sun giveth light to the body, so God hath provided light for the soul; and that is, first, the light of nature, which teacheth us that this is a just thing, *ne alii facias quod tibi fieri non vis*: from this light we have this knowledge, that we are not of ourselves but of another, and of this light the Wise Man saith, 'The soul of man is the candle of the Lord.' They that resist this light of nature are called *rebelles lumini*. With this light 'every one that cometh into this world is enlightened.' Howbeit this light hath caught a fall, as Mephibosheth did, and thereupon it halteth; notwithstanding, because it is of the royal blood, it is worthy to be made of.

Next, God kindleth a light of Grace by His word, which is *lux pedibus*, and *lux oculis*; and that we may be capable of this outward light, He lighteneth us with His Spirit; because the light of the Law shined but darkly, therefore He hath called us into the light of His Gospel, which is 'His marvellous light.'—*Sermons*, 1843 ed., vol. v. p. 319.

III

WILLIAM LAUD

ON

THE AUTHORITY OF HOLY SCRIPTURE

So then the way lies thus, as far as it appears to me, The credit of Scripture to be divine, resolves itself finally into that faith which we have touching God Himself, and in the same order. For as that, so this, hath three main grounds, to which all other are reducible. The first is, the tradition of the Church: and this leads us to a reverend persuasion of it. The second is, the light of Nature: and this shows us how necessary such a revealed learning is, and that no other way it can be had. Nay more, that all proofs brought against any point of faith, neither are nor can be demonstrations but soluble arguments. The third is, The light of the Text itself: in conversing wherewith, we meet with the Spirit of God inwardly inclining our hearts, and sealing the full assurance of the sufficiency of all three unto us. And then, and not before, we are certain that the Scripture is the word of God, both by divine and infallible proof. But our certainty is by faith, and so voluntary; not by knowledge of such principles as in the light of nature can enforce assent, whether we will or no.—*Works*, 1849 ed., vol. ii. p. 130.

INDEX

Acts, 9, 222
Aquinas, St. Thomas, 6, 130, 163, 164, 166
Aristotle, 17 n., 20, 23, 35 f., 80 n., 133, 142, 164, 168, 209, 237
Article I., 85 n.
Augustine, St., 22, 31 n., 56, 88, 238, 239

Bacon, 163, 191, 201
Barrow, v
Bentham, 158
Berkeley, 101, 131 f.
Bernard, St., 56 n.
Boyle, Robert, 27 n., 204 n., 209 n.
Browne, Peter, 129 ff.
Burnet, 2, 116, 188
Butler, 94 f., 158 f., 201 f., 212

Calvin, 8 n., 9 n., 13 n., 61 n., 65 n., 85 f., 106 n., 225
Chillingworth, 27
Clement of Alexandria, 35, 131, 146, 207, 209, 223 n.
Colossians, 81
1 *Corinthians*, 131, 167 n., 243 n.
2 *Corinthians*, 241 n.
Cudworth, 9 n., 14, 83, 122, 127, 133, 143, 182, 211
Culverwel, 83
Cumberland, 163, 169

Descartes, 4 ff., 42, 44, 47, 72, 76, 92, 97 ff., 101, 107, 109, 112, 117 n., 121 ff., 133 ff., 141, 163, 171, 185, 195 ff., 211, 214, 218 f., 221, 227, 234
Dillingham, 162, 164

Edwards, John, 223 f.
Ephesians, 8
Epicurus (Epicurean), 74, 194, 196, 210, 212, 235
Erasmus, 88
Evelyn, John, 40
Exodus, 16 n., 80

Galatians, 32, 138 n.
Gibson, A. Boyce, 136 n.
Glanvil, 176, 177
Grierson, Sir H. J. C., 91 n.
Grotius, 169

Habakkuk, 32
Hallywell, 82 n., 183 n.
Hebrews, 71 f., 117
Herbert, Lord, 179
Hobbes, 3, 16, 42, 91 n., 92 ff., 145, 151, 156, 199, 205, 212, 223
Hooker, 27, 31 n., 47 n., 85 n.
Hosea, 32
Hume, 82, 126 n.

Ignatius of Antioch, 223 n.
Inge, W. R., 142 n.
Irenaeus, 85
Isaiah, 13

Jebb, 133
1 *John*, 80, 91 n.

Kant, 101, 105 n., 183 n.
Keeling, 134 n., 135 n.
King, William, 131 n.

Laird, J., 18, 91 n., 145 n., 163
Laud, 34 n.

Locke, v, 9 n., 97, 127 ff., 151, 152 n., 214 ff.
Luce, A. A., 132 n.

Martineau, 90
Martyr, Justin, 207
Matthew, St., 32, 94
Mitchell, W. Fraser, 4 n., 91 n.
Moffatt, J., 22 n.
More, 73 n., 83, 177, 198, 211
Muirhead, J. H., 4 n., 9 n., 105 n.

Norris, 84 f.

Ommanney, 84 n.
Origen, 83, 168, 182 n., 207, 208, 209

Patrick, Simon, 68, 223
Paul, St., 9, 32, 34, 81, 154, 166, 226, 239, 241 n.
Pepys, 150
2 Peter, 82, 241 n.
Philippians, 21 n., 243 n.
Plato (Platonism), 2, 9, 28 n., 34 ff., 76, 79 n., 82, 96, 106, 121, 122 n., 127, 151 f., 154, 168, 195, 199, 205 ff., 227, 236 f., 242
Plotinus, 2, 70, 79, 142 n., 178, 208
Prideaux, John, 240 n.
Proverbs, 11, 34, 117, 178

Psalms, 105
Powicke, F. J., 35

Romans, 6, 21 n., 22, 31 f., 34, 70, 117, 168, 226
Rust, 83

Salter, 3 n.
Shaftesbury, 3, 18 ff., 22 ff.
Shand, A. F., 145
Smith, 52 n., 91, 108, 117, 128
Stillingfleet, 41 n., 84
Stoics, 84 n., 139, 165, 235 f.

Taylor, 9 n., 82, 177, 180, 183, 211, 223 n.
Tertullian, 207, 210, 223
Tillotson, v, 9 n., 223
Titus, 13
Toland, 129
Tuckney, 3 ff., 11, 27 f., 214
Tyrrell, 151, 157 n.

Ussher, 193

Ward, Richard, 145
Westcott, 31
Whichcote, v, 2, 70, 82, 91, 128, 183, 189, 211 ff., 228, 231
Willey, Basil, 78 n.
Wisdom, 106 n.